LAST
WILD
YEARS

LAST WILD YEARS

Mike Tomkies

JONATHAN CAPE
LONDON

First published 1992
Text and photographs © Mike Tomkies 1992
Jonathan Cape, 20 Vauxhall Bridge Road, London SW1V 2SA

A CIP catalogue record for this book
is available from the British Library

ISBN 0-224-03313-1

Printed in Great Britain by
Butler & Tanner Ltd, Frome and London

Contents

For Jim Crumley

1 · *Astonishing Wildlife*

Never had I known a winter at Wildernesse like this. From day to day it was a bitter fight for survival. The cold penetrated every nook and chink of the cottage, waiting in corners like damp, and loneliness, to assault one's bones, invade the soul. I was sitting at my desk, all alone and halfway up a roadless Highland loch, surrounded by my own weird inventions designed to trap and use every scrap of warmth from a little paraffin heater. Ice was permanent on the inside of the study window. My legs and body up to the armpits were encased in a sleeping bag, yet still I shivered. After eighteen years living in remote wild places, with only boat access to my primitive homes, I wondered if the great wilderness dream was coming to an end. One thing, and one thing only buoyed me up – I was making a wildlife movie that would astonish the world.

By heaven, how I needed that motivation! During the past two years it had seemed as if I was losing everything . . . my father, the gentle Alsatian dog Moobli, my publisher, my best friend, who had died from a heart attack. With each blow my resolve to stick it out had been severely tested. Life had been hardest after Moobli's death, but then I had found the veteran eagle, Atalanta, in a nest that others knew about, so I had stayed on to keep watch over her. So inspiring had that season turned out to be that when eventually I found a new publisher I blew all the first royalty advance on a professional 16mm movie-making outfit and set about filming the rare wildlife around me.

While Atalanta had bred again this year, she was also showing her age. Her wings looked tattered, with two flight pinions missing. She had also chosen her farthest nest, Eyrie 18, which was at the end of what I called the 'Killer Trek', and there was no question of one man carrying all the heavy movie equipment over 12,000 feet of ups and downs to that eyrie. Instead, I had filmed her neighbour, a beautiful young female I named Juno, who with her mate nested on Eagle Rock Mountain, three miles away on the other side of the loch. The trouble was that Juno had chosen a north-facing nest behind a screening ash tree, where the light had been poor. Even so, for the sake of my film, I decided to complete one last eagle season, but before that to spend the worst three months of winter in Spain, where I had also begun to study rare wildlife.

The little pine martens helped me to change my mind about that.

For two years, after months of coaxing, a male marten had been coming to the bird table outside my study window for bread, butter and raspberry jam. Now I looked forward every night to Mickey's cheeky elfin face, his dark eyes gleaming with eager anticipation as he reared up at the window pane in the light from my desk lamp. He even took food from my fingers.

Although the pine marten was brought near to extinction by hunting and trapping at the turn of the century, it is now on the increase, and there is no more attractive wild animal in Britain. About 2½ feet long, with sleek chocolate-brown coat, generous bushy tail, creamy-orange chest bib and rounded fawn-tipped ears and thick chubby paws, the pine marten seems to have been designed for neatness, for sheer aesthetic appeal. It is a fierce little creature when cornered or threatened, but otherwise it generally has a sunny, happy-go-lucky nature.

The excitement I felt when Mickey turned up with a mate, a slim female with twin dark spots on her chest bib – I called her Michelle – was intensified when the two brought their first kit, Chico, to the bird table. The kit remained shy, darting about behind its parents for the scraps they left. When Michelle eventually dared to take food from my hand, it was marvellous to see her delicate, hesitant approach just inside the open window, the sudden brief shrinking back if I so much as breathed, and then the quick, firm tooth-grasp on the morsel held in my fingers before she darted away with it.

The following night both martens came through the window to feed while I took photos, and there were brief '*chrroom*' growls when Mickey got a piece that Michelle wanted; also from Chico, the kit, if his mother did not leave a scrap for him. Chico wanted to venture closer but was just too scared. That evening they seemed so tame that I took a chance and held Mickey's glorious bushy tail as he was scooping up some raisins. I did not hold hard, of course, but he felt it and looked back quickly as if to say – Okay, if you *must*, but I've finished this bit (whipping his tail from my fingers) so where's the next? And of course he got the next, and the next, and the next.

This set me thinking. If only I had electricity, the better ciné gear I needed, the lighting – how wonderful it would be to get all of this into my film. The martens were becoming ever more trusting: maybe I could entice them right inside, where I could concentrate the light from two paraffin lamps and a powerful torch with mirrors and reflectors. If they were given time, perhaps I could do it . . . Well, maybe after all I would stay here for one last winter. I certainly needed scenes of red deer in snow for my film, to show winter's savage effects on the wildlife. The question was, could I survive another winter here, totally alone, or would it see the end of me? There were plenty of reasons for believing such a possibility. It was all too clear that I was not as strong, agile or resilient, now that I was approaching 60, as I had been nineteen years earlier when I gave up journalism for a new life in the wilds.

The real test of my stamina began early in October. After an unusually early cold September snap, the sun burned down so fiercely that I took the opportunity before winter set in to scrape rusty patches off the iron roof and repaint it. With wire brush and a large can half full of green paint, I went outside for the ladder I kept between the woodshed and the cottage wall. This I had constructed by power-sawing lengthways a straight 30-foot pine tree from which red deer had rubbed the bark. It had been a tricky operation, for I had to keep a dead centre all the way down, so as to avoid making thinner weak spots. By laying the two lengths a yard apart, flat sides uppermost, and nailing on stout timber struts every 2½ feet, I had a hefty but serviceable ladder costing next to nothing. Now I set it in place against the cottage wall and began confidently to mount with the green paint. Halfway up –

C–R–R–A–A–A–C–K!

The right side snapped. Only by letting the paint drop and rapidly transferring weight and both hands to the left side did I save myself

11

from crashing to the ground and severe injury. As it was I pulled a shoulder muscle.

I splinted the ladder up with rope and a 6-foot length of two-by-four, and finally made it to the top. As I crabbed about on the roof's apex I felt like an ageing gorilla – heavy, with my shoulder in pain, less sure-footed than I had been in the past. And when I sat astride the rooftop while painting it, the inner tendons of my thighs strained and hurt no matter in which position I placed my legs. Yet I managed to finish nearly half the rear roof, which was fairly good going.

It was while I was sitting thus, for a brief rest, that I became aware of a shape above me. It was Atalanta, flying from west to east above the wood. I was sure she had seen me. Nearer and nearer she came, like a great blackboard in the sky, no white or even dullish fawn showing in her plumage. Some of her great pinions were still tattered, with one missing from each wing. As she sailed overhead, the wind soughing through the mighty wings, I saw her head turn and, for a second or two, her blood orange eye held my gaze. Instinctively, without thinking, I half raised my hand in fond salute, in recognition perhaps of the adventures we had shared, for in that strange instant I felt she was trying to communicate. Precisely what I could not know. She gave two slow beats of her wings and passed on over the larches of the east wood. I thought, she too is getting old, really old. Well, she had been an ageing bird four years earlier, when she and her new and enthusiastic young mate, who I called Melanion, had managed to rear twin chicks. Although she had raised an eaglet in the far Eyrie 18 this year, I had the distinct impression she would not breed any more now. Nevertheless, it was wonderful to see her again, and so close that surely it had been intended on her part.

I left both ground and roof ladders in place, although I would take a few days off to let my tired old tendons recover, and went indoors to listen to the radio news. I was appalled to hear that 'The Greatest', the brilliantly clever heavy-weight boxer Muhammed Ali, had been diagnosed as suffering from Parkinson's Syndrome and would never fight again. Shocked as I was, I also found the news strangely comforting. If an athletic genius like Ali was all washed up at 42, then I need not feel too much shame about the declining strength of a wilderness man in his late fifties.

When the rains came, I was glad I had patched up the rust on the roof. I still made myself complete the rough kilometre walk each morning right round the woods. It took me no higher than 200 feet, but as I stumbled along under a 50lb pack I felt it kept my legs strong for the Hill. I would try to track the movements of the pine martens and searched the woods for their den. While they usually ran off to the west under the huge rhododendron tangle, it was clear that after that they headed east and north east. There were two trails, one ending near the great beech trunk that had fallen across the burn, the other at the rocky slabs below the waterfall. I was fairly sure their main den was somewhere in the steep rocky woodlands in the east.

Early one morning I was woken by a vole gnawing at the roof timbers near the door. '*Ric-rac, ric-rac.*' I got up, banged on the ceiling with a broom, and went back to bed. Within seconds the noise began again. The day before a vole had run across my bedclothes as I was thinking about getting up, and I found that another one had been chewing at my wildlife files on the floor. When I was woken by the pitter-patter of warmish liquid falling on my face, and looked up to see a thin stream coming through a tiny gap in the wooden ceiling boards, I realised it could only be coming from a vole having a pee. This vole plague had gone far enough. I got up and sleepily set two traps with cheese. In about twenty minutes there was a loud SNAP, and the vole had its skull staved in. Later, when back to full consciousness, I felt guilty. I was doing to voles what I criticised some sheep farmers for doing to foxes. I set no more traps, but the dead vole was not wasted. I put it out on the highest moss-covered pine post of the bird table complex, and that night the pine marten Michelle was the first to reach it. It has been recorded that martens were kept by the Romans to catch mice and rats in their granaries. All I know is that, as mousers, or volers, my three martens were quite useless.

It was my practice at this time to take my racing bike on supply trips and, after shopping, to do a time trial of 25 miles or so to keep my legs strong for the Hill without straining the joints. Once, according to the little computerised cyclometer on the handlebars, I covered a ten-mile stretch in 28 minutes. I felt childishly chuffed by these small achievements for they allowed me to think I was not yet totally decrepit. And the benefit showed, for on my first stag trek of the rutting season, I portered 56lb of ciné gear right round the Big Corrie, climbing up to 1,800 feet and down again for some five miles with no strain at all. It proved still too early for the stags, but in the clear autumn sun I took some fine panning sequences for the film, showing the formidable peaks and glens of my eagle territory.

As I was returning from the next stag trek, down the tussocky steps above Wildernesse, I happened to look to my left and there, beating along the rockfaces to the east, came a huge dark eagle. Frantically I unpacked the movie camera, clipped on the battery, set it all up and just got on to her for a short flying sequence before she went into soft focus. I was using the heavy rigid 500mm kinoptic lens that day, and it took time to adjust the focussing ring in front. I was sure the eagle was Atalanta for she turned and flew right over my head. Just then a male eagle also came up from the north east, circled round her, looped up until they grabbed each other's talons and held on with both feet. It was a truly fantastic sight, for they performed one complete and very slow somersault, held on a little longer and then let go, to drift round each other freely again. The camera could not tilt far enough to keep on the eagles as they swept right over my head.

Never had I seen golden eagles perform this complete roll together, though I had watched bald eagles do it in Canada. The pair looped up, extended their feathered tarsi towards each other and then grabbed talons again, but this time they did not somersault. These were the eagles for whom I had dragged deer carcasses from the woods up into the hills to help them in winter. If they were not putting on this show, this glorious pair bond display, just for my benefit, why else did they perform it so close above my head? Suddenly I realised that this was not Atalanta and Melanion, but Juno and her mate, for her wings were in perfect shape, not tattered at all. When later I thought about it, it seemed odd that these two should appear so boldly on what had always been Atalanta's territory.

The two began to fly across the loch. I had to wait for the right angle, and then I took a superb long sequence of Juno flying towards the distant hills, flapping and gliding casually in the sun, but making tremendous speed. Once over the loch, she turned west, and I filmed her going into a brief dive, as if spying prey below, but she changed her mind, swerved up again and carried on to the west in the direction of her own Eagle Rock Mountain. On and on she went as I watched her through the lens, passing silent sentinels of old tree snags on the hills, rock faces, a forestry fence, a boggy area, a patch of shimmering birches. Just as the 100-foot roll of film came to an end, I saw her join her eaglet, which she must have spotted from my side of the loch, and which had clearly seen her coming.

In dry periods, I finished repairing and painting the roof. While I knew my days there were coming to an end, I still loved the place and wanted to leave it in good shape. At the end of the last athletic day of climbing the ladders I went out before dusk to look again at my handiwork. My attention was soon distracted by an extraordinary battle between two stags which I could see taking place on a small ridge across the burn to the north east, just above the level of the roof.

The lower stag was with six hinds and he looked black after daubing himself in peat. He had taken umbrage at a lighter-coloured stag that was standing higher on the ridge and looking enviously at the hinds. Slowly the black-daubed beast walked towards the rival, which just stayed still and watched it approach. Then down went the heads . . . CLASH . . . and they were striving with strength and agility to assert dominance. The dark stag seemed to have underestimated his opponent's strength. Perhaps because he was on the lower side of the slope and thus had gravity against him, he soon began to lose ground. The light beast shoved him back on to his haunches until his backside touched the ground and he rolled over, toppling down the side of a rockface in a full backward somersault. The black stag hit his head hard on the ground, and I saw one antler break off as he rolled awkwardly on to his side. I felt sure he had broken a leg. But he got up, struggling to find his feet, and walked slowly away, badly shaken by the encounter. The victor watched him leave, apparently without further rancour, and then moved back among the hinds which were now his own 'harem'. It had been too dark to film any of it, dammit!

A producer at Tyne Tees Television, who had shown interest in my films and was sending me reels of negative and developing them free, had urged me to take seasonal material, and to film myself going about normal chores, for they wanted the human element too. I panned the camera across the cottage, the woods and hills in their blazing autumn colours, then tried to film myself at the seasonal task of gathering firewood. There was an old larch tree which had fallen across another in the east wood; I would cut it up. I got the powerful chain saw going, started the first cut, then after sighting it up, I set the movie camera on a rock and pressed the motor button. When I dashed back, seized the chain saw and continued the cut, I was surprised to find that although there was no-one about, I felt highly embarrassed! I made an error of judgement and, for the first time in many years, got the saw pinched so badly in the trunk of the tree that it seized up with a choking noise, leaving me unable to extract it. I certainly would not let anyone see that amateurish mistake. I hurried to turn off the ciné camera, then had some hard and dangerous work with a bucksaw to complete the cut, drop the larch, and free my chain saw. That was the first and almost last time I ever tried to film myself doing anything.

It was growing colder by the day. While I was sitting at the desk one afternoon, my hands felt strange and I was astonished to find that the tips of all my fingers had gone chalky white and had lost their feeling. What on earth was this? I lit the paraffin stove, set it close by my left side, and thawed them out. Slowly they returned to their normal colour. From now on, when I was writing, the stove would have to be lit all the time. I noticed that Mickey the marten ran down the logs like an arthritic hare, so it was not just me who was beginning to feel old.

On my next trekking Sunday I woke to lashing rain and northwest gales and, in my frustration, I kept going out at intervals to see how the weather was. After lunch, I climbed up the side of the raging burn to above the waterfall and looked up to the 1,000-foot crests. Flocks of ravens were flying near Eyrie 1, the closest nest to my home but one which the eagles never used. This was odd. I raised my new binoculars and saw something red to the left of the eyrie, below a short but sheer cliff. It was too big to be a gralloch (the gut contents of a stag left on the hill by hunters) and its whitish surrounds indicated it was possibly a dead sheep. There were two ravens on it. I went back to the cottage, and from there saw that an eagle had now landed on the peak above the eyrie.

I raced indoors, carried out the movie gear (fortunately already set up for the martens) and had just got the great bird in focus and taken a few seconds of it perched when a raven mobbed it with swooshing dives. Off it went, with lovely slow flaps. I could see the white wing patches denoting an immature bird. Maybe it was Atalanta's eaglet of the year; certainly the raven knew it was a youngster and kept up the pursuit until both went over the crest. Seconds later the eaglet came back and landed lower down. I shifted the tripod and got it again, flying off as two ravens mobbed it.

If only I could film eagles at a carcass, to heck with rutting stags. I could film them at any time during the season.

Donning my trekking clothes, selecting movie equipment carefully to get the backpack's weight down to 52lbs, I began the hard hike up the ravine of the burn. With that weight on my back the deer path leading along the top of sheer 40-foot drops to jagged granite was dangerous. I came out safely, negotiated the steeps above the western tributary, clambered up through the birch groves, over the tussocky dells and stalked my way up to a ridge that was topped by tall clumps of browning bracken. There were some flattish rocks. I found a low one at precisely the right slant for my tripod. What luck! I set up, poked the long lens cautiously through the bracken, focussed on to the carcass – an old ewe – and waited. Two hooded crows flew over. Ravens quarked gutturally afar off, and I spent a cold hour in the hard wind before I saw one raven flying towards the carcass.

I pressed the button, eye to the viewer, just in time to film the raven sail in, land and tuck into the flesh. Then came another, hovering, hanging in the sky like a black bat, beak and eyes staring down in the sunlight. A third came, a fourth, and finally there were five ravens at the carcass, tugging away with their beaks, constantly changing positions, flying up, and down again. It all looked superb. A buzzard came over, landed on the eyrie peak, and my heart pumped faster as I thought I was in for a bonus, but two ravens chased it away, damn them!

When the ravens had gone again, I hiked on up the almost sheer turfy ground, my calves aching from the weight. I was over the first tops at 1,500 feet, plodding through soggy tussocks, sure I had not the steam for a ten-miler this day, when I heard a brief bull-like roaring ahead over the next ridge. A rutting stag stood with three hinds not more than half a mile away. I stalked him, crawling through wet grasses at the end, and found another flat rock, slanting at just the right angle. What luck again! I filmed him staring at a lying hind, tongue leering from the side of his mouth, as if willing her to get up and stand for him. I went on to record stags running, roaring, backing away from each other at the last moment before an actual clash, hinds grazing in attractive positions, and much other useful footage before starting the knee-cracking descent home. It had been a fabulous day!

I paid for it later, however, with pains in the centre of my gut. While I was stumbling round the estate with heavy backpack in driving rain on my early morning drill I heard a number of ravens croaking in the east wood. I went to investigate and was astonished to find eleven ravens circling the trees. I had not seen such a large gathering so close to home before. They hung over my head, but I could find no carcass that might have attracted them. The atmosphere was gloomy and ominous, and I remembered with foreboding the ancient legend that held the sight of a raven before breakfast to be a signal of death.

A short time later all the ravens assembled in the west wood. When I arrived on the scene, they took off slowly, one by one, and resettled in small trees on the hillside about 500 feet above the loch. It must have been some kind of autumn ritual, the like of which I had never seen before.

More days of incessant rain followed. After baling the big boat and hauling it out of reach of the rising loch, I saw Atalanta almost over my head. She was coming along the shoreline from the east, flapping a lot and gliding little. Again I noticed the tattered wings. When she turned her head to look down at me, she resembled an ancient flying reptile. She swerved out to centre loch, then began to circle back. I tried to race up to the cottage for the ciné gear but my legs would not move at the speed I wanted. I was horrified, for I knew that this was the harbinger of the time when my running days would be over for ever.

The following morning I noticed a strange black dot on the nor-nor-east skyline. Through the binoculars I saw that it was Atalanta. I went in for the movie gear and focussed on her. She seemed rather weak and shaky and was being blown about in the wind as she tried to shake the rainwater from her feathers and then preen them with her beak. I knelt there for a freezing twenty minutes before I got film of her flying off, turning south with her tattered sails wide open, then vanishing to the east.

The martens came early when the rain ceased two nights later. Michelle arrived first, while the light was still good, and took a titbit from my hand. I threw out some more, then went to the kitchen to start preparing supper. Suddenly there came a tremendous crashing noise from somewhere at the back of the cottage. Was there a stag wrecking something out there? I dashed out with a torch and the paraffin lamp and found the two adult martens haring up the roof-painting ladder, running along the apex of the roof, then sliding down the far side on to the porch roof, bouncing from there to their feeding table and finally to the ground. Either they were looking for somewhere to break in for more food or they were going to make a hell of a noise until I went out with some. So much were they eating now that sometimes I felt like an overworked waiter.

18

Once more Sunday began fine and clear and I set off over the burn with the heaviest pack I had yet taken. In it I had stuffed a tape recorder as well as all the filming gear. On hearing a great roar from the higher north-east slopes, I climbed to a smooth cliff wall where I saw an eaglet heading towards me from the west. After frantic unpackings I got fine sequences of it beating away to the east, swerving down, then up, before landing on a high pinnacle. I was about to switch off when it flew again, circled and vanished over the ridges. Before I could pack up the gear and set off again Atalanta herself zoomed over the crests above me. As I focussed on to the great bird I realised that it was in fact Juno. Not only were her wings perfect but as she circled in the sun, casually and slowly dipping a wing to turn this way or that, I could see her pale orange eyes staring down and the thick light golden mane which had always been her hallmark. It seemed odd to see her over here, further into Atalanta's territory than I had ever known her.

After threading in a new 100-foot film, I climbed up the steep turfy sides of the wall-like cliff, only to come up against an 8-foot rockface. Back down I had to go, then up the other side until I reached a 4-foot face over which I could peer through the yellowing autumn grasses. There was my stag, a fine young reddy-orange animal about a hundred yards away. He was lying down and all I could see was part of his back, head and antlers. As he was a good deal higher than me, and the breeze was coming from the west-sou'west while I was approaching from the south, I had to cut up to the right, up to over 1,000 feet. The pack felt really heavy on the almost sheer ground. I headed due north below a long ridge, turned west to a huge rockface, crept along below its south side, then stalked back over the tops. Short bracken helped to conceal the last slithering crawl until I reached a flat rock beside which I slowly erected the tripod and adjusted the lens.

The stag was lying in a cleft, the form of which still allowed me to see only his head and antlers. I filmed them moving about, then waited. After half an hour, the wind more than nippy, he still did not move. I whistled. It had no effect. I shouted. One of his hinds got up, so I filmed her. Then the stag rose to his feet, and I got them both looking my way before walking and finally running off. I clambered on, to the right and into Big Corrie. I was met with total silence and, at first, no sight of a stag or hind. Hell!

I staggered on to the north, then saw some hinds away to the north-east. Up with the binoculars. Yes, there was a big stag with them, but he too was lying down. Perhaps I could get him up, shift him into view. As I stalked round two knolls they picked up my scent, as I had hoped they would. The stag was up and moving slowly with the hinds over a small ridge. I waited and, sure enough, they emerged on the next ridge just a little further away.

While I was filming him turning gracefully to his right, a second stag came bounding over the ridge from the north, saw the rival, and the hinds, and came to an abrupt halt. I then filmed an extraordinary sequence. The first stag turned towards the intruder, the two put their heads down as if to fight, then apparently thought better of it and started walking beside each other to the south east. As if by some unseen signal they came to a sudden halt and turned towards each other again. The new stag began tearing up divots with sideways gouges of his antlers, sending them flying into the air. The first stag just stood watching this, but when the newcomer advanced towards him he put his antlers down. The other did the same. Then both raised up their heads, presented antlers down again, but did not touch. The first stag began to paw the ground with his right front hoof. He made a sawing up and down movement with his antlers at the same time, and that seemed enough to put the intruder off, for he turned slowly and walked away until he was over the ridge, out of sight. I had the distinct impression that the two beasts did not want to fight, were in fact 'pals' in that they knew each other, had spent the summer together in the same bachelor herd.

I plodded on, first up, then down, crossing peat hags, little water-falls and small chasms and filming three more stags. One was roaring on the skyline, another chasing a rival away, and the third rounding up a hind with loud '*but but but*' barking sounds.

It was another wonderful trek, but the best thing about it was that I felt no knee or hip pains at all. Four years earlier I had been diag-nosed as suffering osteo-arthritis, due to the damp conditions, yet now I was carrying more than 60lbs, three times the normal pack weight, and there was no longer any sign of it. It seemed that one of my little wilderness philosophies – 'Get tough or die' – had some validity after all. I applied the same thinking to my stomach, despite admonitions from a friend with a degree in hygiene (or some such discipline) about the dangers of 'salmonella' and how I should never mix raw, cooked or frozen meats, or eat meat that was even slightly off. With just a tiny calor gas fridge, I had been doing all these things for years with no ill effects apart from occasional loose bowels. I believe that just as it's good to give muscle a lot of work to do, so it must be all right, in some degree, to give the gut some problems to solve too. In that way it learns and adjusts.

Speaking of stomachs, I was amazed the following night when Mickey came through the window and stood on the inner shelf, licking raspberry jam from the titbit in my fingers. After a few seconds of this, with the cold air blasting through into the study, I said quietly –

'Eat it all, fool! I can't stand here for hours in the cold while you just LICK!'

He did.

The following Sunday also dawned fine after two days of rain and gales, so I toted the gear up to the tops and filmed three more stags. I was halfway round the east rim of Big Corrie when I saw two ravens diving at a rock on the skyline. The binoculars showed me an eagle perched there, and I saw her pull her head tightly down into her shoulders as one of her tormentors whizzed close over her head. I set up the camera quickly on an awkward-shaped rock and filmed the eagle flying off. The great size and tattered wings told me at once it was Atalanta. One of the ravens performed an aerial dive on her and she turned on to her right side, thrusting out her talons to try and grab it. She missed and vanished over the far ridges to the east. I was about to press the stop button when the two ravens sailed into view and one after another landed with awkward wing flaps in the strong breeze on the rock from which they had dislodged Atalanta. They were clearly looking for grallochs and were not going to have any competition from an eagle.

A great wall of white was moving in from the south west. That meant heavy rain. So I backed down and made for home. On the knee-cracking descents I fell over once and sprained a wrist, but I was glad that yet again I had suffered no knee pains, despite carrying so heavy a pack such a long distance. The rain held off until I was a hundred yards from the cottage, then . . . WHOOSH . . . I ran the last few steps.

I listened to the BBC nature programme on the radio while I swabbed down in the kitchen. It had reached a new low. The naturalist-host and a celebrity guest were at a pond in Finchley in north London, looking for newts. They managed to see one frog! 'Was that a snipe we heard?' said one. I had offered to show this programme nesting eagles, black-throated divers, buzzards, as well as otters, wildcats and deer – all on just one trek, or nature trail. They had said in reply that their schedules were full, but they would contact me again next year. They never did.

Yet eventually they made the sort of eagle-trek programme I had suggested – six years later and with someone else.

2 · Source of All Harmony

The monsoon was back. Torrential rains tumbled from the sky for two days and nights, and I struggled out to film the two burn waterfalls which were at their most spectacular. They were belching spouts, globules, pullulations of thundering tawny liquid on to the immoveable molars of the rocks beneath. Fallen ash and birch trees were being tossed about on the outermost edges of the seething upper pool, soon to be torn free and crashed down the front of the falls to the river below. Both the main burn and the secondary one were shooting rivulets and waves out a hundred yards or more into the loch, like two exhaust tubes from a giant boat. Glittering yellow scum was mounting up the twin islets and a lone cormorant, like a ballet dancer in Dracula's evening cloak, stood on a lone tip of rock, as if knowing that fish would come into the turbulence to catch the foods thus washed down.

The loch itself had risen 12 feet above its summer level and was nearly up to the log gateposts. The 15½-foot semi-cabin boat, tied to its wooden runway, was awash but still afloat. I nearly broke my legs while stumbling between tree roots, up to my thighs in turbulent water, as I struggled to remove the big engine for its pre-winter service. No sooner had I got it disconnected than the wind increased, and as I retreated up the slope with the engine on my shoulders, great watery animals came crashing against the shore, liquid monsters angry at being cheated of their prey.

23

I really needed supplies, having run out of meat, eggs, milk, tea bags, and with only one loaf of bread left (the martens were scoffing three a week), but I funked making the trip this day. The mountain of mail there was to be posted would have to wait.

Although there were fine periods next day, I had to struggle to get the boat out in the strong breeze that was churning up the surface of the loch. Once I got the bow to the waves I would be all right, but then, after moving only 300 yards, I saw a great black wall coming towards me from the west-nor'-west. The gale sprang into a storm, the loch frothed and raged, and I was caught in the heaviest downpour of the year. I could hardly see where I was going, and soon my rainsuit and trews were soaked through. I reached the far side safely, but the shingle bay of summer had disappeared altogether, and the water was so high that I could swing the boat round and rest the stern gently on two tussocks. I tied up to a tree a mere yard away.

With the shopping completed, I made the hazardous trip home and managed to get the keel on to the trolley on the wooden runway at the first attempt. I leaped off, tied boat to trolley, again risking damage to my leg bones as I splashed through the tree roots, and began hastily to winch her up. After only a few turns the winch tore out of its mountings on the ash tree. I used the biff of the next wave to haul the 500lb-boat a little higher and dashed to wedge rocks beneath the trolley wheels. I placed a heavy boulder on the bow so that the stern swung up in the air and kept free of the waves. As long as it did not rain too much and fill up the cabin it should be safe enough overnight.

It was a sunny start on October 24 as I set out again for the tops. Above the burn ravine I slipped and fell. I scrambled up and stumbled on, peering at the ground, panting, hot and ready to call it a day. I reached Eyrie 1, trudged over the top and another mile after the chute, where I took some fine sequences of dozens of ravens zooming over the peak above the 2,000-foot wall that I would have to descend if going the whole length of what I called the 'Killer Trek'. The ravens were diving and performing their odd screw-turns. I decided to film them giving their comical '*gloop*' and '*boing*' calls but found I had left the ciné filter behind. The film would have to be colour-corrected, a costly process. The ravens seemed to be pairing up, the young from various nests choosing mates – or at least companions – for their first winter. I filmed a hind and its calf lying down on a turfy ridge, the hind reaching her long neck back so that she could lick her rear. Then I saw the two eagles heading in from the east. I got on to them just in time to see Melanion dive on Atalanta. She turned upwards, as if to grab his talons, but they did not connect. Her wings were still tatty and her movements clumsier than usual. It was all too brief and soon they had disappeared to the south below my sight.

The wind had switched to the north-east and my hands were freezing from contact with the cold metal of the film gear. I saw a group of red deer far ahead, but with the light fading I turned back. As I ended the film on bright scarlet fungi a vast shadow passed over the one of my head and shoulders. It was Melanion, and while I struggled to thread in a new reel of film I saw Atalanta flying along to the south, level with my head. With her was their eaglet of that year. They soared round and round the huge youngster, Melanion making token dives. It seemed as if they were teaching the eaglet to quarter the ground, to search for prey, and, if any were seen, to perform the kill. I was torn between watching and trying to fit the big telephoto lens to its support platform. Too slow, all I ended up with was a short sequence of the eaglet beating a few flaps and gliding away.

Brrrrh, it was chill up here at 2,000 feet! The lower I went the warmer it became. It had been another notable trek until a moment of carelessness put an end to my pleasure. At the burn I took a large step on to the top of a conical rock, slightly misplacing my right foot which slid off to the right, and, with a gasp, down I went. The rubber patch on my left elbow took much of the shock, as did my right hand which I slapped down on to the rock by my left shoulder, but the inside of my right knee swung over and slammed into the rock. The pain was so intense I gave a yelling roar, sure the joint was broken. I lay there for some seconds, oblivious to the cold water running around my left buttock, until the pain eased slightly. Then slowly I got up and with considerable difficulty hobbled the remaining forty yards home.

It was exceptionally cold in the east wind at dusk. I lit logs in the oil barrel stove and made plenty of hot water for my usual swab-down. What a marvellous invention! It was hard to believe that this rusty 44-gallon diesel drum had drifted up on shore eight years ago and lasted so long. (A manufactured wood-burning stove of similar size would have cost over £400.) It grew so hot that I had to open the window.

As soon as I did so, up came the martens. I was glad to see Chico, who had not appeared the last three nights, back with his parents. All three were scrambling at the panes, rearing up and showing their creamy bellies. As they leaped about the dark air outside seemed to be full of martens. I would soon have to start filming them in earnest, but tonight I was too tired to set everything up. By the end of the month the increased cold clearly made the martens hungrier, for Mickey and Michelle began to come right on to my desk – a good yard and a half in from the window – and ate from my hands. Chico, however, would go no further than the sill. Eventually, to increase the light from the hissing paraffin lamp on the desk, I rigged up three candles and a torch to shine and with a remote control cord (so as to avoid scaring the martens by turning round) I operated the movie camera positioned behind my left shoulder. The whirring of the camera motor did not seem to trouble them at all.

When I ran out of matches a few days later and could not get any of my broken-down lighters to work, I found the loch too turbulent, with waves pounding onshore, to launch either boat safely. Instead I nursed a candle flame all day so as to be able to light the stove, the cooker and my pipe – far easier than rubbing two sticks together for the means of ignition.

Early in November I decided to make an entirely new complex for the martens. I dug up the posts of the old bird table, and the Y-shaped runways which rose to it from the west, and reversed everything so that the martens could run up directly to the study window as they came out of the east wood. Two huge flat slabs of pine, from which I had intended to make a table, were bolted together and set on stout posts to bridge the resited bird table with the outside window sill. I covered the platform with earth and went in search of some really good moss. I found a thick carpet of it lying over a huge flat slab of rock a quarter of a mile away across the burn and carefully cut it away, keeping the roots intact, before staggering back across the burn with the heavy load and arranging it neatly over the soil on the platform. There were even small seedling trees growing out of the moss and, when I inspected my handiwork from inside the study window, it all looked perfectly natural, just like a woodland floor. Would the martens accept it, I wondered.

At 6 p.m., when Mickey came bounding along, he did not even hesitate but ran up the reversed runways and across the mossy platform as if the whole contraption had been arranged like that all the time. It was only after taking the first morsel from my fingers that he became momentarily confused, attempting to run off to the right until he realised that the Y-shaped runways were now facing east.

Chico did not appear. After feeding the two adults I switched on the battery radio and heard an interesting and controversial discussion about the existence of God. When one pundit asked 'What is the sound of silence?' the answer came to my mind immediately: silence is the *language* of God. In ancient silence comes intuition, inspiration, possibly even certain conclusion.

Though this thought came to me instantly, I have always had trouble wrestling with a concept of 'God', for I reckoned that man's finite mind can never satisfactorily define the Infinite. For me, God has to be the Creator of all the Universe, the root of all being, the source of all harmony. It cannot be a master that watches over billions at the same time, rewarding and punishing according to a degree of obedience, and certainly cannot have, as we arrogantly assume, sexual gender and be 'He', or for that matter 'She'. The Red Indians saw 'God' as the Great Spirit, with lesser deities and spirits of forest, river, waterfall, mountain, sea, all with powers linked to the Great Spirit. After a lifetime studying nature, which provides no evidence whatever of a loving or forgiving 'God', this makes more sense to me. If 'God' is the source of all harmony, it is only by living a loving, creative life that one can 'tune in' to that source, that force, and align with the original impulse of Creation. For myself, I can think of nothing finer than to study what I consider to be God's real kingdom – the last wild places and the creatures that live in them. Not just for their sake but because of the spiritual insight, the uplift, which such places give to man. Studying the rarest creatures, the last of the natural world, is for me a mission that has a real religious feeling to it.

I would soon have to make the final decision – to go and pursue the wildlife of Spain or face one last winter here, alone at Wildernesse. Perhaps I had already answered the question when I spent all of a sunny Fifth of November cutting up fallen larch trees for firewood. One 2-foot thick specimen had been blown across the secondary burn and become hooked up in another at the top. It was dangerous work cutting it away in 5-foot lengths, with the

27

trunk crashing down as I leaped backwards over the jagged uneven rocks to avoid being crushed each time.

By dusk, after wheelbarrowing ten loads of logs up the slopes, the woodshed was over a third full, the butts looking far bigger inside than they had on the woodland floor. It was hard, heavy work and I suffered pains in my chest and shooting twinges down my left arm. I hoped I had not overdone it.

I rewarded myself by putting more logs than usual into the barrel stove. By 6 p.m. the air outside was like that in a giant freezer – minus 5 degrees celsius and black, with hoar frost covering everything. Suddenly a bright light appeared by the stove. It had got so hot that the logs beside it had caught fire! I moved fast, threw them into the red hot stove and dashed for water to douse over the rest before I shifted them further away.

Two days later I had another firewood day. This time I felt dull pains in the middle of my chest, enough to make me stop work for a cup of tea. The first snow had fallen and was lying on the hilltops. Looking up at them, I noticed a sudden, strange sensation, something I had not experienced before. My once great desire to climb up there had gone altogether. It was just not there any more.

At the end of my next supply trip I arrived home without my keys. I had never lost them before. I searched the path, the rocks on the shore, and in the end had to break a back window, like a burglar, to get in. I was surprised by how easy this was. Increasing onshore gales made it impossible to recross the loch for some time and I was tortured by the thought that I might have left the keys in or by the van, making it open to theft – though who I thought might drive it away from so remote a location on a wild night like this I cannot now imagine.

I slept badly. Strange pains troubled me for most of the night, high up in the solar plexus and at times in my left shoulder. I also had toothache.

In calmer weather I later boated over and, to my great relief, found the keys lying on the shingle of the far bay. But the omens were not good. With chest and gut pains and aching teeth, with hands going white, with felling trees so badly, unable to climb as I used to and the will to do it disappearing, with the loss of my keys and so on, it was clear that I was not as good at the wilderness life as once I was. I rowed over to the van with some gear and back again, easing the aches and pains only for them to return at night. I began

28

to worry, and one evening actually wrote out my Will in my diary, in case I should not wake up. I began seriously to think it was time – if I survived – to find a small quiet place with electricity and other modern amenities where I could retire from the hard life and just write. Then I caught a cold and my left ear went partially deaf.

I stumbled round the woods each morning feeling old and frail as I squelched in and out of the boggy peat bowls. It was the sightings that kept me going when I wanted to give up – a pair of blackcaps, which were rare so far north; a hefty young fox above the west wood; a great spotted woodpecker hopping backwards down a tree trunk, its red 'skirts' hiding its feet. I cheered myself up by taking it easy and editing down the film I had already shot on a little hand-winding machine. I found I enjoyed this more than writing. I didn't bother to go chasing after the stag with poor antlers when I saw it on the skyline with four hinds in which he was showing no real interest. Chico came on his own at night, never with the others, and I was concerned to see a small wound on his back. Perhaps there had been squabbling and Chico was now expected to find his own territory.

Things did not improve. I was still suffering from stomach pains at the end of November, particularly at night when often they kept me awake, and for the first time in twenty years I decided to con-sult a doctor. It had been gut trouble then – when I had been carted off to hospital with internal haemorrhage and was given two pints of blood. No ulcer was found and it was concluded that I had ruptured a small vein due to unusual violent exercise. (The osteo-arthritis had come to light at a dinner party when my publisher's physician son had given my sometimes painful knees an impromptu test.) Now I saw the stomach pains as a severe warning, and with the hypochondria that can so easily afflict the lone wilderness dweller I began to think I was in real trouble. With no help in my situation I could be a goner. Perhaps I had cancer – my grand-father, after all, had died of cancer of the aesophagus.

It took me two days to ferry my most precious belongings over to the van. If the diagnosis were dire, I would not be able to return. I felt like death hauling the big engine up the cliff from the far shore, doing it in tiny stages, a foot at a time, to make sure I did not rupture my gut. After a careful two-day drive, I stayed with my friend in Surrey who put me in touch with her own doctor. He laid me down, poked, probed, listened and asked questions. Finally he confessed he was puzzled. He could find no sign of an ulcer, and the only unusual thing about me was that I seemed to be extremely fit and strong for my age. He suggested a private X-ray to avoid a six weeks wait for one on the National Health.

A few days later I was put through my paces by a Japanese doctor and his radiologist. Placed between two plates of a giant machine, I was asked to turn this way and that, and twice the machine itself turned me almost upside down. Now I'll hear the truth, I thought, but while the doctor pointed to areas on the huge photos he declared that everything was completely clear and healthy. All he could find to be slightly concerned about was a mildly over-active duodenum, which could cause pain at times, and his remedy for this was to eat more regularly, and not as late as my customary 11 p.m., to worry less and to cut down somewhat on the home-made wine and the drams of whisky. He assured me that my lungs were clear and my spine seemed exceptionally strong.

'What about my heart?' I said.

'That's your heart, there.' He pointed to a little triangular tube.

'It's a bit small isn't it? What's wrong with it?'

The doctor laughed. 'That's how it *should* be! If it were in a poor state it would be enlarged. How old are you?'

'Fifty-seven.'

He looked surprised and pointed to it again.

'That is the heart of a twenty-year-old!' he said. 'I am amazed. I would have said you were thirty-six, forty at most. Do you run marathons?'

'No,' I said, 'but I live a fairly hard physical life.'

I went skipping through the wooded grounds like a schoolboy. Now I would certainly spend the whole winter at Wildernesse, not to prove I could still take it, for I had survived too many in wild primitive conditions as it was, but to get that *film* of wildlife in adversity. Above all, I wanted golden eagles at a carcass.

I had everything serviced – van, boat engine, movie camera; I had my ears syringed and my teeth drilled. Then I stocked the van with winter supplies – lentils, pulses, beans, peas, dried milk and potatoes, flour, rice, a spare 12-volt battery to be powered by my little windmill, and plenty of wine kits!

It was in the gathering dusk on Christmas Eve that I found myself recrossing the 1,000-foot pass that separated my loch from my home village twelve miles away. It had begun to snow in the dark, forbidding valley of Glencoe, and as the van gamely struggled to the top of the pass in first gear, a misty sleet was falling here too. It was too dark to start taking gear across the loch. I manoeuvred the boat engine down the cliff, fetched the petrol tank from its hiding place in the woods, upturned the boat, heaved it down to the water's edge, and camped in the van overnight. There, in that deep cleft, I could get nothing at all on the radio, and the silence was broken only by the hissing of my pressure cooker and the occasional sputtering of the two little hurricane lamps. It was not much of a Christmas Eve, I realised, but there was a sense of high mission about my return.

All Christmas Day was spent ferrying gear across, mostly in drizzle borne by fresh sou'westerly breezes. I pushed the old sea boat out and screwed on the big engine. I dared not load more than a third of the van's contents into the fibreglass hull which was ancient, frail and flimsy, and could have split in two halfway across in the jolting waves. When I reached mid-loch, a blue patch appeared above my head and I got back to Wildernesse in perfect sunny calm. I visited Moobli's grave and carried the loads up to the house. By the time I started to unchain and untie the big boat high on its wooden runway, the rain had set in again.

Back in the summer I had made a new second runway but, having over-estimated my strength, I could barely lift it. I had cut it in two. These 7-foot half runways were now too short to fit together over the irregular rocks on the high part of the shore, so I had to use them – along with logs and other timber – as trestles over which to drag the big boat, inch by inch, down to the water. After struggling to transfer the engine from the small boat, I crossed the loch for the rest of the gear. I hauled it all down the cliff and packed it under plastic tarps on the shore, drove the van the half mile to its parking spot (where I could see it from the cottage), hiked back and loaded everything into the big boat. The most important items went under the semi-cabin to keep dry.

It was one hellish hard day. Altogether I carried 22 loads up to the cottage, 44 trips on foot, sometimes with sacks weighing over 100 lbs. The older I became the more I seemed to accumulate – ciné gear, films, cameras, records, tapes, players, clothes, books, files, cases, diaries, typewriters, stationery, ornaments, personal valuables, huge photo albums, slide show containers, projectors, cans of fuel, sacks of food, bedding . . . oh, heck knows what else! I hurt both my 'exceptionally strong spine' and my 'healthy' stomach when swinging sacks on to my shoulders and, despite the cold, sweated like a stevedore.

A gale was blowing when I tried to extricate the big boat from the loch. With the winch handle broken, I had to lever it out over the runway trestles from the stern with a 6-by-2-inch baulk of timber. When twice the timber had snapped in two, the boat slipped back, and I was too tired to try again. I had to wedge up its stern as well as I could and hope for the best. I was too exhausted to celebrate Christmas. Apart from a few drams while I read some of the half-sack of mail I had received from readers. I managed to get the oil barrel stove roaring to dry out my bedding, and pushed down some hastily-roasted chicken with unpeeled baked potatoes. As I collapsed into bed at midnight, there was one thing of which I was sure: I should not have come back!

The veteran eagle Atalanta was showing her age, her mighty wings
looking tattered.

A bird's-eye view of Wildernesse and the west and east woods.

Having decided to endure another winter for the sake of the pine martens, I made them log runways up to a new feeding complex. Chico (*above right*), the first marten kit, began to come alone but was always more shy than the parents who sometimes bounded in through the window covered with snow.

The first winter gales made the loch treacherous to navigate and me a virtual prisoner at Wildernesse.

The first winter freeze-up made it possible to track down the martens' den but it was the severest test I had ever known.

Strange goblets of ice formed in the slow whirlpool – ideal for scotch-on-the-rocks.

When the burn falls froze it was necessary to wheelbarrow water supplies from the loch.

3 · For Sake of the Pine Martens

When I awoke, there was an odd glowing light everywhere, suffusing everything. It was a total white-out. Snow blizzards overnight had blanketed the land and closed the pass. I had struggled through in the nick of time. One more day and I would have been stranded on the wrong side of the mountain. I made the usual tour of the estate, found no marten tracks anywhere, but filmed my first snow scenes.

This winter, I decided, I would live like an old bear – early to bed and late to rise, maybe getting in ten hours sleep a night. I would work on a new book only during real daylight hours, which could be as few as five with the surrounding hills at this latitude. I spent a day sorting out my paraphernalia and making a new plastic tent to keep the heat round my legs under the desk. Later I tried to work out a way of getting more from the little paraffin heater. Taking away the heavy top and outer casing, which absorb so much of the heat, I screwed an old frying pan to the chimney and bent the curved pan over at right angles so that it received the direct heat and deflected the fumes. On the bottom of the pan, now facing upwards, I set a saucepan of water to heat. This worked well for a time. Then I removed the lefthand desk drawer and nailed a platform of stout wire netting in its place, on which I installed another broader pan of water, with the heater (minus the deflecting frying pan) placed directly beneath it. This contraption proved even more efficient at heating the water and deflecting the fumes. The broad pan prevented the desk from catching fire.

I could do more. I set two 25-litre balons of home-made wine to ferment in front of my knees inside the desk tent. I also hung laundry to dry on wires fixed along the sides of the desk inside the tent trap. So now I had warm air around my legs, a constant hot water supply, an airing cupboard and the wine cooking – all on half a gallon of paraffin a day. Only when the temperature dipped below freezing did I also light the firewood in the barrel stove.

By 10 p.m. on that first night of the snows there was a total freeze-up, with no water at all coming through the pipe from the burn pool. Fortunately I had siphoned off a few gallons earlier and used heated snow for washing up. It was so cold – minus 9 degrees celsius, the radio said – that, for the first time, I had to use the sleeping bag under the blankets to keep warm in bed. Strange little goblets of ice, such as I had not seen before, bobbed in the upper pool of the water-fall when I went there next morning. They clinked together with lit-tle musical sounds in the current produced by slow-melting snow, and I hurried down for the movie equipment. It was difficult to get across the frozen burn and I had to stamp through the surface ice to gain a firm footing on the non-slip rocks beneath. I removed a few of the three-inch goblets after filming them and kept them in the calor-gas fridge. They were perfect for drinking whisky – a fine example of 'scotch on the rocks'.

Mickey had turned up at the study window shortly after six on that first evening, and within half an hour was coming through the open window to feed from my hand as if I had never been away. In the past it had taken him four days to re-establish contact after my absence. Michelle would not at first take food from my fingers when she turned up the next evening, though she was the first to accept bread soaked in chicken fat. I expected them to have driven young Chico away by this time, to find his own patch, but I was mistaken, for soon afterwards he turned up with them, though he remained below, milling about nervously on the old wildcats' cage-trap. Only after his parents had gone did Chico poke his head over the mossy platform outside the window, scampering off into the bushes with each morsel he could reach without actually setting foot above the edge of the platform. This nervousness continued, despite the parents being as tame as ever, even venturing on to my desk and allowing me to film them inside. After a while Chico appeared beside Michelle who seemed to leave scraps for him, which suggested that the youngster was not yet being firmly driven away.

On the morning of New Year's Eve I attempted to snow-track the martens. To my surprise, I saw that they had headed down to the south side of the west wood. With little snow remaining under the trees I skirted round the outside and picked up their tracks again in the north-west corner where they ran out on an open, boggy, snowless area near some rocky cairns. I disturbed a hind and its calf grazing there and searched the snowy tops of the great cairn boulders, but nothing did I find. They were more exasperating to track than foxes.

I did not follow my usual New Year ritual of camping out in the woods to renew my commitment to the wilds. I had come to see time as indivisible, each day as the start of a new year, every hour of every day meaningful, instead of just one man-made marker every 365 days. I swizzled the hands of the clock round so that I should not know when it was precisely midnight, ate supper indoors, played some of my favourite music and went to bed when I felt like it. I had a little more to do in these wintry hills but knew the end was approaching.

Wood chopping had to be done in the morning. Full coffers in both the kitchen and the study had run out after only nine days, and this without the barrel stove lit all the time. I set up the chopping block and went to work, but the axemanship in which I had taken such pride seemed blunted. I puffed, missed shots and often got the axe-blade stuck. Was I out of practice or just in the grip of advancing age?

By January 3 I needed to post some letters and, knowing that it would be impossible to negotiate the steep icy pass in the van, I decided to cycle to a letter box I knew to be only three miles from the loch shore opposite. Instead of the rainwater that usually needed baling from the boat I found a solid three-inch block of ice, which I merely lifted out. It was even colder on the other side of the loch under the north-facing mountain slopes which the low winter sun (when there was any) never reached. All the trees here were covered in hoar frost and the frozen vegetation on the cliff climb to where the van was parked cracked and snapped off underfoot. It was the coldest bike ride I have ever known, the frozen ruts in the rough forestry road doing everything to hurl me off the machine. My fingers were

35

white after the first mile, despite two pairs of gloves. Under a new balaclava helmet my ears lost all feeling and I dismounted to try to warm my hands in the crook of my knees. On returning, I could not face sitting in the open boat before I had driven the van for a couple of miles in first gear to get the heater going so that I could warm up.

That night I made the martens work harder for their snacks. With the filming gear set up in place, I held out whole slices of bread to Mickey and Michelle as they came through the window, keeping a firm grasp so that they had to tug hard to dislodge just one mouthful. On the previous evening I had succeeded in filming Mickey licking margarine and jam from the tip of a knife. He then licked the remaining smears off my hand and even took titbits from the centre of my palm, standing there to chew them and dropping crumbs back into my hand as if it were a bowl. When Michelle did the same after watching him, she took a sharp bite at my finger. It did not break the skin and was certainly a mistake on her part for she never bit me again.

Chico appeared once more but stayed below on the box cage. He ate the chicken scraps I had thrown out and took some bits from my hands at the window sill. This went against all the books which maintained that young martens cut loose on their own by late autumn – though he kept out of the way of his elders.

The martens arrived just after 5 p.m. next day and I took the best head-on shots of them coming through the window by putting the camera tripod where my typewriter normally stood. Chico appeared over an hour later and I put out some bits for him, but Michelle snaffled them first. I gave her a big bit and put out more for Chico, but she came back again and then drove him off. Not until she had been gone for a good ten minutes did Chico return. He was far more nervous now, dashing in circles over the mossy platform, on to the sill, down to the old trap, back up to the moss, as he worked out where precisely the food was. Then a quick snatch in his teeth, and he was away with the morsel. Once he managed to get a whole slice with jam and nut remnants. He paused briefly when taking it, as if he could not quite believe his luck, then looked enormously pleased as he galloped clumsily away under its weight into the gloom.

I spent the whole of a sunny Sunday outdoors shovelling fine earth from molehills into the wheelbarrow, putting some on the vegetable garden and some in the giant compost rotovator. I layered it with raked-up leaves and the contents of my non-chemical loo. I took out many small trees and runty bushes that were about to take over my front pasture, leaving only the best young oaks and birches. An hour was spent cutting off new brambles. I chopped a few barrow-loads of firewood and carried a couple of big logs up from the east wood before it began to grow dark. The weak sun had briefly melted my waterpipe, so I filled up the kitchen containers before it froze again during the night.

After a good deal of procrastination I had begun a new book, mainly about eagles, which was to become eventually *On Wing and Wild Water*. I loathed starting a book, the awesome concentration needed to marshal facts into a pithy and interesting narrative, the business of actually sitting there with a blank piece of paper in the typewriter and nothing coming into one's head, and was not feeling in a fit state to be called to arms again at this time. In the first day somehow I got down 750 words which, if not in final form, at least broke the agonising spell. I suffered shooting pains down my left side in the night as well as aching hips – no doubt the result of the icy bike ride. Working in the wintry sun helped to loosen me up and I was back at my desk, at work again on the book, when Calum, the estate's new young stalker, called next morning after culling some red deer hinds in my vicinity. He told me he had taken only 11 stags from the 9-mile ground instead of the usual 15. I was glad to hear this for, while red deer have been increasing overall in the Highlands, the ratio of good stags to hinds in my particular region had gone down. He gave me his recent fox sightings, two of which coincided with mine, then I walked with him to the far end of the west wood.

That night the martens came an hour late, well after 6 p.m. They were exceptionally hungry, leaping over each other on to the desk, and could hardly wait for me to cut up the jammy squares. To my amazement, Chico came while his parents were there and tried to join in. I did not see them actually persecute him but he was still smaller, weaker, more hesitant, and just got brushed aside as they shot in and out of the window. Once, when Michelle was trying to back away through the window with a titbit in her mouth, Mickey appeared to mount her and started making what looked like copulating movements. At first I was sure he was trying to mate with her, but then realised he was trying to scrape her backwards beneath him with his paws in order to shift her out of the way of the food. When the adults were satiated – about twenty squares each – I made sure that Chico got all he wanted, a mere six pieces.

In showers of fine drizzle next day it turned mild enough for me to remove two of the four sweaters I now wore at my desk and go outside for a break. While in the east wood I was thrilled to see a male eagle wafting past Eyrie 1 with a twig in his beak. My attention was distracted, however, by a thudding noise at my feet. I looked down to find a huge hen pheasant pecking at my boots. The involuntary step backwards that I took did not seem to alarm her, and she carried on pecking among the leaves. This was ridiculous! I had heard that the estate was starting pheasant shooting, and Calum must have dropped off this bird in my woods. He had probably reared it from a chick and the bird had become *too* tame – a pest around and in the house – and so he had off-loaded her on to me. Though she was clearly not afraid, every time I bent to pick her up, she hopped an inch or two beyond my outstretched hands. Well, there was no point in wasting a chance like this. She might disappear as quickly as she had come. I went in for the movie gear and got some fine shots of her.

There was no sign of the pheasant on my rough walk next morning. I had just settled back to the book when I saw her strutting past the bird table. I threw out some lentils and pearl barley, which she pecked up avidly before settling down for the day in my porch. She wouldn't last long with the martens around.

I decided to risk a supply trip after two milder days. Thank goodness I no longer had to endure the 13-mile round boat trip in winter to my old landing place near the lower end of the loch. Having crossed the water and got the van over the pass, I decided to take a hard hilly 12-mile ride on the bike to keep my legs in good trim. When I pulled up to greet Allan Peters as he stopped his car, I forgot that both my feet were strapped into the pedals, could not get my hand down to release the straps, and CRASH, over I went on to my left hip. As I struggled to get a strap undone another car pulled up with a gravelly screech. It was the local doctor. I said I was not badly hurt.

Part of Allan's beat as forestry keeper over some 50,000 acres took in the loch's highest hill, the one I called Eagle Rock Mountain, and he told me of an interesting eagle experience he had had recently in the region. One afternoon, after shooting one more red deer hind than he could take away, he had sought to protect it from ravens until he could collect it the next day by covering the carcass with pennies, boxes of matches, even toilet paper.

'The birds will hover over our heads while we're dealing with the gralloch,' he said, 'and in half a day and half the next morning before I could get back, they could wreck the beast.'

Delayed by an urgent job, he was unable to drive his multi-wheeled Argocat back to the spot for a day and a half. When he finally turned up to collect the hind, he found two golden eagles on it, with the ravens all standing around a short way off. The ravens seemed angry at being displaced by the eagles and, as he watched, kept dive-bombing the great birds without ever daring to go too close. Suddenly the male eagle took off, flying higher and higher, quite slowly with the ravens following and mobbing him. When they were about a mile away, the eagle broke off and zoomed down in a power dive, straight back to the hind. He left the ravens so far behind that he and his mate had a full minute to themselves at the carcass, free from the pesky ravens.

'I would like to have filmed that,' I said. 'I haven't found a single dead deer this winter – no carrion anywhere. I really want to put up a hide near a carcass and entice eagles down to it.'

Allan looked thoughtful.

'Mmm. It won't be easy . . . I can't just shoot a deer and give or even sell it to you. It's all strictly controlled . . . every one has to be accounted for. But if I ever do get or find one dead that's of no commercial use, I'll let you have it.'

The pheasant seemed to be waiting for me by the porch when I got home. I did not really want her killed by the martens, so I laid a trail of grain into the kitchen. She immediately pecked her way along it, but as soon as I appeared in the room she threw herself at the window and began flailing at the glass. I thought she would soon tire and settle down, then she could spend the night safely indoors. But she became more and more frantic to get outside, so I caught her like a chicken. She went calm, did not try to peck and I let her go outside. I tried to keep watch on her, to see where she would hide, and last saw her on the path near the rhododendron bush. When I looked back a few seconds later, she was gone. I went out and searched. There was no sign of her anywhere. A pheasant's ability to hide, when it decides to, is extraordinary. On picking her up, I had also noticed she had no smell at all.

I was worried when the martens came because Mickey kept sniffing the air to the west. I wondered if he were somehow picking up the pheasant's scent. He came back for third helpings at well past eight o'clock and I reckoned maybe the bird was safe for another night. He came trundling across my desk, his dark eyes intent on what I was holding. I could not resist stroking him along the back with my left hand. He felt it, gave a brief '*chhrem*' huffy growl but did not snap at me or my hand. Chico came along later and, for the first time, crossed the sill to take a bit from my fingers, making several tight agonising circles before he plucked up enough courage.

By mid-January it was colder than I could ever remember, and at nights I sometimes found myself shivering inside the sleeping bag under the blankets. Once, before dousing the paraffin lamp, I looked round at the shelves of animal skulls I had collected – the wildcats, otters, martens, foxes, badgers, and the five sets of red deer stags' heads and antlers. They represented thousands of foot-trekking miles, all these skulls, and all seemed to be staring at me. I shivered again. Mine will soon be among them, I thought.

To hell with such sentiments I told myself next day, which dawned calm for a change – and to hell with the desk. I packed some 50 lbs of movie gear, took the small boat with the 4-hp engine and boated down to the second bay. I hiked up the steep loch-side ridges and came to a huge dip which I had forgotten. I groaned and plunged down it before climbing on up again. I wanted to see the main eyries, 27 and 28, still a good mile off, the first at about 1,200 feet, the higher crag at nearly 1,600 feet, rising almost sheer. The great corrie in between was filled with ice sheets. When I could not work my way round them, I trod very carefully indeed – a fall with a 50lb pack could be dangerous. I was nearing the far side, ready for the steep climb up to the nests, disappointed that I had seen no eagles and that the light was getting worse, with pale violet cloud piling in from the south east, when I saw her.

I had just taken the first steps up through the frozen tussocks when Atalanta came beating along from the west. She sailed past both eyries, as massive and dark as ever. I slung down the pack, feverishly extracted everything and just got set up on a flat rock when the eagle swooped up with great folding sweeps of her huge wings and landed on a skyline boulder, like some mythical gorgon. I got on to her and shot forty feet of film of her facing away from me but looking about, raising her tail twice and finally ejecting faeces. I had found no deer or sheep carrion, but she must have been eating *something*. So as not to waste film, I pressed the stop button. The eagle immediately took off! But I got on to her fast for a flying sequence as she vanished to the east. I was far from sure that it *was* Atalanta. The eagle was too far off to be certain. I took good sequences of the eyries and cliff faces, then climbed up to check Eyrie 28. Nothing new on the nest there, so I scrambled down, using my hands to steady myself on the steep frozen ground. I then went to check the long ledge of Eyrie 27, which was excellent for filming. (It was the one on the cover of the first edition of *Golden Eagle Years*.)

It looked good, with plenty of white winter grass laid across it, but when I went further round and saw the birch tree roosting site, my spirits really rose. Preened eagle feathers were everywhere on the rowans, birches and clinging to old bracken and other vegetation. There were fresh white splashes on the ground, but the icy conditions prevented me from climbing up to the ledges for regurgitated winter pellets. My reward for getting halfway up was a superb broad secondary eagle-wing feather to add to my collection. So as not to spoil its delicate membranes I shoved its quill through my bush hat and lodged it in my hair. The three fox dens below the cliffs were all empty.

The arthritis that had plagued my knees until I trebled the weight in my pack two years ago had not returned to trouble me. But, by heaven, all the small bones in each foot were hurting. Little granite rocks, or rock ends, stuck out at all angles from the steep turf, and I could never put my feet down the same way twice. Yet I moved easily and began to feel that I was the human monarch of these hills. The youthful years were over but I was more canny now. Before setting off I worked out precisely what I was looking for, decided what I wanted from the start. With such weight to carry there could be no more idle wandering. What I needed was a pair of youthful, quietly-garbed helpers who would do *exactly* what I told them. Then great film could be taken.

After an icy slow passage home, I hurried up the path to get the barrel stove going. Near the top the pheasant I now called Phyllis appeared. At first she seemed nervous, but the moment I stretched my hand out towards her, she came running over. She had a comical way of asking for food. She would start looking all over the ground, up at me, back down to the ground, and up at me again. I slung her a handful of soup-mix seeds and went in. Blocks of ice had formed inside my windows. I stoked up the stove, filling it as never before, got it roaring and had three big pans of water heating up along its top. I had never used up all the shed's logs in any winter and there was no sense in being a miser with firewood when I had so much of it around me. The task of cutting it, transporting it hundreds of yards, chopping it up and getting it into the house, however, was becoming a bore.

Every night now, after working on my book, I persevered in trying to make the martens tamer. Soon Michelle tolerated my briefly stroking her back, sliding my hand along her tail, but both martens growled if my hand went too near their heads. Once Michelle, who took food far more delicately than Mickey, went so far across the desk I could easily have cut off her escape route with an arm. These little moments of exceptional trust from completely wild creatures were always heartening. Chico, who now always came alone, never tolerated being touched by me at all.

When Sunday January 20 dawned fine, I launched the small sea boat again and used an easterly breeze to help me the three miles to Eagle Rock Mountain. I wanted to film its snowy peaks, ice falls, frozen crevasses for a majestic winter sequence to match those I had of the mountain in summer and autumn. As I lurched along, I saw a huge eagle soaring eastwards above Eyrie 27 with a twig in her talons. Through the field glasses I could see it was lighter-coloured Juno. Once more she was on Atalanta's territory. I saw her drop the twig (not on the eyrie!), turn towards me, swing to the north east, then head north west before disappearing below the skyline. Was she making a new nest somewhere over there?

Beaching the boat, I slung the pack on my back and began the long hard climb. Above 700 feet snow covered everything, making all the little tufty ledges slippery. I reached Eyrie 30 in the main gorge (Juno's best because one could look down on it) and took the main panning sequence I had come for. I hiked further into the mountain's heart to film a huge icefall, and even some fox and badger tracks in the snow at over 1,000 feet. I checked below the male eagle's two main roosts for pellets for the government's eagle survey – vital in determining what eagles ate in winter – but did not find any. I could not cross the deep iced-up gorge at that point so I traversed back half a mile down it, crossed the frozen burn, and headed back up to check another roost high above the gorge. It was being used and I picked up a brand new chest feather. I cleared a fair amount of snow with my feet and hands but again found no pellets. The ground was almost sheer here and the 48lb pack made me top heavy. One slip on a snowy ledge and one would be away to a cold, bouncing, gouging death, so I took it really slowly.

To reach the lower Eyrie 34, the one I had filmed last year, I took a new route and kept coming to icy little cliffs. I had to keep cutting down to the south and back up to the north to avoid them. I was heading round and below the rough steep rock buttresses that bulged to the west of the eyrie I wanted when I found a nest I did not know about. This, Eyrie 41, was an old nest which would be fine to film for there was a deeply heathered knoll opposite it. I climbed up and found another roost but still no pellets. I headed on down to check Eyrie 34. There were no new sticks but the birch tree roost was certainly being used. I found one feather and one pellet, the main constituent of which was sheep wool. This was a surprise, for most of the eagle pellets I had found north of the loch had deer hair in them. With the light fading I hiked straight on down to the burn, climbed the last Forestry Commission fence and wended my way back through the tussocks to the boat.

The little engine seemed fine at first, but the wind had switched to a very bitter north-easter and become strong. The boat began to bang about, making little headway. I cut over to hug the north shore and had just passed Sandy Point when an eagle, which I took to be Juno, came flying along from the west, in the same direction as myself, just above the lochside woods. She looked like a giant prehistoric pterodactyl in the gloaming. I gave my usual '*keeyoo*' whistle and wave, and she dived right over my head. She turned her head to have a good look, then soared up and up in tight spirals until about 500 feet high. Then she escorted me for over a mile, right above me but slightly to the north, before turning off back in the direction of Eyries 27 and 28. It was an amazing experience. Clearly she had been out hunting in the dusk. I had found no carrion on any of her territory this year, so she must have been hungry.

The wind grew worse, and then the engine failed. I rowed for a quarter mile, heaving with most of my strength on the oars but making only about one mile an hour. I tried the engine again in rocking waves. It fired but cut out again after a few hundred yards. Once more I took to the oars in mounting waves and began to feel desperately tired. A strange lassitude came over me, and I longed to pull the boat into shore and just curl up in the bracken and sleep. I knew, though, that if I did I would die, just fade out in last beautiful dreams as the mind lost consciousness and the cold overcame all. I stopped rowing. My head hung hopelessly, my eyes unseeing. I just let the waves rock and buffet the boat, driving me back. At length I forced myself to my feet and tried the engine once more. By some miracle it fired and kept going for the rest of the way home. I was shivering with cold, my fingers all gone white, and it was all I could do to pull even the small boat out a foot at a time.

I forced myself to cut some shavings and got the barrel stove going. Almost out of fire logs, I had to plod wearily to the shed and carry some back indoors, where I chopped them up in the light and warmth of the study. It was only later, thinking about the eagle while I made supper, that I wondered if it could have been Atalanta, with her wing feathers grown again? In the dusk it was impossible to be sure.

Low mist hung over everything next day, and the bluish look to the clouds told me that more snow was on the way. I wrote not a single line but cut up fallen trees all day and barrowed the firewood bolts up through the woods to the woodshed. At times I could hardly get the barrow up the steepest slopes for even my new steel-studded boots kept slipping on the snow. I worked until dusk, my last task levering up a 23-foot section of larch so that I could slide a log under it and cut off bolts without my chain saw blade hitting dirt, and possibly a rock.

After the two physical days, I took my rough walk next morning without a pack and saw the stalkers' boat pulling in below the long wood over half a mile away. While it was true that the activity of shooting hinds was likely cause disturbance to eagles renovating their eyries, Calum would get two or three hinds today and leave their grallochs on the Hill. In this bitter snowy weather those grallochs would keep the eagles going for a fair while. In less than two hours, after I had heard three shots, I saw the boat pulling away to the west again. It was well loaded down. Being an excellent shot, he must have got his quota.

Before dusk a real blizzard set in. Now I would be trapped again. Dammit, I had meant to head out for supplies tomorrow; I would need to be careful with food, though I reckoned I could last another two weeks. That night the radio reported that blizzards had blocked many roads in the Highlands and 70,000 homes were without electricity.

'Seventy thousand and ONE!' I yelled.

These regular winter headlines amused me, for I had been without electricity for 19 years. When the martens came through the window later, I got some unusual pictures, for their backs were covered in snow. I was a little worried, though, when Chico failed to show up. By 10 p.m. soft hailstones were landing with breathy thumps in the deep all-enveloping carpet of snow. Now, surely, I would get all the snow scenes I wanted for my film.

The entire morning was spent snow-tracking the martens. Their prints showed they had been all over the east wood, round the rhododendron bushes by the path and along the eastern edge of the west wood, but not among the trees. Nor had they gone up to the jumbled cairns of giant rocks to the north west which I had long suspected contained their den. I went back to the east wood and found many trails leading to the burn – yet there were none on the opposite side. I was perplexed until I came to the giant double bole of a beech tree which had snapped off and crashed across the burn. Their snow tracks proved that they used this great trunk as a bridge, to come to Wildernesse from the east. Once I had crossed the burn and was amid the branches on the far side I soon picked up their trails for they seemed to have been all over the place.

I tracked them through all the snow-covered tents of broken bracken, following many leads as they had diverged to scoop up insects, or whatever, out of the snow, but none of them ended at any den. I fixed on a higher more definite track, lost it in a marshy area, and then picked it up again on the far side. I followed the prints over many high, precipitous ridges, losing and finding, losing and finding. I backtracked occasionally, making sure I did not step into any of the prints in case I needed to backtrack a second time in order to decipher which way they had gone and why. As they could leap three or four yards and the terrain was rough and rocky, it was not always easy to pick up their tracks again. Finally I traced them to a huge, steeply sloping cliff that was composed of giant squarish granite rocks jumbled on top of each other and flanked and draped with the upturned roots of fallen trees. The tracks went down, from rock-top to rock-top, into a small tunnel about three feet up from the bottom. There were a few tracks after this on the ground, but they petered out and turned back.

So, I had found the marten's den at last! Without the snow I could not have done it. The den was about half a mile from the cottage, giving them a return journey of at least a mile, a long way for small animals. Judging by their running about in the woods too – for their

45

tracks quite often deviated a hundred or two hundred yards from a central line – they must have covered another half mile at least.

I hiked back for the ciné camera and filmed as much of this as I thought interesting, particularly the den and the tracks over the fallen beech across the burn. Then I repeated the process with my Olympus single camera. One set of smaller tracks led up the west side of the burn, past both waterfalls, to the big roots of a tree overhanging the burn. I felt sure they were Chico's and that he had found himself a closer den, somewhere on the steep snowless sides of the burn's ravine, but I could not prove it.

As if to indicate that my theory about Chico was wrong, all three martens came together that evening, all fed together amicably, and there was no squabbling at all, although Chico was still slightly shyer.

Another tremendous snowfall overnight obliterated their new tracks. Some red deer hinds, which had used the west wood as a dormitory, were now grazing in fair sunlight on the ridges above. I could not just sit at the desk. I assembled the movie gear, sneaked down to the shore with it all over my shoulder (tripod legs closed up) and then had a tough stalk under and over the great fallen fir trunks in the wood until I reached the north edge and could set up to film the hinds. They were suspicious, kept looking up, and I had to keep freezing motionless so they would not see me. Finally, I got fine shots of them scraping away snow with their feet, shoving it aside with their noses, scrubbing up heather, their necks stretched to full length as they cropped sparse shoots sticking up above the snow. Then I saw another herd of hinds way over to the west, some sitting down, some grazing below leafless trees and a beautiful gorge. I did not want to disturb the hinds, so I sneaked back with the gear through the wood and found a fine smooth rocky pinnacle high above the shore to the west which gave me a splendid view of the new herd. It also took in a wide panorama of the loch and ridges of the hills that lined it too.

While I was filming I heard a bang. The hinds began to run. Then stalker Calum appeared left of picture, climbing up the hill. He bent down to something, obviously the hind he had just shot. He then sat on a rock to eat his lunch. After this bonus I guiltily returned to my desk and completed four more pages of the book. Before dark I would have to wheelbarrow some containers of water back from the burn as my water system had frozen up again.

On January 25, a bitter but brightly sunny day, I went tracking the martens once more and was surprised to find them foraging among the trees over 400 feet above their den. There was a raven on a rock above the spot where the day before Calum had gralloched a hind or two, and another in the air. I heard '*krok krok*' calls above me – three more ravens were heading in from the east. They clearly had wonderful eyesight. Although they would not be able to see the grallochs on the ground, they could clearly see others of their own species gathering excitedly, and wanted to be part of any feast that was going.

The next thing I saw was an eagle. It landed on a low ridge nearer to me than the gralloch area. I stumbled up through the snow to fetch the movie gear. When I returned and set it up, the eagle had gone, but a raven was in its place, with others flying overhead. I may as well take a few feet of them, I thought, and started filming.

As I followed the flight of two in the sky, the mighty form of Juno appeared in the lens. She sailed gloriously in the sunlight, showing the myriad fawns, creams, beiges and browns of her great wings, ignoring ravens which chased and dived on her as she performed circles, soared towards me and turned back again. Then another eagle joined her, as big as herself, showing big faint white patches on its underwings. The eaglet! Once again, contrary to received wisdom, my findings that eaglets sometimes spend the entire winter with their parents were proven. They glided round each other, never once bothering to turn on the ravens. I got a brief glimpse of the male too, though he was about a quarter mile farther away. I kept the camera turning as Juno finally came flying towards me, beautifully outlined against the snowy peaks she was passing. On she came before turning away to my right and passing through a cleft above some leafless oaks and birches to the north. What a superb sequence, and all occurring by chance! I had the impression the eagles were not hungry. They had probably already eaten from the grallochs which would be much easier than normally for them to locate against the backdrop of white snow.

4 · *Battle for Survival*

Just one day later, despite an hour of weak sunshine, I knew that I was engaged in a real battle for survival. The temperature plummeted. My feet were cold despite wearing boots lined with sheep's wool. While at the desk, my legs were encased in a sleeping bag. I sat in two pairs of socks, four sweaters, two pairs of trousers, and even gloves, from which I cut the finger-tips so that I could still type. Both paraffin and barrel stoves were lit. Every so often during the day I went out and chopped logs like a crazy man. Cutting wood to keep warm, and thus alive, was far more important than keeping to some self-imposed writing schedule.

At night I put six sweaters, all sent to me by readers, over the five blankets on my bed, and still I shivered. The radio said it was 15 celsius below zero, the lowest for 30 years. In the mornings my towels indoors were stiff with ice. Outside, on the daily heavy-pack trek, it was painful to breathe, my nose constricting with the cold, and my eyes hurt at the edges as if about to freeze up between blinks. This constant bitter cold, accentuated by the damp, could kill anyone in my situation who was not prepared to anticipate it and work very hard physically to combat it. I could not get water from the burn now because it was frozen over, with little depth in the tiny trickle that still ran. Instead I had to wheelbarrow containers up from the loch. A few more days of this and the loch itself would begin to freeze over. The only bonus was that I could save costly calor gas; my

48

fridge was now a tin box shoved into a deep bank of snow. I felt more alone than ever, for now there was no chance at all of anyone walking or boating in. If I fell ill now, death would follow without any doubt. But . . . so what? I had almost done my work here. What was not yet published lay in my diaries. After nearly twenty years I had really had enough.

Nevertheless, I kept filming . . . a wonderful shot of the iced-up waterfall, with some water still trying to push its way through . . . a dramatic sequence of huge 'organ pipe' icicles, some six feet long, and enough to kill a man if they fell off and spiked him. I made the hard snow trek up into the frozen cauldron of the hills, to Big Corrie, for the best wintry scenes I wanted. I wore the leather-soled, metal-studded rubber boots I had inherited from Geoffrey Kinns but they slipped on icy ledges as badly as rubber wellingtons. Sometimes I had to turn my feet sideways when climbing, like a skier fighting his way back up the piste. No two steps were the same, for often the snow was crusted so hard that I had to stamp each footstep through it. A slip on the steeps and I could slide or bounce back many yards, and all the time I had to pay attention to the weighty pack with the movie gear so that it did not suffer damage in the stumbles and falls.

There were big fox tracks between those of the deer as I climbed up to the north east, and I followed them for a quarter mile hoping to catch a glimpse of one, but then turned back down to the south east, heading for the lochside woods far below. Near the top some snow drifts were deep and I probed with my stick to avoid being swallowed up. At last I was over the edge and the whole panorama of Big Corrie lay around me. It looked like the Arctic! I did an almost circular pan of the icy cliffs, but there were no deer, nor eagles, nor any other sign of life up there.

The best way back was to follow in my former tracks and I made good time, especially as I kept sliding down as if my boots were mini-skis. I reached the burn again and filmed more marten tracks, a scat on a snowy rock, and a tunnel under some tree roots which clearly they were using as a temporary den.

By the time I had got the barrel stove roaring, all the warmth generated by the exercise of the trek had gone. I funked my usual bath in the icy kitchen. Once the study had warmed up a little I spread newspapers on the floor there, set down the hot water bowl before me and knelt like a monk on a prayer mat. It was still far too cold to strip naked. Instead, keeping my sweaters on, I washed my feet and legs, dried them, and put on socks, trousers and boots. Only then did I strip the top half and wash my arms, chest, neck and face. Last of all, with all my clothes back on and a tea-towel tucked round my neck to catch the drips, I washed my hair! I tell you, it was numbing.

After this weird ritual, as I was gathering up the sodden newspapers, I saw Phyllis the pheasant standing on the martens' table. There had been no sign of her for three days, and I was sure the martens had bumped her off. But there she was, as large as life, and looking very hungry indeed. I stretched my hand towards her; she leaped from the bird table on to the window sill. By the time I reached the front door with handfuls of barley, oats, wheat and lentils she was waiting beside it. She picked up the individual grains with her beak so fast that her head and neck appeared just a blur.

The martens were hungrier with the cold and even tamer than usual. I could mix my hands among them as they raced in and out, and it was enjoyable to feel their tough furry bodies brushing heedlessly against my fingers. Due to the martens' great appetite I was running out of bread and had to harden my heart until I could get over the pass once more. I cut down to three slices between them each night.

At last, at the end of the month, milder rainy weather drifted in from the south west and the snow began to melt. When I saw forestry vehicles passing along the track on the opposite side of the loch, I knew that the pass was open again. There were a lot of supplies to replenish. I also wanted to recharge the 12-volt desk battery on the van's dynamo as there had not been enough wind lately to turn the little windmill. I packed the boat and set off across the loch.

To get the desk battery, empty calor gas canister and the paraffin jerricans up the cliff to the van entailed two climbs. I was still breathing heavily as I set off along the forestry track. Round the first bend came my keeper friend Allan Peters in his Land Rover, beaming with anticipated pleasure.

'Remember what you said about a deer I couldn't use for venison? Setting it out for eagles with a hide over it?'

'Aye.'

'Well, I've got you a roebuck. Poor beast was killed on the road this mornin'. I've taken the horns off, and that's all I want.'

I thanked him, but he was disappointed when I explained that I could not set up the buck on Eagle Rock Mountain with him right now. I simply *had* to get paraffin and more food, and, besides, I only had the small boat and engine in the water today. It would take ages to get to the mountain and back in that. We arranged that he would drop the buck on my cliff path, so that I could take it over to my side of the loch and set it up where I liked. During the next week he would shoot an aged stag that was foraging on the lower slopes and would not last the winter, and we could work that one together from a hide.

It took most of the day to catch the ferry and drive to the big town forty miles away and purchase all my supplies. Before leaving I visited the main bookshop, to see if my new book *A Last Wild Place* was in stock. There were four copies on display and, as I looked at them proudly, a good-looking blonde woman of about thirty slipped one out with a gloved hand and began thumbing through the pictures. Here was a chance, an ideal opportunity to meet an attractive woman, and one, moreover, who was obviously interested in wildlife. I wanted to tap her on the shoulder and say, 'I'll sign it if you buy it!' But I did not. Although my heart began to pound, I did nothing. I was as shy as when I was a country-reared youth of 19. The lone years in the wilds had driven away any expertise I had learned with women. She put the book back, and the moment was gone.

Back at the lonely cliff I carried and hauled everything down the muddy steeps, including the roebuck, took it all over in the boat, then lugged the lot up to the cottage. I left the buck spread-eagled in the stone porch. It was dark by the time everything was in place and I had got a meal going. I wanted to bath down but was too tired to carry pails of water from burn or loch.

South-west gales began to blow next morning, bringing milder air and intermittent showers of fine drizzle. This would discourage eagles from soaring as much as usual, so I should be able to get the roebuck up to about 500 feet without being seen by them. As I got out of bed I heard the harsh loud croaks of ravens passing overhead. The legend that if you hear ravens before breakfast someone in the house is going to die, makes some folk fear ravens but I had never seen them as harbingers of doom. To me they are the wilderness clowns.

I filmed the roebuck lying in grass and short broken bracken, then bundled it into my backpack. It weighed only about 50lbs but it felt like 100 as I weaved slowly up the ankle-wrenching, foot-busting, tussocky steeps with it. I plugged away, sweating in the drenching drizzle until I found a gently-sloping open plateau of short heather and grass. I had already cut a thick hazel stake, using the swollen joint of a two-branch junction to hold down the thick cord rather than cutting a notch. I drove in the stake with a rock until its top was no longer visible, then tied the buck's rear leg tight down to the stake with the cord so that there would be no loose play. The carcass was arranged with the head lying downhill to the south east, where I would be in the hide, and the line of the belly facing south west. Thus, if the eagles stood below the belly (which I thought they would), I would have a perfect view. But if they stood uphill, behind the backbone, I would still get good film. If foxes or badgers gnawed through the cord I would have to restake it with wire.

After hiking back down, blissfully light with the pack empty, I busied myself with outdoor chores. There was the hen pheasant to feed, for she kept following me round like a dog – even running behind me down to the shore when I went to retrieve a jerrican of paraffin I had left there the previous night. Seizing a crowbar, I climbed up to the pool in the burn to free my blocked waterpipe, first undoing it at the junction near the cottage and scraping out the gravel and vegetable debris that had come down it. The raging torrent had piled rocks over the end of the pipe, which now lay two feet under the surface. I balanced on the slippery boulders and prised the rocks away. Holding up the end of the pipe – with the funnel jammed into it – as high as I could with one hand, and scooping up jugfuls of water with the other, I managed to get the siphon system working again. Prising the rocks back over the pipe with the crowbar – to hold it down again – was even harder, and once I slipped and almost went over the 30-foot falls. Not until the pipe was secure could I relax and look round. There on the bank stood the daft pheasant! She had followed me for more than a hundred yards through the wood and presumably had watched the entire operation.

Now I could have a much-needed bath. With the thinnest and driest chopped faggots I lit a fire in the barrel stove so that it would heat up quickly and placed a cauldron of water on top. While waiting for the water to warm, I set two 4-gallon containers of red wine to bubble in my under-desk tent. The air lock on one was too high to fit under the desktop and I had to lean the container to one side and prop it up. To avoid the cold of the kitchen, I washed my hair and swabbed down on my knees in front of the hot barrel.

Afterwards, as I typed my diary, feeling refreshed in clean clothes, I suddenly noticed Phyllis standing on the bird table outside the window. She turned her head on one side, cocked an eye upwards and stared at something in the sky. I hurried out. A large female buzzard was flapping against the increasing wind towards the west wood. Was she going to the roebuck carcass? By now it was getting dark, and once she reached the north edge of the wood I lost sight of her in the gloaming. Well, good old Phyllis, I thought. She's actually proving useful! What baffled me about the pheasant was how she constantly escaped, or avoided, being murdered by the martens, for all three were still coming most nights to feed.

After giving the pheasant a handful of maize, I watched her carefully through the window. As dusk fell she crept slowly towards the cover of the big rhododendron bush by the path, keeping her head down deliberately. Then, having looked stealthily about with slow head movements, she made a tremendous dash into the herbage, almost quicker than the eye could follow. Once hidden, she gave off little or no scent. After dark the gales blew harder and the martens were over an hour late. I fed the two adults before Chico came alone, made a nervous jerky run over the mosses, seized one small morsel and fled. Within minutes Michelle returned, took care to fit four pieces into her mouth then rushed off with them. I was sure she was going to feed Chico, which again went against the books. Finally, with the wind blowing my desk papers everywhere, I threw the rest of their food outside and kept the window tight shut.

In the early hours I was woken rudely by a loud thud, followed by a liquid *glup*, *glup*, *glup* sound. It took about three seconds for me to realise what it was – the big wine ballon I had propped up on its side had fallen over, and my precious wine was leaking over the study carpet. Despite the freezing cold, I moved with surprising speed to mop it all up and set up the ballon more securely.

The rainstorms persisted for two more days, but I took many breaks from my desk to glass the roebuck with binoculars. Ravens flew over occasionally, and one circled above it but then carried on to the west. When the wind died down on the second afternoon, I felt it was time to put up the hide. I was reserving my best and biggest one for working with Allan, and the only other I had in the cottage was a canvas and brass rod affair which wasn't altogether satisfactory. The rods held the canvas taut but its bright shade of green was wrong for this terrain. For this reason I carried it up to the 300-foot level and set it inside a triangle of large rocks so that it could be seen only from overhead. I tied on wads of heather and old brown bracken stalks to obscure the roof, but the two front rocks were so close together I had a rather narrow field of view – about three feet on either side of the carcass. It would have to do, and at least the rocks were on a slight rise so that – in theory at least – I could make a long crawl into the hide without being seen from the carcass.

Next morning brought better weather, the low sun even peeping shyly between the clouds at times. I went into the rear bedroom to glass the buck. There were two hooded crows at it. Well, hoodies were better than nothing, and maybe the eagles would see them at the buck and come down too. After a hasty breakfast I climbed up to the hide. The hoodies had gone by the time I got there but returned after a freezing cold hour. I filmed them waddling about and tugging to little avail at the carcass which had already lost its upper eye. I had not expected it to be so cold. Without gloves and with the hoodies gone and no sign of other birds in the sky, at noon I gave up.

I was rather proud of the placement of the buck and the hide – so that I could glass them both from the rear window without having to go out of doors. I could now dodge out of my self-imposed morning ritual walk round the woods with heavy pack because the sight of me would have kept any eagles away from the area. For the same reason I could avoid gardening without any feeling of guilt. The trouble was that I had almost run out of firewood and could not chop any on the usual block beside the woodshed. Instead I wheelbarrowed logs into the kitchen, removed the carpet from the concrete floor, protected the window from flying faggots with wire netting, and after an hour had all the coffers full. Nothing appeared at the carcass all day.

Next morning, as I was putting a pan on the calor gas stove for tea, I heard a faint tinny hooting. Allan's van was on the far shore, his lights blazing straight at me. I rushed out, gave him two blasts on my old brass car hooter to let him know I was coming, scoffed down some bread and jam, wrestled the big boat into the water and went over with the hide.

Almost an hour later we were climbing up the eastern shoulder of Eagle Mountain with the ciné equipment and the hide. Allan had shot the old stag dead in a deep gully which was almost sheer on three sides the day after we had last met. Twice he had seen a pair of eagles at the carcass, which must have been Juno and her mate because this was in her nesting area. The second time he had seen them actually chase ravens from it, and after that the biggest members of the crow family stayed away until the eagles had eaten their fill. How I would like to have filmed all that!

The best hide site was thirty yards across a small burn and uphill from the stag. A huge old birch tree had fallen, raising a 5-foot semi-circular wall of mud and rocks with its roots, and all we had to do was rig up my netting hide as a roof to bridge the top of this wall with the steep hillside. We stuffed it with heather, grass and other herbage until it was impossible to see from the air anyone sitting inside it. Then we cut a square hole through the mud of the root tangle which would hold the movie camera at right angles to the stag without the use of a tripod.

All seemed perfect. When I inspected the stag closely I found the meat smelly, already going off, and felt that maybe the eagles would not come back to it again. Allan said that if the eagles peeled back the skin they would find fresher meat. Neither he nor I had found any naturally dead deer this winter, so the eagles, ravens and crows must have been hungry and well used to feeding off grallochs. Allan, whose job it was to clear the excess of roe deer from the nearest forestry compartment suggested stalking a couple and putting their grallochs beside the carcass to entice the eagles back. We had to move quickly for he had to be home to feed his cows before dark at 5 p.m.

Allan went ahead with his neat .270mm rifle, which held five rounds. He stalked as I did with my camera, against the wind, scanning every ridge, cliff and gully for deer before moving on. After a quarter mile we saw two roe does moving up a high ridge to the south east. He dropped to his belly, but felt that due to a slight rise in the ground they would still see him. We moved round to the right, then up again until we saw the does on top of a small sheer crest. Allan crouched slowly and looked back to make sure I was behind and below him. I knew he was a good hunter when I saw how much time he took to ensure he got a clean shot. He shifted position several times as one of the does moved haltingly, then stepped over a small gully near some birch trunks. BANG! The doe half leaped, crumpled, fell, and rolled over and over down the almost sheer gully.

By the time we got to it the beast was dead, shot through the heart, behind the shoulder. Allan did not even look at it. He *knew* it was dead. He said he had seen the other, a younger doe, head south west and then lie down: he was going after it. I was sure it had run, and kept running, and he would not get it. He climbed up a sharp heathery runner for a further 150 feet and vanished over the top. He could be away an hour, so I followed quietly – just in time to see him spreadeagle himself between tussocks and again take his time to aim. BANG. Allan went off, signalling me to follow. This doe was shot through the head. He bled it there and then, cutting through the jugular in the centre of the neck above the chest cavity. I dragged the beast back to the first and after he'd bled that too, we hauled them both down to where he had parked his Argocat, a brilliant little caterpillar-tracked machine which he used for taking red deer off the Hill. We bounced and jerked along his route home until we were nearer the gully with the stag carcass, then he gralloched both roe and we carried the grallochs up to the stag and arranged them naturally for my filming tomorrow. He wished me good luck and trundled away.

As I hauled my boat out of the water and plodded wearily up the path to light a fire and make a meal, Phyllis, who had heard my engine, had stationed herself by the porch, waiting to be fed. I threw her two handfuls of soup-mix pulses.

I did everything by the book. Up early, in the dark, I boated out with all the movie gear and two sandwiches, left the boat more than half a mile from the closest landing point and hiked up to the hide, approaching the gully with great caution. There was nothing to be seen at the stag, but when I got closer I spotted the deep hole, six inches across that had been pecked out behind the ribs. Both grallochs had gone. The eagles must have come in twilight, although foxes could have taken the deer innards. A quick look to ensure that the sky was empty, and I climbed into the hide as a bitter east wind began to blow. Although I encased my legs in an old sleeping bag I soon cooled down. A raven came down after an hour, landed on a broken alder snag and then flew off again. All that came to the stag carcass to be filmed was a little great tit that pecked and guzzled away at the meat. I tried to read a book. After six hours I was shivering constantly, even whimpering with the cold. Both my gloved hands were white, my right foot went to sleep and I began to see black dots at the sides of my vision. Once, when I turned from the book to try and stuff grass round my legs, I came over dizzy, drowsy, and almost passed out. I knew then that hypothermia was setting in and to stay any longer would be death. Moving like a man made of Meccano, I

56

managed to pack up and leave. Never was I so glad to quit a hide. I was only half warmed up by the time I reached the boat, and I shivered constantly in icy winds as I burbled back to Wildernesse. I should have got Allan to take up some warmer clothing in that machine of his. At least I could see one eagle now, drifting in circles above the Eyrie 28 peak. At first I thought it was Atalanta, but as she flew higher and higher, lit up by the sinking sun, and then went into a jet glide back to Eagle Rock Mountain, I realised it must be Juno.

After landing, I slogged up to the roebuck carcass, largely to get warm again. I was crossing some steep stuff at the 400-foot level when I saw a log with ear-like projections on a ridge above. It was a fox, a dog fox to judge by the width of the head, and it had the whitish-grey chest patch of the last fox I had photographed. I knew Cedric was dead and this animal – maybe Cedric's son – had taken over his territory. Well, it would be quite a bonus to film *him* at the carcass. Trying to be friendly, I called '*Rowl!*' a few times, in fox-talk. He twisted his head from side to side, like a dog listening keenly, but he made no reply before turning round and vanishing, brush-last, through a gap in the rocks.

Apart from the missing eye and a few tufts of hair, the roebuck was still almost untouched, the hoodies having made little impression on it.

Back at the cottage I could hardly muster enough strength to chop firewood. I felt weak as I typed my diary, my fingers, toes and ears sore from the cold. All that shivering weakens one. Making a meal seemed an impossible chore. But one is what one *eats*, as much as what one *thinks*, and I forced myself to knock up a quick chicken and tinned prawn paella in the pressure cooker. I was not looking forward to going into that far-off hide in that frosty sunless gully again.

Next morning I decided I would not. An icy north-east wind was blowing and I saw snow showers covering much of Eagle Rock Mountain, whereas there were none over the hills round me. Allan was welcome to its exclusive use! I had thought the stag meat 'off' anyway, so I would do better to keep a closer watch on my own carcass.

I worked on the book, and glassed the roebuck before lunch. There were two big ravens at it. As eagles often locate carrion by first seeing ravens at it, and I had seen Atalanta – or Juno – in the area yesterday. I grabbed the big pack of ciné gear and stole up to the hide. I filmed one raven tugging at the anus. Another perched on the belly, pecked at the ribs, gave up that and hopped gawkily to the head, where it tugged at the nose and lips, and no doubt the tongue. I was surprised to find I was still too far away. At two hundred yards even the excellent but heavy 500mm Kinoptic lens could not capture the detail for top class film, and as I could still only afford a normal pan-and-tilt tripod and not the heavy tripod legs and fluid head I needed for total stability, I dared not use the lighter 800 or 1200mm Novoflex lenses in these winds. The ravens made some headway for they jerked back tiny morsels of the flesh before flying away. Immediately, the two hoodies which had been waiting on a rock nearby flew down and pecked from the places the ravens had opened up. After they had left I endured only two more hours, for the hide was extremely small. Because of the tripod legs I had just two positions — on my knees sitting back on my heels with one tripod leg between mine, or sitting on a one-inch plastic foam pad with the leg between my knees, which I also had to hug to prevent my back hitting the rear wall of the hide. Changing from one position to the other without shaking the hide was also excruciatingly difficult. I wished I had taken this one to the stag and kept the bigger netting hide for working the roebuck. I also began to think that the site was still too near the cottage for the wary eagles. When all I got next day was film of one raven pulling at the rear end, another one landing nearby, and being chased off by the first, I became convinced of it.

I passed Moobli's grave as I clambered down to the cottage and saw that the grassy mound above it had now sunk to normal level. His body fluids, nutrients, and his dear flesh would by now be eaten away, dissolved. Only his bones now lay under the sods. A primitive instinct wanted me to dig up those bones and skull and bury them in a civilised place, a 'haven of rest' so I could visit them easily in later life. Even as I formulated the thought I knew I could never bring myself to do it; and I knew, too, that part of me had already decided not to stay on in this harsh isolate place for very much longer. I had begun to drink more. While I stuck to my old rule of 'never before 6 p.m.' the one about 'no drinks at all on Sundays, Tuesdays and Thursdays' had gone by the board more than a year ago. I was making wine at a cost of only 30 pence a bottle and a drink seemed all I had to look forward to at the end of a day.

5 · Eagles at the Carcass

Sunny spells arrived on February 9. I climbed up to the hide early and finished a film on a raven leaving the carcass. As I threaded in a new roll I saw it joined by three others, then they all swerved oddly about the sky. I closed the side of the camera and looked through the viewer.

There was a socking great golden eagle on the roebuck! And I had missed filming it flying in and landing! I pressed the button as the eagle – standing uphill near the roebuck's spine – seized a chunk of skin and fur at the middle of the ribs with its huge beak and pulled. The skin held. The eagle then grabbed the upper leg, raised it up a few inches and let it drop. It stepped on to the carcass and gave a few tugs below the ribs. This not having the desired effect, it went to the back again, grabbed the ribskin and tried to heave the buck over. Wings out, legs and feet braced, it hauled and jerked, making the 45–50lb carcass almost dance about. The buck was four times the weight of the bird. In no time at all my film had ended, the fastest three minutes I can remember.

I fitted in a new 100-foot roll, but even before I looked through the viewfinder I heard two loud 'k'yew k'yew' calls, then another eagle sailed in. I missed that landing too, though I managed to capture the first eagle beating away. It was obviously the male for the new bird was bigger and more powerful. I thought this might be Atalanta but it was hard to be sure at that distance, and the male had seemed a little too dark in colour to be her mate, Melanion. The male had torn tufts of skin and hair away with his last heaves and Atalanta seized on the ribs opening, braced her legs and HEAVED. The power of her neck muscles was staggering . . . pull, *pull*, PULL . . . and she actually shifted the whole front neck and head of the buck a few inches uphill. She delved her beak into the hole, pulling off big red scraps and jerking them back down her throat. Enough of that. Ponderously she rose into the air with heavy wingbeats, then literally danced on the rear of the buck . . . up, down, . . . up, down . . . twisting her body and outstretched wings to right and left before she landed back on the rear leg and began again pulling flesh from the holes she had clearly made with her talons when performing her weird but beautiful dance. Once, by pulling hard on the thigh flesh, she lifted the whole leg up to the height of her breast before the morsel tore out and the leg fell back again – just as my film ended.

Heck, it was bitter cold. My fingers felt as if they had suffered frostbite, and I had to have a break from the achingly cramped positions. I slipped out of the back of the hide and stole down to the cottage to warm up and refuel with a cheese omelette.

I went back in the afternoon and filmed the male at the buck. Again he seemed too dark to be Melanion, but perhaps that could be explained by the fact that the sun had gone in. It was interesting to note that it had taken eight days for ravens to go to the carcass, and ten for the eagles – probably after they had spotted the ravens flying down. It was all going so well I decided to leave the movie gear in the hide overnight.

Back home, I was lifting my training weights (which I do to keep strong for the hard life and not to become Mr Universe) when a shadow fell across the window. It was Mickey marten, for the first time in full daylight – just when I had no film and no camera. The little devil!

There was nothing happening at the buck next morning, and in need of some leg exercise, I strapped on the heavy pack and walked round the east wood. Returning along the lochside, I saw both the eagles in the sky, above the west wood and heading towards me. *Damn!* Amid the leafless trees they had spotted me, of course, and they angled their wings back, hovering like huge buzzards while taking a good look. Quite casually I turned north and sauntered into the cottage. I could not afford to be seen outside for a while and spent the next two hours spring-cleaning my study. When I saw from the rear window that an eagle was at the carcass, I crept up to the hide.

I was not sure which eagle it was because as soon as I pressed the button it began to perform – leaping round the buck, tugging it and shaking it as if about to turn it over, and finally flying off, facing me and giving me a nice panning sequence to my left. The sun came out a few minutes later. I happened to be looking through the viewfinder when a shadow crossed over the ground from the left and I shot a superb sequence of the huge female flying in, landing a few yards away, pausing to look all round for danger, and then flapping to the carcass. She stuck one set of talons in the neck, the other below the shoulder, and tugged bits off the foreleg. She did this so hard and fast, just an inch from the joint, that the leg looked like the slowly flapping wing of a dying bird.

After a while the male glided over the west wood and called to her, a sound similar to an eaglet's call but much deeper. Ravens flew nearby too, but clearly they dared not go down while an eagle was in possession. One of them dived at her in frustration, shooting upwards at the last moment in a rush of air, but the 'bird-queen' took no notice. Having completely opened up the roebuck's shoulder, she delved her beak into the red hole at many different angles and pulled off shreds of flesh. Finally, having eaten her fill, she walked clumsily some three yards to the side, her gut looking full, wiped both sides of her beak on the grass, then started looking casually around. I now had film of the male flying off, her flying in and landing, and I dearly wanted her taking off too. I waited . . . and waited . . . four, five, six minutes went by and my arm began aching from holding my finger up to the button. I let it down – and immediately she took off!

Well, the eagles would be away for a siesta now and would not be back until late afternoon, if at all again today. Even though I was a little too far away, I had some good stuff, what I called 'insurance' material. Could I possibly get really close footage of these majestic wild creatures on the last few films I had left? I would have to take one hell of a big chance.

Dismantling the hide, I climbed up with it until I was slightly higher than the roebuck, then negotiated a steep and tricky tree-covered rockface until I was only 45 yards from it. There I found a grassy shelf below a little granite cliff, with a stout but stunted holly tree growing some four feet away. The earth was too shallow to hold the hide's corner stakes securely but the holly tree would act as a bracer. At least it was a fairly windless spot. Quickly I erected the hide and did my best to disguise its awful bright green colour. I tied cords over it and wove bracken and heather through them, stuffed some camouflage netting with vegetation and fastened that over part of the front and roof. Rocks placed in special bottom pockets for the purpose held the hide down firmly and ensured that there would be no flapping canvas in a high wind. Even so, I could do little about the vivid greens of the outward side and the back. It was quite the worst hide I had ever set up and I was sure the eagles would not come down while it was there.

I went back to the old site, dismantled the ciné gear and put it in the big pack, then tramped over to the slopes above the gorge of my burn and headed home. As I emerged by the little waterfall and pool that held my water pipe, I glanced up at the roebuck plateau. There was an eagle already back at the carcass. Through the binoculars it looked like Atalanta. Either she was totally disinterested in the hide or else she was colour blind. I was amazed!

The eagles usually came in the morning between 11 a.m. and midday, so if it was fine tomorrow and I got up there by 10.30, I should be in good time. I cleaned all the movie equipment, loaded the camera, then assembled as much of it as possible so as to minimise movement in the hide. Towards dusk I went out for another look and, blow me, the male was now at the carcass. He looked down at me, paused for a few seconds, then carried on eating.

Only when I went back indoors did I realise my day had been so filled with action that I had forgotten all about lunch. Well, I would make up for it with a big dinner. As I put all I would need next day into the big backpack, including plastic foam, a book, scissors, tape recorder, stills camera, and even a slug of Christmas pudding to keep my energy level high, I weighed the items. The lot, including the pack, came to a surprising 64lbs.

While I was eating my ears began to itch. I found great chunks of skin were peeling off, while hard lumps had formed in the flesh round the edges. They must have suffered frostbite in that bitterly cold hide and on the icy boat trips.

Early next morning I struggled up with the gear and assembled ciné and still cameras on two tripods, so that there was even less room than usual in the hide. I tied myself in, only to find my view of the roebuck through the huge 500mm lens partly obscured. A loose strand of heather had somehow swung across the glass. *Dammit!* I had to undo the hide's rear and show myself by going out to stuff it back. I just hoped no eagles were in the sky. After almost an hour a hooded crow landed, walked to the rear of the buck, tugged off a few snippets of meat as the camera whirred, and flew off. At 12.28 p.m. I heard the loud '*k'yew*' cry of an adult eagle, then some softer, more musical, '*howlk howlk howlk*' calls, rather like louder and slower bubbling notes of a cuckoo. I had sometimes heard these sounds at eyries over the years but had never been sure they were made by the eagles.

I looked out through a side hole and saw both eagles flying over the ridges, coming straight for me. As they loomed nearer and nearer in a casual glide, I realised that here was the perfect situation for that costly 300mm to 600mm zoom lens I had been told about. The first eagle landed on a rock above the buck with two backstrokes of its huge wings, then the male landed on another. They stayed there, peering in all directions, very wary and clearly checking all round the carcass for danger. I could not see them through the ciné lens but dared not move the camera.

At last the large female flew to the grass above the buck and I took fine footage of her tramping down to the remains of the carcass, heaving it partly off the ground as she ripped the skin back further and tore off chunks to swallow. Now that I was closer, she looked enormous, her power even more obvious. Now I could see that it was not Atalanta, but Juno! There was no doubt about that wide cowled head, rounded, dome-like, a vast marmot when she looked at me head on. The unusually light gold of the mane at the back of her head and neck and the big orange eyes confirmed it was Juno. My heart pumping hard, trying to get material on both cameras in case this would be my only chance, I completely missed her flying off with either of them.

A few minutes later came the '*howlk howlk*' calls again, and the male landed. He also heaved at the carcass, less strongly than Juno, and when he turned his rear to me to pick at the lower gut, his talons kept slipping down off each side of the buck, as if he were trying out some weird dance or imitating the side-to-side stomping of a chimpanzee. He was the same dark-faced male I had filmed at the nest, Eyrie 34, the previous year, so this would help continuity in my film.

Suddenly there was a brief swish of great wings, a light thump, and Juno had landed on the grass above him. I panned from one to the other as she looked up into the sky. She preened her wings and patiently watched him feeding. She did not barge in beside him. It seemed as if, unless really hungry, golden eagles will await their turn at carrion, a notion borne out in later observations. I took pictures of the two eagles with the stills camera but the movie lens was far too strong. Luckily, I was behind it when the male finished eating. He took two steps to the side and flew off. I managed to follow him on film but not far, for he went off unusually fast.

Juno was in no hurry and just sat for many minutes looking about. I was running short of film. I waited until she moved, and filmed her tramping down, lifting her huge pantalooned yellow feet high over the grasses so as not to entangle her talons. She paused for a few moments, then bounced on down at a gawky run, wings flapping slightly to maintain balance. She peered at the carcass, as if working out how best to tackle it, the sun glinting like fire in her fierce eyes, and put one foot high up on the buck as she looked down at it. Evidently there was no flesh showing for she removed her foot again, braced both sets of talons below the roebuck's backbone, lifted her long tail clear of the grass, grabbed the skin at the edge of the hole that had been made in the ribcage, and heaved. Now she really meant business. I was more in awe than ever at her sheer power, the strength in her back and neck muscles. Heave, *heave*, HEAVE . . . each jerk repeated quickly after the one before, her feet climbing backwards, wings beating for more force, she lifted the entire carcass – all but the back legs – right off the ground and hauled it more than a yard uphill! It was an astonishing feat to witness, and to film, for what was left of the corpse must still have weighed over 30lbs, three times her own weight. To me, she was more like a winged tiger than a bird.

While she fed from the new flesh exposed beneath the skin she had ripped back, a hooded crow landed nearby, waddled cheekily to the rear of the carcass and began to peck bits off. Juno seemed only slightly put out, and each time she twisted her head sideways to give the crow a warning glare, it flew off a few yards, then walked back. Finally Juno lost patience and made a fast uplift of her great wings. This sent the crow away for good. Just as I decided to capture some of this with the stills camera she finished feeding, stepped to the side, wiped her beak on the grass, sprang into the wind and beat away. Never mind, if all came out well, I thought, I now had six minutes of film which would astonish the world.

I had been in the hide for only 4½ hours and it was all over by

Although the temperature plummeted to new lows, the dry cold enabled more deer to survive than was usual in prolonged wet conditions. Trying to film them on the tops with the heavy movie gear was an exhausting business.

An old stag lay down for long periods, dying. The carcass would have helped with filming the eagles feeding if I had managed to find it.

Instead I hauled a dead roebuck up to 600 feet and filmed the female eagle Juno waiting her turn to feed while the male rent the carrion (*top right*).

Juno's greater size and strength was obvious (*below*) when she began to haul the 32lb carcass uphill with heaving jerks.

At first Mickey overlooked the great tit that had killed itself flying
against the kitchen window, preferring the bread and raspberry jam,
until at last he made off with the bird.

3 p.m. I packed away the movie gear and slid out of the hide. The male eagle was hanging in the sky above me. I grabbed the stills camera, still attached to its telephoto lens, and took his picture. He was not at all bothered, as neither eagle had been by the bright green of parts of the hide. I was sure they knew I had put the carcass out for them. As I staggered down under my heavy load I was glad I had not succumbed to the temptation of tracking the winter wildlife in sunny Spain for I would have missed this unique experience.

I could not work at my desk while the fine weather lasted, so next day I paid two long visits to the hide, both abortive, for nothing at all came down. Maybe the eagles had found a fresher dead deer somewhere else. There was little flesh now on the roebuck. I left all the gear mounted in the hide for the morrow.

At dusk I saw a weak yearling red deer in the east wood, looking grey, sad and pathetic, but I did not know whether it was a staggie or a hind. Such young, or very old deer, infested with such parasites as nasal botfly and lungworm, weakened by starvation when grazing is at its worst, soon become too weak to climb into the hills each dawn to forage with the herds and die of pneumonia. I would keep an eye on this one for its carcass could replace that of the roebuck.

February 14 saw the sort of short but blazing sunny day that February often bestows on the Highlands, and I shot easily up to the hide, carrying just a tape recorder. It was another fabulous day. After a long wait, the male came in with high 'kee' calls, plucking a few bits off before flying away again. Then I filmed Juno landing, clumsily hop-running down to the buck remains with her great wings held up, so large I couldn't get them all into the frame. She hauled the carcass about again, ripped open the head, twisted off an ear and dropped it before delving into the ribs, her great beak working like the precision tool of a master sculptor. I even filmed her flying off and stayed on her for several seconds.

Despite the bright sun, it was cold in the hide for the holly tree shaded it and a chilling north-east wind blew constantly. When I tried to get up to leave I could not straighten my right knee and thought it had locked shut for good. But a few minutes in the sun and some hard massage brought life back to the leg again. It had been clamped tight for as long as all the hours I had sat on my right haunch. Despite more than one reviewer describing my books as masochistic, the truth is I hate being either too cold or too hot, but I will put up with almost anything to get on close, even intimate terms with rare and magnificent wild creatures.

The question that bothered me now was where in heaven was Atalanta? My knowledge that she was old had been replaced by a fear that she might be dead. Otherwise she would surely not have allowed Juno and her mate to stay on her territory for so long. Maybe when an eagle becomes old and she breeds less often, or stops altogether, her territory dwindles and portions are filched by younger, more vigorous eagles. Eagle 'boundaries' cannot be fixed in law, surveyed on a map, and must be under a constant process of change. At the same time, when a young eagle returns to take over a territory on which it was born, it may not use the same eyries as its parents. Perhaps some memory gene is triggered and it uses one or two of its grand or great-grandparents' nests which its parents never used.

I wasted five and a half sunny hours in the hide next day after ravens had woken me by flying over the cottage croaking. The complicated behaviour of a group of ravens at carrion would have been fascinating but I was not rewarded. After lunch I went round the east wood to see if the yearling deer had died. I found it over the burn, and when it saw me, it ran uphill between the old alders of the east bay with what looked like a healthy enough gait.

I spent the rest of the day reducing to firewood another 'widow maker' larch tree which had blown over and become dangerously hooked up into another. I cut off 5-foot lengths, having to leap out of the way each time the top portion of the tree crashed down until it was almost upright again. Normally the tree then falls away from the one it is hooked up in, and you get a couple of seconds to see which way it's going and leap out of the way. This one did not do that. It remained bolt upright, held in place by a few minor larch and beech branches. It was impossible to cut it any further and was now far more dangerous than when I had started. The next south-west gale would send it crashing across the burn; meanwhile I would have to avoid the site. I cut the three 5-foot lengths into one-foot bolts and wheelbarrowed five loads back to the shed. By the time I had axed enough of them into firewood faggots to fill the coffers in both rooms I felt thoroughly exhausted. There was no doubt about it, my energy level was dwindling.

Just as I barrowed the last lot into the cottage, out of the woods came Phyllis the pheasant. I had not seen her for days, and still the martens had not got her. I fed her, admiring her ability to survive.

Both martens came shortly after dark, ignored a chicken carcass I had set on their table and fell over each other to take titbits from my hand. When Chico came alone later, three times he picked up the carcass, decided he did not really want it, and ran off without it. In the morning Phyllis was up on the table pecking away at the bones. Cannibal!

A quick glance informed me that there were four ravens up at the roebuck remains. I gulped down a cup of tea and some bread and jam, but as the sun rose over the hills the ravens all winged away, circling the cottage with raucous croaks. I knew it was probably hopeless, but I hiked up and put in four more uncomfortable hours. I could not read a book as I had forgotten my spectacles. I tried to while away the time in meditation. As usual, when I sat down and deliberately tried to meditate, I started to fall asleep. Any insights gained have always come suddenly, in moments while trekking in the mountatins – a quick effusion of feeling, of sentience, awareness of all, that here and now is the answer, that 'hell' and 'heaven' and 'paradise' are in this moment NOW, and all plotting and worrying about the past or the future are stupid and meaningless . . .

The sky grew dull from the south west and spots of rain began to fall. I packed everything up and carried it all down to the cottage. I hoped a weather change was on the way. While the dry sunny days were fine for filming, the bitter cold caused problems. Sometimes the calor gas would almost freeze in its bottle and so not work. Though the gas fridge didn't matter, and was in fact turned off, I still needed gas for the cooker. I was also fed up with water rationing.

I barrowed five containers of water from the burn to the kitchen, then went out with a pan of hot water and poured it carefully over the lower end of the frozen pipe. Long thin rods of ice came out. I dashed to the other end with more hot water, axing away the ice covering the rocks that held down the inlet in the pool below the waterfall. After pulling free a length of pipe and warming it I managed to get out more thin poles of ice. I tried syphoning water down the pipe but it was still blocked somewhere in the middle of its 100-yard length. I tried shaking and bending the polyurethane pipe in places where it was exposed, to crack the ice inside, but that didn't work either. I left the top end of the pipe on the bank instead of putting it back in the icy water of the pool. It was becoming more than a nuisance and I would have to find a way of freeing it soon.

Two days of south-west gales followed, the rain falling as snow on the hills above 1,000 feet. I noticed that some of my thousands of photo slides were developing an odd damp bloom on the protecting glass. I stoked up the barrel stove with twice as much fuel as usual and spread the slides all over the cleaned floor, replacing most of the glass mounts with plastic holders. The room became so hot on the second night that I left the window open, and Mickey and Michelle had a fine time demolishing six slices of buttered bread and jam on my desk.

Suddenly I noticed that the room was full of smoke. It came billowing out from beneath the barrel stove. I shone a torch under it and found that the rusty bottom had burned through and debris from inside was alight on the floor below, the flames spreading swiftly. The whole place could go up! I dashed to the kitchen for a pan of water and sloshed it under the stove. Small explosions came from within, followed by loud hissing. There was steam everywhere. But soon the fire was out.

The old barrel stove had lasted for nine years since I had found it washed up on the shore a mile down the loch and had laboriously cut the outlet panels with a coal chisel and hammer. Now it was useless, and I would have to make another stove. But I never did. Instead I put a piece of curved metal inside the barrel to cover the hole and went on using it for the remainder of the winter. It was a sign that I knew I would quit the harsh life in these Scottish hills once my film was finished.

I returned to the water pipe after a supply trip in heavy rain. Having carried the last load up from the boat, I went up to see if the thaw had melted all the ice. As I was replacing the inlet pipe back under rocks in the pool the wind died down and clouds peeled away, the setting sun casting pink rays through the trees. Even then I could get only a trickle of water through the pipe. I pushed some quarter-inch piping up the kitchen tap and placed the other end so that it would dribble water into a 10-gallon container. I retired to the study to read the mail and feed the martens. Could Michelle be pregant, I wondered. I poured a drink and became engrossed, forgetting all about preparations for supper.

The hallway floor was aflood when at last I returned to the kitchen, and I had to exert some force to open the kitchen door, behind which a thick rubber draught excluder was holding back the three inches of water that covered the kitchen floor. The remaining ice in the pipe had melted and water was flowing freely once more. I put on rubber wellingtons and began scooping up water in a dustpan and tipping it into buckets. I was too tired to finish the job and went to bed reckoning that it would all drain away naturally.

The thaw ceased as fast as it had come in the bitterly cold night. As I stepped into the kitchen next morning I slipped and nearly brained myself on the concrete. More than half the room was like an ice rink, even freezing over the thin cord carpet that covered the centre of the floor. It was as well I had filled the water containers for the pipe was frozen again. I chopped up some of the ice and pushed it into the turned-off fridge before going out to feed the pheasant. Phyllis was dancing coquettishly on the bird table, bucking her tail down and performing sudden hops to left and right. Was she feeling the onset of breeding instincts?

I heard a whir of tiny wings as I went back indoors and then a sickening thump. A great tit, which had come in through the open door, had panicked at my entrance and killed itself trying to fly through the glass of the closed window. Birth, death, and trials in between.

The boats were the next problem. I found the big boat completely underwater, while the gales had overturned the small one so that it lay upside down with the engine in the water. I wrestled it back on to its keel and carried the engine up to the cottage to dry it out. The only way I could find to haul out the big boat was by propping up the port side and then baling it out faster than the waves could fill it up again. I kept running to the bow to lug its slowly emptying bulk an inch or two higher. It took two hours to get the boat out of the loch's reach.

I felt weak, exhausted, hopeless. By going into the wilds nineteen years ago I had pronounced my own sentence. And now, it seemed, it was being carried out. Age, the loch, these hills were wearing me down. And for all the rewarding and moving mail from my readers, it was not as though my books were earning enough to make life much easier in future. Ah, hell, what was the use of whining . . .

At dusk I saw the weak yearling deer wandering through the front pasture on its way from the west to the east wood. I stalked and watched it for twenty minutes. I could easily have run the poor creature down and put it out of its misery. But I would never again kill any animal if I could help it, either for food or to feed the eagles so that I could complete my film. It was important to let it die in its own time. Nature would doubtless soon take its course, and I would have to work that much harder to discover *where* nature had taken its course.

There was no sign of the deer next morning. It had certainly not perished in the east wood in the night. After a spell at my desk I went out again but could not find the deer.

I began to see some odd lights when I returned to the kitchen. I rubbed my eyes to remove a jagged pattern well to the left of my vision, but it did not go away. The pattern, which looked like the zigzag shape of an old-style electric light bulb filament, grew into three quarters of a circle which I could see with both eyes shut or one open. I sat at my desk, seeing nothing to the left of centre except the lights flashing like sparklers, unable to focus the typewriter keys properly. How on earth would I get out of here if I went blind? I forced myself to stay calm and felt my way back to the kitchen to make more tea. After an hour the lights began to fade and finally went away. It was a severe warning.

Stress – if stress it was causing the trouble – surely came from the constant loneliness and having to do everything myself. I thought I had become inured to that, despite the physical tiring. I sank myself back into my writing.

6 · Feeding Mouth to Mouth

I found the sick deer on the lower slope of the west wood on my morning pack-trek. It was walking away from me, looking back anxiously with bulging eyes. The long-lashed eyelids closed very slowly, making the eyes move loosely in their sockets – the familiar look of a dying deer. I went back for the ciné camera and filmed it moving disjointedly up a green spit in the rocky cliffs below the wood. I tried to cut it off and make it walk the other way so that it would not fall over the cliff. It did not have long to go now.

After lunch the next day I took the camera out again to look for the deer. It was lying in a pool of water on the south-east edge of the wood only twenty yards from where I had left it the day before. Its head was turned back on its body and bloody flesh was oozing out of its nose, probably due to a combination of lung worm and pneumonia. It was not a yearling but a small adult hind weighing about 120lbs. Somehow I had to get this dead weight up above 500 feet for the eagles.

I made a harness for my waist from a thick old army belt and tied a hand rope round the dead deer's neck. Slowly I dragged the carcass up through the gullies, over the bogs and rocky ridges to the top of the wood. Then I hauled it, inches at a time, up the almost sheer terrain to the roebuck site. It took an hour and a quarter to negotiate a mere 400 yards of treacherous tussocks, my twisting stomach taking the weight.

All that was left of the roebuck was a stinking bag of skin and bones which I threw away. I staked down the fresh hind in the same position, so that I could interchange film shots. I freshened the hide with new vegetation, then returned home as fast as I could. After baling the boats again, siphoning off a barrel of red wine and having a swab down, it was gone six o'clock. Few would imagine that a man alone in the wilds has never enough time to get everything done.

I had gut pains in the night and hoped I had not done any serious damage. With internal haemorrhage I might not wake up. There were two hoodies on the carcass next morning, but with only 200 feet of unexposed film left I ignored them and got on with writing a difficult passage in *On Wing and Wild Water*. At 4 p.m. I went up for a closer look. There was an eagle on the hind. It stood, legs astride, facing away from me and seemed to be trying to pull up the deer's backside. Then I spotted something black, flapping in front of the eagle – a raven. It was beating its wings as though struggling to get airborne while one of its feet were trapped, perhaps beneath the hind. At last it broke free and dived down over the small crest beyond the site.

I returned to the desk but could not settle and instead took to cleaning both cameras and cutting primitive new lens filters from gelatin. In fading light I kept glancing up through the bedroom window while I packed everything for the morrow. A hoodie was chased over the west wood by a bigger black bird which had a forked tail. Then I remembered the raven with the eagle at the carcass and realised that this was the same bird, having lost two or three feathers where the eagle must have caught its tail. Imagine filming that tussle and the raven's escape!

Just before 6 p.m. I took another look. An eagle was back on the hind. After all the food I was putting out on the hillside in this poor winter for carrion surely the eagles would use one of the three nearest eyries – all very suitable for filming – when it came to the breeding season. With no sign of Atalanta, it was clear that Juno had now annexed at least this southern part of her territory.

The restful day restored my energy reserves, and when I carried the 60lbs of filming gear up to the site next day I felt no strain at all. I set up everything inside the little hide but refrained from pushing the front of the huge lens through the elephant-trunk aperture in the canvas while heavy clouds were heading over, promising a shower. But I could see enough through it to be able to adjust focus. I twiddled the moveable barrel – and received a shock.

72

The huge form of the eagle Juno was standing close up to the new hind carcass. I had still not completely concealed myself, and my backside, ankles and feet were protruding out of the back of the hide. Even so, she had come down and there she was. I could not film her without pushing the lens all the way through the camouflage netting and arranging the canvas round it to screen it from view. I was cursing, almost aloud, when the male eagle came floating in, gliding at almost stalling speed, and landed, light as thistle-down, right next to his mate. I felt enraged at such awful luck.

Recalling how they had accepted slight lens movements before, I reckoned I could get the lens through the canvas hole safely but the camouflage netting outside had been disarranged by recent winds. When I had carefully manoeuvred the lens through the canvas, I found that the male eagle had gone. With the lens bringing in only two thirds of capacity I filmed Juno in case she departed too. I then waited until she was looking away to the west and shifted some of the netting. She moved round the carcass digging flesh from the rump.

At least I had something to show for my efforts. Now I had to get the lens totally clear, though I couldn't move out of the hide while she was there. My gloved hand was too thick to get through between the lens and the canvas, so I took a foolish chance and removed the glove, poking my raw fingers through, knowing that my hand flesh would show, but hoping she would not spot it. By the time I had cleared the lens fully she was gone. I could see her hanging in the sky to the west, apparently unperturbed. Neither she nor the male returned, however, until I had left after 5½ more painful hours.

There was only 65 feet of film left but I was determined to use it all. I also wanted to capture sounds on tape. I took another chance and, at dusk, carried up the remnants of an old canvas hide with two hazel poles and a sailcloth needle. Carefully I sewed this on to the back of the main hide and strewed grass and bits of old bracken over the top of it. Now I could lie down and so put in longer vigils.

It was soon clear that I had taken one chance too many, for during four more long visits, until March 3, not once did either of the eagles or anything else come down to the carcass. My hopes rose on February 28 when I was in the garden and saw one of the eagles land on the highest ridge above the hide. It seemed to be watching me with great interest while I fed Phyllis. It did not go to the carcass.

One morning I saw the male eagle sailing over the nearest ridges to the west, mobbed by a raven that flew first above then below him. Suddenly he turned and chased his pursuer, which dodged all over the sky to get away. The eagle soon desisted and began to soar away, but the raven's mate appeared and kept dive-bombing towards his back, zooming upwards again at the last moment before impact. The three of them flew around for some seconds before the eagle landed on the high peak above Eyrie 1, directly up from the cottage. The first raven, which had been following, now hung over him, hovering in the cold east wind, with its claws extended downwards towards the eagle. It landed some four feet below him, just as the second raven sailed in and landed close to the left of the mighty bird. Before long they all flew off and both ravens mobbed the eagle together until finally he turned on them, forcing them to swerve many times at sharp right angles to the ground, until they vanished from sight. Of course I could film none of it for the movie camera was up in the hide.

I went out twenty minutes later to see the eagle on the tip of Eyrie 1 peak again, and once more the ravens landed nearby, but the eagle now seemed more interested in staring down at the carcass. There appeared to be no real animosity between eagle and raven. If you could not call it symbiosis, there was a definite interaction, as if this aggressive play were meant to help them to accept each other within the same territorial boundaries. It was quite extraordinary to see the ravens so close to the eagle without it showing any inclination to pounce. Soon the ravens were up in the air again, hovering over him, both with their feet stretched downwards. They were certainly telling the eagle that this was their territory too, and that their nesting rights were equal to his.

By this time foxes and badgers were destroying the hide carcass at night, and I finished the film with some dim footage of a badger snuffling about and chewing morsels I had set out round the remains of the deer. Surely now I had sufficient interesting film to secure a backer from one of the major television stations. Even if the Tyne Tees producer had lost interest. First I needed to go south and get the recent footage developed.

The behaviour of the martens at this time was becoming even more interesting. Martens are of course carnivorous animals, and I had thought Mickey might appreciate the delicacy of a great tit (the one that had met its end flying into the kitchen window) and so I had set out the brightly coloured corpse among the jammy pieces inside the study window. To my surprise, he sniffed at the jam, then at the fresh tit, before running off with the preferred raspberry jam. Twice more he took bread and jam and left the tit. Not until I placed the bird in front of the jammy bits did he take the tit – just as my camera flashed.

For three days only Chico came to be fed, with no sign of what had kept his parents away. It made me think again that they might be breeding once more. When they returned, Michelle was very hungry. She came less often after that, and sometimes, when she did not appear, Mickey would pile up several pieces at the end of the mossy table and, after he had finished feeding himself, would bound off into the darkness with them, as if taking them to her.

One night there was a bit of a squabble when both Mickey and Chico turned up. Huffy growls and muffled squeaks could be heard in the darkness outside as they settled matters in the long grass.

I tried to get Mickey to take pieces of bread and jam from my mouth. I could make him see the pieces of bread dangling from my lips and he would come close, but he kept turning away as if scared of such close facial contact. I made a longer strip of buttered bread with jam and held it in my fingers close to my face. He came hesitantly, ready to flee at any sudden movement on my part, and tugged it away. I repeated the process with my fingers actually touching my mouth. Again he seized the other end and took the strip out on to the mossy table. When he returned for the third time through the wide open window, I gently waved a gooey strip up and down in front of him. Mickey's head also went up and down as eagerly he followed its movements. Slowly and ostentatiously I put one end between my lips and eased my head forward. I tried to hold my breath. My heart was pounding with excitement, and maybe a little fear. What would happen if he lost his nerve at the last moment and bit my nose, or scratched my eyes? Too late now . . . Nearer and nearer came the sharp nose, the dark brown eyes, until they were out of my focus. Then, with a delicate nip of his white teeth, he eased the strip from my lips and took it just a yard away to chew it up.

I suppose it doesn't matter a damn whether I can feed a wild pine marten mouth to mouth, but it gave me as great a thrill as when he had first eaten out of my hand. The trust this act bore witness to brought to mind a passage I had read in *Mountain Monarchs* by George Schaller, a true trekking naturalist whom I admired:

75

Man is modifying the world so fast and so drastically that most animals cannot adapt to the new conditions. In the Himalaya as elsewhere there is a great dying, one infinitely sadder than the Pleistocene extinctions, for man now has the knowledge and the need to save these remnants of his past.

I had written something similar in my own first wildlife book, *Alone in the Wilderness*, published a year earlier in 1976. Reviewing the possible future effects of pollution, over-population, too much tourism, deforestation, mining and development in the last wild places, I had been extremely pessimistic, and emphasised the inspirational powers of the wilderness. I no longer felt quite so gloomy.

What we forget is that however much we rape, pillage, pollute and damage the world about us, we will never destroy this planet entirely; only change the environment temporarily so that we destroy ourselves. And when we are gone again, the latest pinnacle of evolution, or the highest creation of a minor 'god', nothing much will have happened. In a few hundred years, a blink in time, all traces will have been obliterated.

After all, wildlife has returned in abundance to Bikini atoll [where the first atom bomb was tested] . . . everything with which we pollute the earth came from the earth itself. It is in our *concentrations* of these substances that we do the damage. Eventually the earth, our planet, can re-absorb all. Nature will take over and erect the truth of the real 'God' of the universe. And we, mankind, the naked strutting cockerel who had pretensions to 'knowledge' and 'understanding' and 'philosophy' will be gone.

Michelle arrived one evening *before* dusk. I had gone outside to obey a brief call of nature when I heard a thump. The marten dived off the mossy table and disappeared round the side of the cottage. I gave the usual calls and whistles, and up she came hesitantly. Then she panicked at seeing me outside and took flight once more. I hastened inside, threw open the window, whistled and watched her return. She was very hungry and I was able to get her also to take food from my lips. Such a little thing, but how it cheered me up.

Both martens came late, after 11 p.m., at the end of an appalling day of frustration preparing the boats for my trip south. Although the water was as low as it was usually in summer, I had to ensure that they were out of reach of any possible rise in the level of the loch while I was away. The short runways were almost useless in the shallow water. The new nylon rope kept stretching, acting like elastic, pulling the boat out of my control and off the runways when I was 30 yards away at the pulleys. It was an almost impossible task for one man, and I lost count of the number of times I had to run up and down resetting everything. 'Leave the lot and GO,' my body cried out.

Chico had come earlier, snatching all that he could at once and then making off. Then the two parents came tumbling over one another to take jammy bits from my desk. Again they let me stroke them without protest, though I cannot pretend they *liked* it. Mickey took two pieces from my mouth, and after a day like this I felt sure that but for the martens I would have given up this hard life at the end of the last season.

Next day, in south-west gales and light rain, I tried once again to get the big boat higher. It was too close to the ash tree on the left of the boat bay for me to use the block and tackle without the rocks being in the way. I got behind the boat, put both hands on the stern, and PUSHED. Forgetting that the trolley wheels no longer pointed straight up the runway, but instead were jammed into the side rails as a result of yesterday's fiasco, I shoved the boat right off the trolley. I cursed. Without water high enough to float the boat there was no way I could get it back on to the trolley. By the time I had manoeuvred the useless trolley out of the way the boat was lower than before. More curses. I could have shifted the winch from its winter position, but that would have entailed the impossible task of pushing everything out into the loch and somehow floating the boat back on to the trolley and a runway while the water was raging in the strong wind. I was raging too, but I tried to control myself as I set another runway above the boat. I went behind the stern again and gave a collosal push. The boat shifted a yard higher, even without the trolley, but a great pain shot down my back, making me cry out. I must have squashed something and had better unsquash it fast. I moved carefully to the ash tree, held on to a branch and swung there, dangling, in the hope of stretching my spine a little. The pain eased.

I had to figure out a way to get the boat higher. Eventually I moved a big rock to each of the four corners of the runway, then with a fence stake levered runway and boat up together until I could insert smaller rocks under the corners. If the loch came higher than that while I was away, then so be it.

Now for that bloody engine! I managed to get it the short distance to the rock steps below the gateway. With a bunched-up sweater on my right shoulder, I manoeuvred the heavy motor on to my back while kneeling on the grass below the steps. From that awkward position I found I could not get up with it – the strength was no longer there. This was the moment I had dreaded. I held my breath, made a supreme effort, and managed to stand up with it, only to be struck by a blast of wind as I started walking. My foot hit a rock the wrong way as I staggered, and down it came off my shoulder. CRASH! the carrying handle smashed on the bottom step, rendering it useless.

I stared at the wretched machine lying on the ground, at the dark sky, and felt beaten. After resting on my knees for a long time I decided to have one more go. I scrambled the engine up on to the highest step where I could get into a better kneeling position. Down on my left knee, with the right one braced in a crouch position, I heaved, wavered, and finally stood up under the appalling weight. I had no further trouble carrying it up to the cottage, but when I knelt once more to lower it to the ground I was done. Legs trembling, heart pounding, back and shoulder aching, I had to rest again for several minutes. No doubt about it now, I thought. Age *is* catching up. Five years before I could have carried two engines at once, one in each hand. I hate it. I *hate* it . . . !

A laughing, bleating sound seemed to mock me. Five unmarked sheep which I had chased off the front pasture each morning were back again. I had begun to hate their stupid leering faces, their stink, their persistence in finding ways through my fence, their destruction of my plants. I herded them out again and returned to tie up the boat and gather up the crowbar and other tools. It was the moment for Phyllis to emerge from the woods for her lunch after a three-day absence.

Who would believe what it takes to leave a place like this just for a two-week business trip? I now had to repair the old small sea boat with fibre glass before making the crossing, then dismantle the hide . . . clean the cottage . . . switch off water and gas canisters . . . carry to the lochside essentials for the journey – photo files, projector, films, diaries, food . . . As if they knew I was leaving, the adult martens came together again, taking morsels from my lips and scuffling with each other on my desk. Chico arrived alone and very late to gather up the bits that were left. He looked small, thin and, yes, depressed. He was finding it tough in a lonely world. I left them plenty to eat.

It was calm for the crossing. I walked the half-mile to fetch the van, carried everything up the cliff to it, hauled the boat out, turned it over and tied it to an alder stump, then buried the engine in plastic sacks high in the conifer woods. It was already 5 p.m. and beginning to get dark. I turfed the bike out of the van, padlocked it to a tree and camped there for the night.

In the morning I spent a while glassing Eyries 27 and 28. There was definitely an eagle on Melanion's roost to the right of and above Eyrie 27. I drove away with high hopes for good nesting shots on my return with which to finish my film.

7 · A Kind of Cheating

It was not as if I had gone into filming totally inexperienced. Before taking up the wilderness life my work as a journalist had been bound up with the film world and I had lived in Hollywood in the mid-sixties. Soon after I had settled at Wildernesse a BBC team had come to make a film of my new lifestyle, called 'Keeper of the Wilds'. We worked hard for a week, and I was given a colour print of the finished programme. I wondered then if it had been a way of justifying the modesty of the £100 fee that I was paid. Years later, when *A Last Wild Place* was shortly to be published, a crew from BBC Television Scotland journeyed up from Glasgow to make a ten-minute documentary about my wildlife work for a 'news' magazine programme. They also gave me a video recording, but this time no fee. It would help to sell my books was the rationale.

My belief from this experience that I knew roughly how the television media worked proved wholly naive. The films, when processed, came out superbly but they were not even to be viewed by the Tyne Tees producer, who told me the project was off; he was leaving the network to sign on at the Labour Exchange. Channel 4 claimed to be booked up with natural history projects for the next eighteen months and would not be able to look at my material, though I was given the name of a small company which made wildlife programmes for the network. Anglia Television's 'Survival' thought they had covered the Highlands enough but suggested I

Michelle came less often to the bird table in the spring, but it was a great thrill to keep Mickey's company on such intimate terms.

The female eagle relaxing on the ledge while her three-weeks-old chick groomed itself were the rewards for hauling 64lbs of movie gear over these punishing hills.

should write to them in detail, which I did. A leading producer at Central TV said it was most unlikely they could take my film 'on board' but I would be hearing from another of their producers. I heard nothing.

I was approached by the BBC for a programme called 'Scott Free', in which Selina Scott was to profile individuals who had given up urban life for freedom in the country. I couldn't help smiling at the concept of 'free'dom. Was I expected to do this one for nothing too? If I was required to work hard for a week, and to make some of my wildlife footage available, I decided to ask for a modest fee – which amounted to one per cent of the film's budget. But then I was told that the format had been changed to revolve around communities, and thus my life would not fit. Ah well, a 'community' could hardly expect to be paid, I thought. The programme eventually featured a friend of mine who received a good salary from the Nature Conservancy Council for his job as a warden, and who was happy to take part in the film without being paid.

At least I aroused enough interest at the BBC Natural History Unit in Bristol to be promised that someone would view my film material later in the year. By the end of three weeks I was on my way back to Scotland with new heavy tripod and lenses, almost £2,000 the poorer for these and developing costs. And I had no secure salary; only irregular income from my writing.

I took a detour into Aberdeenshire to visit a nature warden friend of mine in north-east Scotland who had shown interest in my filming. Before looking at some of my reels, he produced a bombshell. The BBC Nature Unit in Bristol had been filming sequences in his enclosure for a ten-part series called 'Wild Britain', and some of these he now showed me. He had converted an old Nissen hut near his farmhouse by removing the roof and enclosing the metal support arches with a strong wire mesh. Within had been created a miniature environment – a pool, a stream, little slopes and rock formations amid strategically planted small trees. My friend had kept pine martens for years and these had been filmed in the enclosure, along with a couple of wildcats and some stoats in white winter 'ermine' coats provided by his keeper friends. Wild Britain – in a cage?

I said it all seemed like cheating to me. Filming real wildlife in genuine wild locations was all that interested me. He agreed that, in a way, it was cheating, but how else, he asked, could one film such wary creatures as the pine marten or the nocturnal wildcat at close quarters, especially in their dens? I could see the logic of his argument that what mattered to viewers in their homes was the quality of close up images on their screens. To see close up animals and birds that most people normally have no opportunity to see in real life was obviously the point of my film-making as much as anyone else's. I have no quarrel with any television film of tamed birds of prey or animals kept in pens so long as they are not passed off as a record of the behaviour of WILD creatures in a totally WILD habitat, going about their business as they would when the cameraman is not there. Making creatures appear to be wild and free when they are not is a deceit unless it is made clear to the viewer – or so it seemed to me.

My warden friend thought my films were not far from the magic formula – one part in ten of usable film! He felt that, though the eagles at the carcass was excellent material, it was no good just filming random sequences. One needed a script and some organisation. But all I was doing, I said, was gathering material to show to potential backers.

As I drove away I began to think I might be wasting my time lugging 60lbs of gear up into wild and inhospitable mountains. How could I possibly compete with enclosure filming? Anyone can go to Richmond Park in the suburbs of London with a tripod and photograph a tame stag roaring, even win a 'Photographer of the Year Award' with it. It takes something more to trek a total of 80 hard mountain miles to photograph wild eagles from a precarious hide on a ledge 30 to 40 yards away. Of one thing I was sure – if the eyries closest to my home were not occupied this year, there was no way I could get my hide and all the film equipment to the farthest nest sites at the end of what I called the Killer Trek.

I reached the shore opposite Wildernesse in light rain and rescued the engine from the woods. It took eight sorties to get all the gear to the loch shore. I loaded the boat, covered the cargo with tarpaulin and crossed safely. I saw that the sheep had been all over the place, leaving their shit everywhere, even in the porch. Phyllis came flying out of the woods to greet me and peck at my boots. My bed was wet with accumulated damp and before dusk I had to boat over to fetch the dry sleeping bag from the van. It took all next day to chase out the sheep, launch the big boat to collect the rest of my gear, sort it all out, and set up the 12-volt windmill generator again.

I was going through my notes for a slide show and talk I had reluctantly agreed to give for charity in the village hall, more than a dozen miles away across the loch, when Michelle arrived at 8.21 p.m. There was nothing wrong with her memory, I thought as she fed from my hands. She looked slimmer. I hoped it meant she had young cubs. Mickey did not arrive until the next evening, an hour after his mate.

Allan Peters told me when I joined him for a cup of tea before my show that the field worker who was looking at the eyries on Eagle Rock Mountain for the Nature Conservancy Council's Eagle Survey had found no nest occupied and only one – Juno's best, above a small gorge – that had been built up slightly. Yet I knew from my filming that she was still in the vicinity. My hopes rose, despite the gloomy report, for it might mean she was using an eyrie on my side of the loch.

As the hall filled up I fought off an attack of stage fright by telling myself I was just going to be chatting to a few friends. I was going to have a good time. I went through 306 pictures, got laughs in all the right places, and received a heart-warming ovation at the end. People came up to me for autographs and I sold the only seven copies of my books that I had in the van. I could have got rid of 50! I enjoyed it all and thought I could do more of this when I became too decrepit for the Hill.

It was a calm night when I reached the lochside, and very dark. I sat in the van, drinking red wine to help wind down before settling to sleep there.

I decided to take a careful look at the highest of the nearest eagle nests, Eyrie 28 and the lower 27, where I had seen that eagle on the roost tree. Atalanta had not been seen all winter, and in any case I believed her to be too old to breed again now. She might even be dead. While Juno had usurped part of her territory to visit my carcass, that was a far cry from actually using one of Atalanta's nests. I took only the still camera and the telephoto lens on this reccé.

As I tramped up through the woods the harsh gobbing '*powyow*' sounds told me that the beautiful black-throated divers were back at islet after wintering on the sea. While red-throated divers had been filmed frequently on their high hill lochans, to my knowledge the much rarer black-throats had not.

I felt the full effects of last night's nervous excitement and the late wine on the first and steepest 500 feet of this trek, but I kept up a pace just short of pounding heart and worked through it. The arm-chair-shaped Eyrie 33 had not one new stick on it, so I headed on up for a tiny rowan that marked the cleft through to the high crags above Eyrie 28, still more than a mile away.

Suddenly an eagle soared over from the east, far smaller than Atalanta and too dark to be Melanion, her mate. It circled above the high eyrie, came back twice as if to inspect me, then treated me to eight glorious yo-yoing 'golden ball' dives, three of which I photographed. I perspired on, the damn trek far longer than I recalled it. I passed over the tops, intending to go a quarter of a mile further so that I could look back on the eyrie from a safe distance. Another eagle headed out from the cliffs below me. Had it come off Eyrie 28 after all? It circled south and back, and I took a good picture of it with talons down and neck bent for a closer look at me. It was not large enough to be Atalanta, and there were light patches under the wings. I climbed down below the eyrie and across a scary narrow ledge above the void to view the nest from the eastern side. No new sticks or vegetation were to be seen. If eggs had been laid in there, it was very cunning to make the nest appear unused. I reckoned I had better get out quickly so that the eagle could return if needed.

I hurried down to Eyrie 27 and saw that a great deal more tussock grass had been strewn over the 9-foot ledge that housed this nest. Cautiously I edged my head round a rock buttress and saw the huge beak and golden-maned head of Juno. So she was here, where the cliff faced south, and the hide site lay perfectly between rocks to the west, enjoying the best possible light for filming! She walked to the edge and soared off into space.

Juno circled, watching me. I did not attempt to take out the camera. I could just see the tops of two eggs in a nest bowl under the rocky overhang, almost three feet in from the edge of the ledge. I hurried away. From 300 yards, before turning for home, I saw her flap back to the ledge and waddle in to the overhang and her eggs.

I had begun to think that the activities of the increasing number of fish farms – in both sea and freshwater lochs – were beginning to effect the breeding patterns of the eagles in some of the hills, forcing them to use higher eyries that were prone to fail in late snows. The new barytes mine between my loch and the village twelve miles to the south would only exacerbate the problem, though I had to admit that the ugly open cast workings across 20 acres of open hillside was but a flea-bite out of a pair of eagles' hunting territory, which would extend to some 12,000 acres. I had been told that the local fishing club was up in arms over the mine for releasing the waste water after washing crushed rock and ore indiscriminately into the river. Complaints had been made to the Nature Conservancy Council to no effect – indeed no reply. However, news that the N.C.C. had acquired from the Ministry of Agriculture a 1,300-acre area of mossy wetlands – home to greylags, white-fronted geese, greenshank, among others – on the south-west shore of the loch suggested that the region might be better protected in future.

The fish farm was a threat to wildlife in more ways than one. I was not alone in thinking the three sets of fish cages that floated along the south shore of the sea loch were a blight on the former beauty of the landscape. Two local businessmen I met while returning with Allan from a trip to film some otters there reckoned the tending of fish cages had driven two known pairs of otters back into the woods, or further to the west, for their holts near the shore had been abandoned. I heard that an otter had been found dead on the road, its head crushed so that no-one could tell if it had been shot first. The fish farm staff had alleged otter depredations on the crowded salmon smolts in the cages. Only one person, it appeared, had objected under the planning laws to installation of fish tanks in the sea loch where otters were once plentiful. Allan also told me of the new forestry road being built through the glen that housed Eyries 6 and 7, both on a long ledge immediately above the roadside. The birds would not be able to tolerate that and breed properly. 'The end is coming here,' I muttered as I headed back over the pass to my home loch. All the more urgent then to film Juno and her mate at the easy Eyrie 27 while I still could, once any chicks were ten days old.

Next afternoon, while I was working on my book, I heard a powerful boat-engine whining nearer along the loch. I could see a dark-haired young man and a blond woman talking behind the windscreen of a big white boat that stopped just outside my boat bay. They drifted while the man raked my cottage and the surrounding land with binoculars. I did not show myself. They restarted the engine, gunned the boat over to the far shore and again drifted for about ten minutes. They were not fishing. Suddenly the boat headed back at great speed towards the west. As it passed the long sandy point three miles away I saw another smaller boat with three people in it, also heading west. I felt nervous. Were they folk who had been at the fox dens near the eyries, taking terriers and guns to bolt a vixen and kill the cubs before the lambing season? Or were they egg collectors, spying round to see if I were in or out on the Hill? It may seem like paranoia but there is very good reason to be suspicious in a place like this. As it happened, my suspicion of a nearby farmer was erased when I saw his advertisement in the Royal Society for the Protection of Birds journal, inviting holidaymakers to stay at the farm and see something of Scotland's rare wildlife, including eagles.

On a wet and windy April 12, with snow falling on ground above 1,500 feet, I saw a peregrine falcon fly from a ridge to the north west and wheel away towards Eyrie 1, which was obscured by trees. A pair had hatched chicks in an old crow's nest higher up the gorge two years before, but the martens had got them. Were the peregrines nesting there again? I climbed up next day to look and, on the way, found two sheep trying to get at the spruce I had planted to mark Moobli's grave. I leaped out of the trees at them with a great roar and barking. The sheep went off like greyhounds. Barking appeared to be more effective than chasing. Both the crow's nest and the eyrie were empty, but I found three ewe carcasses on the way, one torn apart by foxes and another right above the eyrie. Measured against only one dead hind found within half a mile radius of my cottage this winter, these deaths were unusual.

That evening the martens gave me one of their biggest surprises. Chico turned up first but refused to come through the window. Then Mickey arrived, grabbing several pieces and taking them down to the ground. I was astonished, on peering out, to see Chico down there receiving them from him. It went against everything the experts said – that young martens leave their parents before their first winter. Could it be that Chico was FEMALE, and that Mickey was more than normally interested in his first-born 'daughter'? The pair returned with Michelle at 9.37 p.m. and all three swarmed over the table with no animosity whatever. Finally Chico came back alone, crossed the window ledge and fed from my hands. I felt sure now that the name should be Chica, for this marten was a good deal smaller than the other two. Altruism is hardly a common trait among fierce pine martens but it was just possible the parents were giving her some support in a time of trouble. But why would Michelle be so tolerant if she had young cubs somewhere?

Gales and rain prevented me from trekking on Sunday morning, so I renewed the wooden stanchions at the back of the kitchen sink. These had rotted where the single water pipe from the burn came through the wall. After a lunch of two boiled eggs and a slice of bread I boated to below the middle of the long wood and, finding one of my old runway planks washed up on shore, hauled the boat out on to it. For the first time I humped the entire new movie gear up to about 800 feet, gasping my way up through tussocks, bogland, jutting ledges and scattered boulders until I reached a rocky ridge, four to six feet high, that overlooked but screened me from Eyrie 27. The sky was clear and sunny, but up there I was exposed to a buffeting wind. I set up. After moving the heavy fluid-head tripod and camera to a flat rock to my right I saw an eagle launch itself from the eyrie face. It seemed too small to be Juno, and from the lightish colours beneath the wings I judged it not to be her mate either.

I got on to it – a superb picture in the view-finder – and pressed the button. Nothing happened! The eagle sailed east, then turned and approached, shaking its wings as if in irritation at seeing me, and vanished over the loch while I was still trying to get the camera working. Could I have been sold a duff battery? I hoped it was not Juno I had seen. Surely she would not leave her eggs when I was a good quarter of a mile away, was well screened. Besides, if it was Juno she knew I was friendly.

Arriving home, I seized the second battery and boated over to the second islet to see if I could film the black-throated divers, or perhaps even an otter. I found a superb spot, behind a thick pine with many low screening branches, pointing south, behind which to conceal myself. After about an hour along came the divers, not far off in the water. I focused, pressed the button – again it did not work. I could not shout curses because of the divers. Instead I stared at the ground and muttered, 'This is the END!' How could both batteries be faulty?

Back at my desk I read the camera manual all through. I had not done this before, and there I discovered the tiny gadget inside, called the 'buckle switch', which had shifted slightly out of position. When I had reset it, everything worked perfectly. There was nothing wrong with either battery.

I was even madder with myself later for forgetting to assemble the flash unit on my stills camera so as to photograph the young marten when next it was joined by its parents – which of course happened that night. I woke just after 6 a.m. next morning to see Phyllis on the martens' table glaring in through the window at me. This was becoming a habit I had to cure, for she defecated over the table and spoilt my marten shots. I hissed at her, threw white rags over her, poked her with a fishing rod. It took a week before she got the message.

The sheep had massed ranks and there were now eleven of them forming daily raiding parties. They bleated me awake at dawn and scoffed my flowers. When I chased them, they split into two gangs. One lot ambled away up to 400 feet while the other raided the woods for tree seedlings. They had 10,000 acres in which to roam for grazing but insisted on my little hard-won patch. They had not come when Moobli was alive. They came to symbolise not the true Highlanders, who did not run sheep, but the Lowland and English wreckers, who brought the sheep to these hills after the scandalous Highland Clearances.

I looked to my fencing. The 250-yard frontage and some of the sides were complete, but I had left gaps into the woodlands so that red deer could have access to my pasture. There was a gap a foot deep all along the bottom of the rear section where I had run out of fencing wire. That would have to be made good. For two days I prized out hundreds of staples, breaking my best screwdriver in the process, and laboured to lower the whole 300-yard rear section to make it sheep-proof. The ground was so uneven that I had to carry up specially cut logs and jam them into the spaces, then nail the lower wire of the fence to them. Without the usual barbed wire along the top, it would now keep sheep out while deer could still safely jump over it.

My spirits lifted on my next supply trip. A producer from the BBC Natural History Unit had been in touch with my publishing editor. They were thinking about two films, one showing me going about my work in the wilds, the second to be my own wildlife film – IF my stuff was good enough. I wrote an enthusiastic letter straight away.

8 · Filming the Fabulous

Filming continued in fits and starts over the next few weeks as the weather allowed. I managed some good shots of the courtship displays of the black-throated divers that had returned to the loch in early April. Eleven cock and six hen chaffinches came once more to squabble over scraps on the bird table. Ferocious gales swamped the boats, entailing the usual heavings and balings, before a snow blizzard put a stop to filming until the melt on Sunday April 21 prompted me to finish the fence repairs and go in search of eagles.

Using the hefty new tripod as a climbing aid, I struggled up to the windy rocky spur where I had seen Juno before. I could see the male eagle performing golden ball dives away to my left while I was setting up the camera in a perfect little recess, but by the time I was ready he had gone. I had only minutes to wait before a huge eagle flew almost straight above my head towards the eyrie. It was surely Juno. With the camera focused on the nest, in she came from the left, preceded by her shadow, and landed with backward sweeps of her long wings. She tramped into the recess. I had seen that she carried vegetation in her talons, probably white grass to keep warm the lining of the nest bowl.

While I filmed all this the camera sounded unusually smooth. I checked the dial – the film had gone past 0. I twiddled the knob of the rear spool. The film was loose; it had all gone through. But at what point? Without my glasses I might have read 30 feet left as 80 feet and missed it all. I sat there fuming. What a useless wildlife cameraman I was turning out to be. The wind was biting cold as I threaded in a new film.

After a short wait I heard crows calling and spotted an eagle flying along below the crest of the hills to the west, with another close by. I swung the camera and took a superb sequence of the male being mobbed by diving crows which he shrugged off with irritated upward flicks of his wings. As he sailed east he once extended his talons for a stretch, pulling them up again like an aircraft's undercarriage. The fluid head tripod was worth its weight in gold for such extended panning shots, but how could one get a proper light meter reading with the action already in progress against a cobalt sky which suddenly became snowy white when the eagle passed a patch of cloud and then went dark against cliffs in shadow?

I wondered what the other eagle was doing here. I looked back to see Juno's head poking above the nest rim. Maybe she was wondering the same thing, for there should not be three eagles in her nesting range, just as she should not be in Atalanta's territory. I began to shiver when a small cloud stopped in front of the sun. Then I saw the male eagle again, just above the crests a mile away to the north west, the other eagle still close by. I swung the camera and by luck got on to him as he went into a spectacular series of roller-coaster dives. As he hurtled down I could see through the viewfinder his beak, his shoulders, the tips of his folded back wings. Then out came the wings to break the fall, a soaring upwards again, a few flaps to regain height before over the invisible helter-skelter he went again, wings folded in like a giant trussed turkey, diving to earth. When he shot up for the third time I got the crest of the hills in frame as he glided away to the east.

Minutes passed. When I glanced back at the eyrie, which was still in sunlight, it appeared empty. If there were eggs up there they would be all right for a short while but, like my fingers, they would soon begin to feel the icy grip of the wind. I was just debating whether to put in a new film spool when two birds appeared against the dark hills to the north west. One swooped up underneath the other and the top one performed an abrupt half turn to its left, as if it were about to fight. They headed south west across the loch towards Eagle Rock Mountain, and it was then that I saw the gleaming, almost circular white patches which indicated an immature bird. The other eagle was clearly Juno, probably escorting her own chick from last year out of her area. There was firm intent about the action but no outright aggression. She would have to return to the nest soon if the eggs were not to grow cold. I focused back on the eyrie, leaving plenty of space on the left of the picture, and pressed the button when I saw her with naked eye approaching. It *was* Juno. The camera whirred as she landed on the left of the long ridge and tramped over to the nest bowl.

If I had missed her landing the first time, there could be no doubt about this fine sequence, and that of the male doing 'yo yo' dives. The gear felt heavier than ever while carrying it downhill to the boat, and that seemed to be made of lead as I lifted it off the washed-up plank and into the water.

That night Michelle looked much thinner than she had when last she appeared. Chica came with Mickey the following evening and he gruffed at her twice, but only when they were competing for the same morsel.

I was visiting the local forestry office on my next supply trip when news came through of a big fire on the south-west side of Eagle Rock Mountain. It had been caused either by a sheep farmer trying to burn off long heather and get a green bite for his flocks or by a careless tourist, and all the foresters were out fighting it. When I reached home, I could see smoke puthering up from the mountain's far side. If the flames spread to any of Juno's earlier eyries over there, they would not harm her now that she was nesting on my side of the loch. On a rough count of one acre in ten each year, burning can be a useful tool in managing long old heather and undergrowth for sheep, deer and grouse. Too often, however, such fires rage out of control and hundreds of acres at a time are consumed. There should be far stricter control of 'muirburn', with harsher penalties for those who inflict wanton damage on nature.

Fortunately it rained all night, and most of the next day, so dousing the fire.

A few days later I saw a big female buzzard drift out of the highest cliff face to the north east, though as it went through that familiar role and lurch upon hitting an air pocket I thought it might be an eagle. If so, could there be a new eyrie up there across the burn gorge? The territories all seemed to be changing round. I climbed up but found nothing new around the 1,000-foot level above the burn. The local Nature Conservancy Council field scientist, Jeff Watson, told me that disturbance from fish farms in the sea loch near Fiunary had displaced a pair of eagles to the shores below Eagle Rock Mountain. It was possible that they were using one of Juno's old nests since she had taken up residence on my side of the water.

Early in May, during a brief warm spell after a late blizzard in which I had counted 1,150 daffodils standing up to their necks in snow, I went to check the eyries on Eagle Rock Mountain. I found no sign of occupation apart from Eyrie 34, which had been covered with tussock grasses, a single white feather resting on them. At first I thought it was from an eaglet, but it soon became clear that this nest was being used merely as a daytime resting place by an eagle hunting on the mountain's northern slopes.

As I strode back down I saw an eagle heading over from the north west. Through the binoculars it looked like Juno's dark-faced mate. By the time I had set up the camera he had been joined by Juno. They circled round each other, crossing and recrossing each other's path in a graceful aerial ballet as the camera whirred in my ear. Then they turned towards me, Juno leading with slow but purposeful flaps, the male beating faster to gain on her. He dived down at her back, levelling out at the last moment as she turned to greet him. She achieved this by pulling in her right wing and giving one hard beat with the left that turned her on to her side, then pulling in the left wing again as he zoomed past, shooting both out again to right herself. Juno turned north, as if to cross the loch to her nest. Once more the male flapped faster to gain height, and I saw the sun glinting on his golden pinions as he dived at her. I could hardly believe my eyes, for this time she made an even more spectacular turn, right over on her back, and I saw their talons touch briefly before she rolled back. I felt sure that this wonderful air dance of the eagles had not been filmed before.

They flew on past their nest site and across the highest mountain miles away to the north. I became concerned for the eggs in their nest. The warm sun would be on the nest of course, but maybe the eggs had already hatched. I tried to convince myself of that.

I heard that an eagle had been forced down into a nearby sea loch by a flock of seagulls. Two men, one of whom I knew to be employed by the World Wildlife Fund, rowed out to rescue the great bird which had vomited and was clearly weak. Analysis of a sample of the vomit revealed the presence of alphachloralose, an agricultural poison used by farmers to control crows, woodpigeons and the like. I voiced my suspicions to keeper Greg Hunter who was looking after the sick eagle until it was well enough for release. In the previous year the Royal Society for the Protection of Birds and the Nature Conservancy Council had published the preliminary results of their joint eagle survey, numbering as many as 424 pairs and 87 single eagles occupying 511 ranges. Could some farmers, who persisted in believing (quite wrongly) that eagles constantly took live lambs, have decided there were just too many predators and be secretly taking 'control' into their own hands? When a fox was found poisoned with the more deadly strychnine in the Morvern area, I could not help wondering if it had been left on the Hill on purpose, in the hope that an eagle would pick it up, so killing two 'birds' with one stone.

Earlier I had taken issue with Jeff Watson's findings that sheep carrion was a cause of golden eagles doing well in the western Highlands. I had always found more dead red deer than sheep on winter treks, though I had to admit that as much sheep carrion as deer had been brought into the nests I had observed over a nine-year period. As it happened, this was the first year in which I found more dead sheep than deer on my side of the loch, the ratio this winter being an astonishing five to one. It seemed to me a case of 'turn 'em loose, collect the subsidies, gather what's left'. You could hardly blame farmers for increasing their flocks in order to gain from the extra E.C. subsidies handed out to support the lamb market, in addition to the £6.25 a year then paid to pure-bred breeding ewes and £4.25 for cross-breeds.*

On the return from a fruitless search of the forbidding glen of long precipitous cliffs, rising to more than 2,000 feet, where once Eyrie 37 had flourished, I glassed Juno's nest across the loch from the forestry track. Two white blobs could be seen on the ledge but there was no movement in the nest. I became apprehensive, and on a sunny May 7 felt I could no longer delay a trek up there to see if all was well. I reached the long saddle above the eyrie with a nagging feeling that I

---

* In 1991 these subsidies, under the Hill Livestock Compensatory Allowance, were £9.39 per breeding ewe on the seriously disadvantaged land (the highest hills), £4.90 on the medium qualified lands, and £2.45 for lowland sheep. In addition, under the sheep annual premium scheme, mainly funded by the EC, farmers received an average of £10 per ewe. Detailed records of each sheep must be kept and under the latter scheme, in 1991 the number of ewes eligible was limited – on a basis of up to 1,000 ewes per producer in 'Less Favoured Areas,' and up to 500 on other lands. At the time of writing there were EC proposals to limit these subsidies further, to 750 ewes in hill areas and 350 in the lowlands. This would hit hard at Scottish farmers who have larger flocks than exist in most EC countries.

was about to discover the worst, but instead of climbing down immediately I headed on up to 1,600 feet by the easier route to Eyrie 28, which I would have to check if 27 had failed. I saw no eagle anywhere in the sky. This seemed odd if there were newly-hatched chicks in the vicinity. The high nest was still empty and unused. I clambered down between the projecting rocks on the precipitous short-turfed slope and received a shock. There, lying on the flat mossy rock where three years before I had found one of the veteran Atalanta's fresh eggs, was the leg of a lamb. Removing the camera from the pack, I photographed the leg before working my way down until I could just see the outer edge of Eyrie 27's ledge. I clipped on the telephoto lens and, holding the camera close to my eye, moved on slowly until the whole nest came into view. Juno was not there, but on the front edge lay most of the rest of the dead lamb. It did not look at all bloody, as it should if the eagle had killed it. With hardly any safe hand holds I made the short sheer climb to the nest. Just as my intuition had told me, it was empty. Juno had made a lovely neat bowl with masses of tussock grass, but there were no eggs or chicks, and no bits of shell anywhere either. Nothing had hatched here in this season.

A weariness came over me as I stumbled down over the steep tussocks. This area had not been disturbed by anyone else. There was no sign of a knee or foot depression anywhere, though of course a professional egg collector would try to eliminate his tracks. Perhaps the late snows had put paid to Juno's incubation. If so, where were the eggs, or the remains of them?

On a supply trip next morning I phoned Roy Dennis, the Highland Officer for the R.S.P.B., to find out what he thought might have happened to Juno's nest. With no evidence of human intrusion, he thought the late snow had forced her to give up and that hooded crows or ravens had later taken the eggs. I had never known hoodies to take eagle eggs, but Roy assured me it had happened when they were abandoned. Ravens were a more likely cause, I thought.

After a day of rain I crossed the loch to check the furthest three faces of Eagle Rock Mountain. I took no gear but the binoculars, my object simply to find another viable nest. In order to search all the gorges thoroughly I virtually climbed the 3,000-foot mountain twice. I saw one shy eagle on the western face making a couple of half-hearted dives to put distance between us. There was no deer carrion to be seen, though I came across two dead sheep – a good-sized lamb with a broken foreleg which had gone over a sheer cliff edge and a ewe that had fallen into the farthest gorge. No eagle or fox had been at either of them. For all my labours I found all the old eyries untouched and the one new nest built up but not used. I moved well, running at times, and came to the conclusion that my recent tiredness must have been due solely to trying to carry too much weight. Maybe I could brave the 'Killer Trek' for one last time on my birthday.

Next morning I gasped with the pain in both ankles as I tried to walk. I had overdone it after all. Although the stiffness wore off after hobbling for a short while, I could not face any real work on so hot a day. I washed some trekking smalls and hung them out to dry before wandering over the burn to keep watch on the islets in the loch. The pair of black-throated divers had appeared in my boat bay one morning recently, making a cacophony of mewing wails and *'powlyow'* gobbles, obviously in distress. I had gone down to investigate and had seen one of them run across the top of the water, beating its wings on the surface. It flew about a hundred yards to the south before slooshing down again. They both stayed close by as I boated out, one coming so close that I could see its red eyes without binoculars. When I returned, both birds began the eerie wailing again. It was as if they were trying to tell me something, and there was real agitation in their voices. As I had not seen the divers in my area for some weeks I had assumed that they had nested on Heron Island, their second site three miles away. If so, had the nest failed, as it did last year? I would check before long, but I saw no sign of the birds on this day.

I was not bored, however, for I found a rock pool, which drained a boggy gully, with caddis flies, tadpoles and even newts in it. I had never seen newts in such small pools before and could not fathom how they had got there. The spawn-on-a-duck's-foot theory would not hold good here for the pool was only ten feet by five and nowhere more than sixteen inches deep. It would dry out in summer and be flooded when the loch rose above it in winter. Perhaps there were newts in the loch and these few had become stranded, but I had seen none at all in loch shallows in hundreds of boating hours.

In the late afternoon I was scything down brambles in the front pasture when I heard a shout.

'Anyone about?'

'Yes, there is!'

I groaned and walked back to the cottage to find four beefy hikers standing at my front door. I suggested that they might keep to the lochside rather than marching through my garden. But they turned out to be nice lads from the university in Manchester. When they told me their route for two days, I realised it was a mile longer than the Killer Trek!

'Have you seen any eagles?' I asked them with more respect.

'Plenty!' said their leader, a doctor of more than 16 stone and several inches over six feet tall.

They were swiftly indoors eating my cake and waiting for the tea to brew while they showed me on the map precisely where the eagles were. It turned out that they had found Atalanta's farthest eyrie, number 18, with a healthy two-week chick in it. Another eaglet had been seen in a nest just outside my area which was checked annually by the Royal Society for the Protection of Birds and the keeper on the land. The doctor told me that he had applied for a licence to observe eagles at the nest and had been turned down on the grounds that someone already had permits for this area. I confirmed that that someone was me, and joked that if Atalanta's chick vanished he could expect the cops to be asking him questions. He laughed, but I could see he didn't like being admonished for going near eagle nests without permission. The hikers bought one of my books and I showed them the easiest route over the hills back to their camp site.

When they had gone, for some reason I began to have doubts. What if these men were not what they claimed to be? They had said that two of them would return: would they go near the eagles again without permission? I decided to inform Roy Dennis of the RSPB, who would check them out. At least they had saved me an exploratory 'killer' trek to find out if that far eyrie was being used. Yet I could not avoid the sinking feeling that my last wild place was dwindling away with the influx of more and more enthusiasts to the Hill.

I was worried too about the divers. When I heard their wails on another sunny morning, I boated down to Heron Island, taking the special screen-hide I had invented for the diver's shoreline nest situation. An ungrazed jungle of bracken, tall bilberry and other vegetation grew up between the giant fallen whitened trunks of ancient pine trees on the island. By rowing quietly into a natural bay on one side I could slide through the green tunnels of herbage without disturbing the nest on the other. All I had to do when I reached the mossy depression behind a huge square flat-topped rock, flanked on one side by a small cliff and on the other by sparse bushes, was to screen off the gap nearest to the loch with vegetation-stuffed netting, and to do the same across the top of the rock to hide my head and the camera.

Having moved as slowly and silently as possible, I raised cautiously my bush-hatted head beside the rock. One of the divers was on the old nest! Now what? In the past I had succeeded in erecting the hide without disturbing the bird on the nest, but that had been on a breezy day when there was plenty of other shifting vegetation as well as mine. Today was windless, and I dared not risk it. I waited, but the diver remained almost motionless. I was just thinking about leaving the hide there and sliding back through the tunnels when I heard an odd, loud call.

'*Peet!*'

It was like an oyster catcher's cry but longer, and it was made every ten seconds or so. It seemed to be coming from the far side of the island. I wondered if it was the other diver, though it didn't sound harsh or metallic enough for that. I kept watch.

'*Peet!*'

It was coming nearer, towards me. Suddenly I saw the diver on the nest pushing its long awkward body in a series of belly-flops from the nest to the water. I had about four seconds – if she swam out to mid-loch – before she could see me from the other side of the bushes. Quickly I hoisted the netting screen across the branches of two baby pines so that most of me would be hidden from her view. I got my head back to the side of the rock and stopped all movement just in time.

'*Peet!*'

It was still louder now. I saw a big 'V' wake pass the diver's nest site and head straight towards me. It looked like the body of a diver with its head under water. Slowly I lifted the glasses. It was an otter! It swam steadily along, still emitting the regular '*Peet!*' calls. I could now see its head and shoulders and the first thick curve of its strong tail – and I had left all the cameras at home!

As it drew nearer I could see its dull unblinking eyes. It was like a furry submarine. When it was immediately below me, it suddenly turned to its left and dived. Only a few yards away from where I lay some bubbles rose to the surface, indicating a circular path, then they stopped. It did not come ashore in my sight. I could still see the form of one dark-freckled olive-brown egg in the diver's shallow depression quite close to the water's edge. The diver must regard the otter as an enemy, for this one had cleared the nest as soon as it heard the animal calling. Whether the otter was actively looking for eggs I did not know. Its quick dive might have been caused by catching my scent. If so, that could be enough to keep the otter away from this part of the island for a while.

The diver had been joined by its mate and was almost at the far end of the lagoon – too far away to detect my moving fingers. I needed only to tie four knots and to weave in a little more vegetation and the hide was complete in a few minutes. I lay down my head for a short rest before leaving and heard a soft *'gowol'* note. I knew this gull-like sound well and looked up slowly. One of the divers climbed out of the water and stumbled awkwardly back to the nest to settle down on the egg. I waited until I could see through binoculars her eyes close and then left, making sure I was always out of her sight. When I reached the pine trees on the crown of the island I heard the otter making its whistle call again and hoped it was heading away to one of the other islets.

After the dawning of another fine day I boated out early to Heron Island with full ciné gear. I took immense pains to manoeuvre it all – heavy pack in one hand, tripod with fluid head in the other – as quietly as possible down to the screen hide. It was wasted effort. The egg had gone. I had no doubt as to the culprit. There was no sign of the divers. Well, I was here, so why not wait an hour or two and see what happened . . .

No sooner had I set up the camera than both divers appeared. I pressed the switch and took a superb sequence of them moving slowly through the shimmering water. They looked forlornly about them, giving me head-on 'cobra' images and exhibiting the bereavement behaviour of divers, putting their heads back under their wings as if to take refuge from the terrible truth.

Moments later I heard voices, and both birds dived simultaneously. It was one of the farmer's yellow boats with what seemed like a tourist couple in it. There was something familiar about the bearded man who from time to time raked the sky with binoculars. They were too far away for more positive identification. I waited until the boat had gone but the divers did not return. The disturbance would be enough to put the otter off for the rest of the day. I left at lunch time.

9 · *Endurance for an Eaglet*

The prospect appalled me. I had doubled the size and weight of my best hide to accommodate all the new movie equipment and dreaded carrying everything up and down a total of 12,000 feet of elevation to the farthest eyrie, the only one on my territory known to be supporting an eaglet. Despite the need to finish the film, and the fact that I had spent my birthday (May 25) at eagle eyries for the last nine out of ten years, it was impossible. At least, I couldn't manage without a helper. I knew I could not count on Allan Peters, who had been moved to an area further south, nor on Jeff Watson, who was still struggling to complete his eagle survey in the worst spring for many years. But there was someone else I could ask . . .

At that time Jim Crumley was features editor of the *Evening News* in Edinburgh. I had written to him after reading his sensitive review of my book *A Last Wild Place*, and days later his tall powerful form had marched past my window while I still lay abed. Since then we had enjoyed a few treks together and I valued his friendship. Built like a rugby forward, modest and quiet in manner, he was also a brilliant poetic writer who loved the Hill as much as I did. He could make more in words of the flight of the cormorant than ever I had done of eagles in the air, and I was not surprised when he was made Feature Writer of the Year in Scotland. Anyone who would sample his unusual mixture of muscular practicality and heady word images and idea associations should read his book on the Cairngorms, called

A High and Lonely Place. He had always wanted to work on eagles with me, so I wrote to him that afternoon, and in due course we arranged to meet on his first free weekend – by coincidence the 24th and 25th of May.

As time slowly passed I grew impatient. I filled two drizzly days writing golden eagle nest record cards for the British Trust for Ornithology. A cold three-hour crouch in the screen hide on Heron Island revealed no new divers' nest, nor any eggs, nor even sight of the birds on the water, though I had heard their wailing calls. I chased more sheep half a mile from a small gap where my fence crossed the deep secondary burn. I found the remains of a dead fox, and saw the year's first checkered skipper butterfly, as well as a pearl-bordered fritillary on a bracken stem. Mickey marten came capering round the cottage in full daylight while my movie camera was down in the pasture, trained on Eyrie 1.

What if – when the time came – Jim couldn't get away? A journalist's time is not often his own. By then the eaglet would be almost a month old – if it was still there. I was angry at the thought of defeat and felt guilty at funking the long, hard trek on my own.

Then suddenly, on a hot sunny day with a cool north-east wind, I had an idea. Although the new Fensman hide I had bought on my last trip south – with its square shape and guy cords – would be too artificial for eagles, I could make a small lie-down hide from just the canvas and three hazel wands. I could endure that for a few hours. I could leave the heavy tripod and fluid head at home and take only a little pan and tilt model. With just the movie camera, two lenses, one battery, three films, notebook and pencil, lunch and a can of orange juice, I got the total weight down to 40lbs. Still more than enough!

I stumped up the steeps on the far side of the burn, which cut out two gorges, and went through the chute and over the lip into Big Corrie. It was a dreary two-mile upward plod to the far end, where I saw an eagle come out of the furthest high cliffs to my left. I hiked up and searched the faces but found no new eyrie there. At last I reached the crest overlooking the river at the bottom of the almost sheer 2,000-foot wall. I was feeling knackered already and the top of the 1,000-foot eyrie peak looked to be miles below me. I lied to myself, aloud.

'Come on. It's only another half mile!'

I began to descend the precipitous slopes. It was like going down a never-ending fire escape of rough turf and tussocks, zigzagging down for ever, sliding on my backside, clinging on to anything I could grasp with both hands on the steeper bits, the river never seeming to get nearer.

It was a long time before I reached the valley floor and stumbled through the peat hags to slake my thirst, drinking like a horse from the flowing waters. Then came the hard, steep climb round the west side of the hill that led up to the eyrie. My knees began to crack and the bones in my feet hurt under the heavy load on the constantly twisting ground. There were no landmarks. Fortunately I got the route right this time and came out by the dead rowan tree that Melanion used as a roost. Beneath it were one old regurgitated pellet and a new one, still wet, and plenty of fresh white splashes. I hiked on up as far as I could before dropping over a short cliff above a rising gully. I turned round. There was the large white chick in the nest. I could just see its head move as it crouched down on seeing me. There was no cover for a hide, no heather at all, only tussocks and short grass. Lower down a green ridge projected along the top of the gully cliff. When I erected the hide in front of that the two greens matched. I had it up in three minutes, shoved a few rocks into its inner pockets to brace it down and slung white tussock fronds over the top to match the terrain. After glassing the sky and the surrounding peaks, to make sure an eagle was not watching, I slid inside.

The chick was already sprouting its primaries in a blue-brown line along the rear edge of each downy wing. It soon relaxed and I began to film. It stood up, flapped its wings hard, and fell over. It backed to the edge of the nest, tilted its white posterior comically into the air and let go a double barrage of liquid white faeces. The first was like a warning shot, the second deluge meant business. I watched it somersaulting down, down, down into the void. I was glad not to be walking under the eyrie at that moment for being splattered by an eaglet is not the most pleasant experience – although, surprisingly for a meat-eater, there is little smell. After a lie down and snooze, the chick got up again and began tugging with its beak at a bloody chunk of lamb. I filmed it heaving hard, twisting its head from side to side to try and pull off some flesh, then its hold slipped and, *flump*, it fell over backwards.

By 3 p.m. the eyrie was bathed in lovely golden sunlight and I filmed the eaglet hauling again at the lamb, then beating its embryo wings hard and bouncing about the nest. It was one of the liveliest chicks I had observed. If Juno lost her eggs because of the cold and snows, how was it that Atalanta had not, for this was her favourite nest, in a far wilder and colder glen? She could not be as old as I had been thinking. Several times the eaglet cheeped after long gaps of silence but no parent eagle came in. No doubt they distrusted the lump of the hide. I was taking chances, certainly, but I had worked with this pair many times, had hauled deer out of the woods into the hills for them during several winters, constantly saw them, and they saw me on treks. I was sure they knew I was harmless.

I was disappointed that the first two items of prey observed this year had both been lamb. This was most unusual. There certainly seemed to be a great shortage of wild prey in these hills. More and more sheep means more and more grass, heather and so on being eaten, and so less for the wild creatures.

As the sun began to sink behind the distant hills I realised I had no food left. My throat was parched, I had no sleeping bag, and while I had stripped to the waist in the baking sun, a cold wind began to whistle through gaps in the hide. I could not spend the night in such a cramped position. I dressed, dismantled the hide and equipment and set off for home.

A red tent had been put up in the glen half a mile below while I had been hidden. Maybe that had put off the eagles. I hiked round on sore feet below the eyrie, over the rounded hill to the south east and down to the river bed. As I stared in the usual horror at the great wall beyond the hags and bogs I knew I could not get all this gear back up there without being caught in the dark. I stashed the hide and tripod under a huge rock slab and covered them with grasses.

After refilling my water tanks at the river I began the great slog, trying to race the shadows of the peaks made by the sinking sun. Sometimes I got ahead, so that the dying beams lit me up; sometimes up the slower, steeper parts the shadows overtook me and plunged me in gloom. Soon the rest of this wall would be in sombre shadows and it would be getting dark for the long haul on the far side. I gasped and moaned. Every time I got near what looked like the ridge I saw another higher ridge behind it, almost perpendicular, and I still had a lot of weight to carry. Once, heart pounding, my legs went wobbly, and I was forced to rest for a minute.

I staggered over the final heights but could recognise none of the landmarks. Somehow I had gone too far to the east. I tried to turn south-west, but with no sun for guidance I did not turn far enough and came out above the glen on the east side of Big Corrie. I turned sharp right and started going faster downhill, the deer scattering. At last I was going down the ghastly steeps of the burn gorge above the cottage, knees very painful now and the sides of my feet more sore than ever I could remember. It was almost pitch black when I staggered into the cottage at precisely 10.10 p.m. Though I could hardly find the strength I warmed water, had a bathe down and made a quick primitive meal. I was glad I had made the trek. Not only had it provided me with wonderful new eaglet material that would fill in a few gaps in my film, it had also eased the depression caused by guilt that I had been dodging it.

The two adult martens came after Chica and were ravenous for some reason, clawing at the window gap and snatching bits from my hand with less care. I was still unsure whether Michelle had produced kits this season. Some days earlier I had seen her romping round the cottage, again in full daylight. She looked very thin, and when I saw her lolloping into the woodshed and start foraging, I wondered if she had kits in there. A later search proved this wild hope unfounded. After that she seemed to become less tolerant of Chica's continued presence, and growling arguments below the table occurred more often.

One night I had heard sounds of a violent quarrel and shone a torch down in the direction of scuffling, grunting and high-pitched squeaking. Michelle and Chica were fighting like cats, rolling over and over on the grass before finally Chica broke away. Michelle then jumped on to the table, licked her front paws, and came in through the window to be fed as if nothing had happened. I could find no marks of battle on her, but clearly she felt Chica should now be finding her own territory.

I was careful how I got out of bed next morning. At first I could hardly move for the pain in my ankles, though the knees seemed to be all right again. I hobbled round the estate without a pack to loosen up. When I saw a few sheep near the rear fence, I could not chase them away. Instead I banged on a sheet of corrugated iron and barked them out. I felt better after lunch, and boated out to post urgent mail.

It was sunny and hot but my legs still felt tired two days later. On my early morning round – again without a pack – I saw a checkered skipper butterfly flitting over the grass at the start of the high marshy path that ran above the cottage to the east wood. In the next 80 yards I counted 17 skippers, the most I had ever seen in so short a time. There were also hairstreaks in profusion and many pearl-bordered and small pearl-bordered fritillaries too. I decided to try to capture these dancing specks of golden sunlight on film, but it proved by no means easy. I set up the hefty tripod and fluid head on an open stretch of the path where single bracken fronds sprouted tall near a muddy patch. After a while a single checkered skipper landed to give me a nice sequence, and a pearl-bordered fritillary alighted on the mud half an hour later, its proboscis emerging as it walked about sucking up moisture. It required patience, but nothing to compare with the long hard treks and waiting in eagle hides. I was practising a pan when a skipper came to a single bluebell that I had dead in focus and began probing for nectar, holding hind wings low with forewings high, the sunlight glowing through them.

I was fearful that we would not be able to make the great trek when Friday turned out drear and rainy, though I hoped Jim would turn up anyway by the broken down pier at the end of the forestry track. As it happened, we met by chance on the ferry as I returned from a hurried trip to the big town 40 miles to the east to buy some decent food and a bottle of whisky for Jim's visit. I boated him home and found that I need not have gone to the town at all. Good fellow that he always was, he had brought with him a twelve-year-old malt whisky, two huge steaks and a cake baked by his wife Val, all designed to put extra zip into our eagle legs. We were both conscious of what we faced on the morrow, if the weather improved, and turned in early.

It was cloudy but fairly bright when we set off, Jim carrying the heavy tripod and fluid head, a battery and a pint of milk. I took the movie camera, battery and lead, three films, two lenses, a book, hide bracers, thin foam bed, a tin of orange juice and enough food for 24 hours. The huge double hide we carried between us. It was hell going up the first steeps and often we had to stop to catch our breath. Once we were over the top and on the long trudge through Big Corrie we managed to get into a sort of rhythm. We stopped only when one or other called out to change his carrying hand to the other side. After hiking the long swing to the north west we came face to face with the last great yawning glen and 1,800 feet of almost sheer descent. Jim agreed that it was a killer. We gained some relief by letting the hide roll down some slopes on its own, easing it here and there over humps and rocks, until we had it down to the valley floor. After a quick drink at the river I went in search of the tripod and small canvas hide which I had hidden under a rock so that Jim could carry them home.

We struggled up to the hide site. The rear section of a lamb, not very fresh, lay near Melanion's roost – no doubt the other half of the one I had seen in the nest five days before. I could detect no smell of poison. I put it behind a rock slab out of sight of the glen below but still visible to flying eagles. To my great relief, we heard the eaglet calling as we passed below the nest.

The hide went up in the previous spot. I worked from inside, forcing the ends of the three thick hazel poles into the earth, while Jim passed through the long slim bracers which I threaded in and out of the netting to make a rigid tunnel. After fixing on the sprigs of heather that we had plucked on the way, we had nothing else with which to camouflage the hide but white tussock grasses. Like badgers, we clawed heaps of it from all over the area, weaving it quickly into the netting, and in less than an hour the hide was completely covered with natural vegetation and moss.

I clambered inside, arranged the thin square of foam to fit my lying hips and shoulders, set up and focused the camera on the nest. Jim disguised the long lens with grass held on with an elastic band. When he left at 3.30 p.m., promising to return in 24 hours, and to be very careful how he operated my calor gas cooker, it began to spit with rain. I did not envy him that hard hike even in light showers and hoped the rain would not come to anything. I soon found that while I had chosen the most level spot on this hill, it was far from flat and small projections stuck into my hips and ribs. I slid into the bag straight away, blew up a plastic pillow for my head, arranged the food and drink in a far corner and settled down to wait.

After twenty minutes the eaglet rose from its prone hiding position and tried to tug bits of meat from the body of a ptarmigan. It kept stumbling about and seemed to be learning for the first time that it had to stand on its prey, hold it down with talons in order to rip off morsels. Occasionally it jerked a snippet down its gullet, and I was glad it appeared to be undisturbed by the whirring of my camera.

To my horror, the rain increased after the first two-hour wait. As the light began to fade and the old canvas of the hide's roof started to leak, one insidious drip right where my head would be, I felt I must be mad. I had desperately wanted to spend my birthday with the eagles, a whole day-and-night stint, for this would certainly be the last time. It had been a 'killer' trek all right, and even with Jim's help I had carried more weight than ever. I was knackered before I got into the hide. Now I faced all night and most of next day in this desolate place and in this awkward position.

It became bitter cold as dusk fell. Rain lashed down and leaks sprang all over the hide. The sleeping bag began to get wet and for the first time I felt panic. I might not survive this night at all and Jim would come back, if he *could* come back with the mountain tops drowning in mist, and find my cold body! Then the rain eased off a little and I prayed it would stop altogether.

At 9.45 p.m. the chick squeaked and I shot up to the eyepiece. The male was just leaving the nest. He had dropped what looked like a large vole and a small dark spiky thing which could have been a bird with torn feathers. I filmed the chick trying – for two or three minutes – to get the vole down its gullet before it slumped down facing in to the cliff, its head out of sight. At 10 p.m., when it was almost dark, I heard another squeak and looked out. The female – which I took to be Atalanta – was at last on the nest, a huge dark boat-like shape, moving her head slowly as she looked back in the direction she had come from and then round the nest. It was too dark to film, but I watched her feed the chick from the ptarmigan for more than half an hour. Then she brooded it, by lowering her chest feathers and left wing over it, and went to sleep for the rest of the eagles' short night.

I could not sleep. It was so cold that I had to pull the sleeping bag right over my head, tie the laces to leave just a small air hole and use my breath to keep my gloved fingers warm. I had even put the rear end of the bag into a black bin-liner to keep some of the wind off my feet. I was afraid I would start to shiver, my teeth to chatter, and lying prone as I was forced to do, there would then be a real risk of hypothermia. I forced myself to perform short-stroke running exercises with arms, hands and feet inside the bag. I tried to think positively and not give in to a feeling of panic or dwell on the fear of death.

The night seemed endless as I lay in the claustrophobic trap. The wind beat and battered the hide, the rain leaked on to my face. I had tied the Barbour jacket hood round my head, so I just heard the sound of it as it dripped on to the bag too. Other leaks splashed my chest and hip areas. In five hours the bag was almost entirely soaked, and then the cold was far worse. A runnel had formed at one point, and water draining from the mountain slopes above me was trickling through under my bum and hips. I lay in one position until I could bear it no longer, then struggled to turn over, hauling the jacket down as far as it would reach to protect that area from the cold sodden ground. Hell, it was cold! When I began to shiver, I ground my teeth, even dreaming up sexual fantasies as a way of holding on, and gradually saw the dawn coming.

At nearly 4 a.m. I took a look through the eyepiece. Atalanta was still brooding the chick. I did not film this, nor her leaving the nest at 4.32, as it was still too dark. The male came in a short while later, followed by Atalanta. I really could not miss this and filmed them both on the nest, glaring out into space and calling loudly. Melanion flew off and came back with the section of lamb I had hidden from the view of the glen. The female fed the chick for a full hour, most of the time with her tail and back to me. Towards the end I decided I had better shoot *some* of it for it might be the only chance at feeding film I would get.

I had just started a new 3-minute roll when suddenly Atalanta turned and began glaring and calling out, and I could see through the hide mesh the male hovering a few yards from the eyrie. He soared in a tight circle, then went higher, circling the other way, hovered again, went lower and lower, rocking oddly from side to side, and vanished below the brow of the hill in front of me. I had tried but had been unable to get on to him; he was moving about too much. I swung and focused back on the nest just in time to see Atalanta calling out again, her opening and closing beak showing in the lens despite the poor light. Then I saw Melanion flapping along from behind me to the nest. He landed on it, dropped something, and flew off again as his mate uttered shrill chittering 'kik kik kik' calls.

It was still stormy, with heavy rain showers, and while I was using especially fast speed film, I had no idea how it would turn out. It would not be perfect, beautifully lit film, but if it came out as the human eye could actually see it I would be happy enough.

This success cheered me up a good deal and I felt happy to have survived the night. I shifted about a lot to try to keep warm, ate the soggy sandwiches with no appetite whatever, drank the pop and started on the milk.

At 11.50 a.m. the male came in again and I shot him leaving prey. At 12.05 his mate returned and fed the chick (from the grouse he had left) for a full 31 minutes, but again she kept her tail and back towards the lens. I became so exasperated that I whistled, gave deer barks, and when they had no effect, I yelled out 'Turn round!' She did not appear to hear me at all. Whenever the chick's beak and face showed I exposed a few feet of film. Halfway through my last 100-foot roll she shifted so that I could see clearly her feeding the eaglet, and at last I got what I really wanted – the plucking of morsels from the grouse and the beak to beak feeding shots, as clear as a mountain burn in good light. I even filmed her leaving, following her flight for a few flaps, before the lens became obscured by the right-hand support of the hide.

Well, a truly great morning, ranking with the best hours at Juno's Eyrie 30 on Eagle Rock Mountain three years before. After all the troubles, determination had paid off and I had the vital feeding sequence I wanted. I told myself I could leave Scotland with honour, if I chose.

By now I was shivering all over, my teeth chattering. The hide, the bag, the foam mat, the grass and earth, everything were soaked through. It was like lying in a wet refrigerator. I began to pray that Jim would come early, if he came at all. The mist was still covering the tops of the great 2,000-foot wall but I hoped it would not be a mile to the east where the cliffs were shorter. Just before 3 p.m. I heard Jim's cheerful shout. Never before had I been so pleased to hear a human voice. I had dreaded trying to carry all that gear back over the killer hill, if I could move my frozen legs at all. I took the camera down and tried to crawl out. It was impossible to move much faster than a sloth. The legs still worked, but stiffly, slowly, like those of some long-buried ghoul emerging from a frozen tomb in a horror film.

We took down the hide and carried it flat up the hill and hid it in a cleft in the land below the cliffs north of the eyrie. It could not be seen from the hide site, never mind from the glen below. Maybe, just maybe, if I could find another helper, I would return and use it one more time. If not, it could stay there until it rotted away. We staggered off under our loads.

At first I was glad to stretch my legs, but on the way up the killer wall the lack of sleep began to tell and Jim took the lead while I kept up as best I could. We stopped often, cursing the Hill for this was one you had to climb the hill's way, not your own. Some hills you can wend your way up; this one demanded you climb up the steeps, bluffs and chimneys with no way round them. When we were halfway up the rain began again, making the hand and footholds slippery. It was hell, but so happy was I that I had finally succeeded with the eagles after all, it did not seem as bad as I had expected it to be.

Mist swirled around the tops as I led the way home. Often we were enveloped completely, so that I had to go by wind direction and instinct. On the level, and even going down at times, I felt glad to be still alive. I began almost running. Halfway through Big Corrie Jim yelled for a breather. I turned round and saw him looking like a drowned beaver, swaying on his feet, even his powerful frame vulnerable. No doubt I looked worse. Jim had done that trek twice in 24 hours, something I had never done, and only to help me; I felt ashamed of my selfishness and apologised.

After a breather, the mist cleared again and I was glad to see we were dead on course for Wildernesse, the mountain cleft above it now showing way down low at about 1,000 feet. Then it was the hell of going down the last precipitous slopes. All the time the rain had been pelting down and I was soaked to the skin everywhere except on chest and back, due to the Barbour jacket. With gratitude we forged twice through the raging burn to cut out a long bend and reached home safely.

While we were waiting for bathing-down water to heat up I dried the soaked ciné gear. Jim tapped my arm and pointed to the kitchen window. I saw a great tit in the willow bush with a green winter moth caterpillar in its beak, twirling from side to side on its feet as it looked round for danger. Then it flew to the nest box I had installed on the window sill and, after a pause, flew off again. Slowly, I lifted the wooden panel I had fixed to the inside of the window, which formed (as far as the birds were concerned) the back of the nest box. We saw the female sitting on eggs, her tail thrust upwards, her black beady eyes filled with determination to stay there and not be shifted. Gently I replaced the panel. I was really looking forward to photographing the adults feeding chicks for it was, as Jim pointed out, 'A bit easier than eagles!'

I felt good for nothing when Jim departed with my grateful thanks next morning. For the rest of that day I did nothing apart from writing up notes and cleaning the ciné gear. I sat on my swivel chair for over an hour, just gazing out of the window without a thought I could remember passing through my mind. My reverie was halted when Mickey came bouncing up in full daylight and scrabbled on the window. All the ciné gear was in pieces on the floor as he took bread from my lips. I set it all up but he did not come again until an hour after I was in bed. I was still tired from the trek so he buffeted in vain.

Next morning, the great tits' nest box was on the ground, wrecked, with one broken egg beneath it. The martens must have torn it down and taken the eggs. They had scratched much of the bark off, no doubt when trying to tear it from its wall fastenings. *Blast 'em!* I had a good mind to stop feeding them altogether. But when both turned up at a more civilised time, 9.05 p.m., and performed their usual acrobatics on the moss and advanced with their perky elfin faces over the sill to my desk, my love overcame my anger at their robbing the nest box. These creatures had been my only companions through the long winter after all.

10 · *Buzzard Persecution*

The Fensman hide was set up and camouflaged in a matter of minutes on a steep woodland slope above the lagoon on the other side of the loch where last year I had watched the buzzard's nest in which I was now surprised to find three new chicks. The nest was in a high fork of a huge oak tree, which nevertheless I could look down on from a ground site higher up the hillside.

Action started almost as soon as I had the camera with its 400mm lens set up. One chick started to preen its neck down while another appeared to attack the third in the deep well of the nest. A few minutes later the female flew in, landing on the right so that she was partly hidden by the tree's trunk. She tore at a woodmouse held in her talons and fed morsels to the preening chick. Then she flew off, letting the remains tumble into the well. The chicks made no attempt to peck at them for all at once the nest became a hub of activity. The biggest chick launched a deliberate attack on his two siblings, stabbing at their heads with his beak. The two smaller chicks were forced to climb the nest walls and sit on the edge to escape, leaving the biggest one holding the nest well – clearly his intention. The medium-sized chick was better able to hold its own, occasionally stabbing back, than the little chick, which seemed totally defenceless. Once out of range, it crouched down with half closed eyes and appeared to sigh.

This sibling rivalry among some young birds of prey (it takes place among eagles too) always seems a tragic waste. It usually ends only after the weakest has perished.

Within minutes of my entering the hide next morning, the chicks were at it again, Big Chick pecking viciously at Little Chick's head, while Medium Chick manoeuvred round behind the bully. (From now on I will refer to them by their initials.) Shortly after 10 a.m. the male flew in with something small and brown, peered round nervously and shot away again, leaving the chicks looking bewildered. A minute later in came the larger mother. She reached down with her right foot to pick up what the male had brought – I clearly saw a shrew – and looked towards the hide in alarm. The 400-foot reel ran rather noisily and so I stopped filming and attempted to blimp it by wrapping a thick towel round the camera. The buzzard began to rip up the shrew and tender pieces to BC. She could hear nothing now. LC managed to stagger round the rim of the nest and pick up a tiny bit that had dropped.

Shortly after midday the female returned again, this time with two voles held in one foot. She let one fall into the nest and ripped up the other to feed the two bigger chicks. When LC tried to approach, BC battered him away so that he got nothing. The mother got into the well and fed a piece of the second vole to MC which had stationed itself between the female and LC. The parent then flew off.

Less than an hour later LC began to fall asleep, no doubt from hunger and exhaustion. It toppled in from its uncomfortable twiggy perch on the nest edge. Immediately BC attacked, pecking at LC's head and attempting to twist each of its white wing stubs off. I filmed it all as LC tried to get away. It scrambled up to the left and collapsed on the rim, flapping in pathetic protest. Minutes later LC fell back into the well and was again harried. This treatment stopped only when the female returned with a frog and alighted on the far left of the nest, where MC, also out on the rim, pushed her way between mother's legs, where it managed to be enough nuisance to be fed one snippet to every three that went to BC. Poor LC made a valiant effort to struggle round to its mother, but BC hauled it down off the rim for another volley of stabbings. The mother paused and watched, but did nothing whatever to prevent it. With my own eyes I saw her as a bystander to almost the complete demolition of LC, yet she did not interfere.

It was terrifying to watch the magnified scene through the lens, to witness the callousness of natural raptorial behaviour, the total lack of

A female buzzard soars over her woodland domain.

The chick looks up expectantly as the male buzzard lands on the nest.

It was terrible to watch the systematic persecution of the smallest of three buzzard chicks by its elder, but this is normal instinctive behaviour among large raptors, and neither parent did anything to prevent it.

concern or pity on the part of the parent bird. My impulse was to wish a bullet put through BC, or to climb the tree and clout him. But that would be foolish. In the predators' world only the wariest, the toughest, the fittest survive. There was no hate involved, no malice, no conscious cruelty, nor even knowledge that they had to reduce the competition for food. It was blind instinct from the egg, implanted by centuries of evolution.

Poor LC struggled to get over to its mother to be fed but she simply ignored the weakling, feeding only BC and MC as they competed strongly. In desperate terror LC gave up and fell down into the well and then clambered out on to the rim on the far right. Ten minutes later it fell in again and BC grabbed the back of its neck and shook it cruelly. LC did not seem able to learn that BC would hurt it, and perhaps that was why the mother made no special effort to feed it. Not up to standard – so let it die.

It was appalling to see all this in close-up, to imagine the constant pain LC must have suffered, to witness the desolation in its eyes, an expression almost of wanting to die, to submit and find peace in death. It had been hatched for only a few days and the only life it had known was one of persecution, hunger and pain. I am not ashamed to say I wept for the little creature. I knew I had unique and dramatic footage but I would have forgone it all to spare that chick. By 3.30 p.m. all three chicks were lying together in the centre of the nest, BC on top of LC. I knew the mite would not survive unless I did something; I also knew that I should not interfere with the laws of nature.

I packed up and walked down the steep slope. It was soon obvious that I could not climb that massive oak and rescue the little chick. The nest was 50 feet from the ground, there were wide gaps between the branches, and one could not reach over the broad nest without damaging it. I was forced to let nature take its course.

Next morning I was installed again in the hide by shortly after eleven o'clock and was surprised to find LC still alive. It even had a little food in its crop. Would it survive after all? At 11.55 the male came in, dropped a shrew, and left again to return minutes later with another, which he kept dropping and picking up for one chick or another to snatch. MC grabbed it twice but could not swallow it. When the male picked it up again and held it between the chicks, it was LC which reached down from the rim, snatched the shrew and swallowed it. It may sound ridiculous but I felt a real sense of elation. All the while, BC sat in the centre of the nest, his crop full. The female returned without any prey, saw there was nothing left in the nest either and departed again. At 1.15 she appeared once more and the male landed beside her. It was the first time I had ever been able to photograph both parent buzzards on the nest with their chicks. They soon left.

The mother came in with a mouse at 2.05 and fed most of it to BC. The last of it went to MC which had got between her legs again. LC stood on my side of the nest, cheeping plaintively. After the mother had left BC attacked LC so ferociously that it could hardly crawl out of reach of the repeated twistings and tuggings. It crawled round the rim to the north while I prayed that it would fall off so that I could rescue it. At 2.23 it tumbled back into the well and awoke BC who drove it to the far south edge. After five minutes LC tottered back down, laid his head on his tormentor and went to sleep. It would not learn, and I knew then that it would not survive.

After six hours in the hide, my backside numb, I boated home.

I don't know what prompted me to contemplate the Killer Trek once more on my own. Perhaps it was the experience with the buzzards. After scything down encroaching bracken I spent a hot day lying out in the sun, conserving my strength and thinking of times past, of wonderful and terrible Highland days, knowing in my heart that they were coming to an end.

I was cutting a hazel walking stick next morning to help me carry so much weight – something I had never used before – when I heard shouts coming from the loch. I went down to the shore and raised the binoculars. A family was prancing about naked on the divers' islet. What an affront it seemed! The two middle-aged adults were overweight, the man bald and bearded. When he bellowed again at two children in canoes, disturbing the peace of this beautiful wild place, rage boiled within me. I wanted to seize my hand axe and dash over to administer a neat circumcision job. Had I not been about to set out I would certainly have gone to order them off. But with nothing to protect – except my unguarded cottage for a couple of days – now that the divers had lost out to the rainstorms and the tame gull Cedwig had been defeated by the otter, I had no really good reason to deport them. I resolved to give the rowdies fifteen minutes, but when I went back to the boat there was no-one to be seen.

I was still angry when I started stumping up the first steeps with the heaviest load ever. I was even forced to carry the heavy ciné tripod and the fluid head for I needed smooth shots of the eagles flying in and out of the nest. Food, milk, films and one battery were in a small pack worn backwards on my chest. As I plodded up and up, heat waves shimmering around me, I felt I was doubly crazy to tackle the Killer in these temperatures. Even my arms grew tired from pressing on the stick. Well, it was really for the last time. If I got good material, that would be the end; if I didn't, it would still be the end.

The chick seemed fine when I reached the hide site and glassed the eyrie. The hide was in the cleft where Jim and I had left it. I plucked heather from the cliff sides and dragged it all down on top of the hide, then set everything up in the same position as before. There were no eagles to be seen in the hot white sky. I slid inside and examined the nest. There was no prey and the chick's crop was empty. Bad signs.

Hours passed without sight of the adults. All I could film was the eaglet preening (chocolate-brown feathers were already growing on chest and back) or trampling the nest while looking out for a parent. After all my years of experience, could I have taken one chance too many and spooked the eagles? I might have been spotted sliding into the hide. I should never have tried to do it on my own, without someone to walk away in full view of the birds. But, I reasoned, this pair 'knew' me well. For many winters I had hauled dead deer out of the woods for Atalanta and Melanion to feed on and had also worked their nests more than once. Had she not fed chicks while I was actually building a hide 40 yards away? I worried about it for half the night. Although I dozed fitfully, I could not get comfortable. At least I was not cold.

After dawn I filmed the eaglet bouncing about and flapping its feathery wings. A great deal of plumage had grown in eight days. At 8 a.m. the chick began to squeak loudly and excitedly. I switched on the camera before looking. The male had landed on the nest with prey by the time I got my eye to the viewfinder. I filmed the eaglet mantling its wings over what had been brought in, its head down in a threat posture, protecting its food from father in spite of the fact that he had brought it in. It was comical to watch this serious attempt to become defensive, Melanion looking on casually with approval. 'That's right, kid. Don't let anyone take it, not even me!' There was no doubt now that this was Melanion, almost a tawny eagle in hue. He stepped carefully round the cheeping eaglet on to the edge of the nest nearest to me, looked down in close scrutiny, then picked up a stick in his beak, transferred it over the top of the still stiffly mantling eaglet and dropped it back on the nest. After a pause, he walked to the front edge, crouched down, and took off. This time I kept on to him and followed his flight right round the cliff face until he vanished behind it to the east. The whole sequence had looked wonderful through the lens and his mighty golden form lit up by the sun as he winged round the cliff was just the fabulous new material I had needed.

My euphoria was dampened when the chick hauled the prey over to my side of the nest. It was the rear leg of a big lamb. It is no good trying to appease the sheep farmer with falsehood. The leg was blooded up and I had to admit the eagles probably killed this one – a rare occurrence in my experience. Once again on this trek, like others this year, I had seen not one golden plover, no snipe nor grouse, nor even a ptarmigan; there was a shortage of natural wild prey. I ended the film on the eaglet facing me while rending the leg, facing the front of the nest, then sitting on its hocks, still pecking at the leg.

As usual, once the chick is six to seven weeks old and well able to tear its own prey, the mother, which has done nearly all the incubating, brooding and feeding at the nest in the early stages, takes long breaks, sometimes three days or more at a time; it is then left to the male to bring in food. Atalanta would be a very old eagle now and I did not really expect to see her at the nest that day.

At 10.23 a.m. the eaglet called loudly, and through the small hole in the hide by the tripod I saw the male winging in. I pushed the button long before he reached the nest and knew I had got him soaring in, landing, dropping prey (a chunk of ptarmigan) and then taking a sharp step backwards as the eaglet seized it and switched its back to him, again mantling its wings. It looked as if Melanion would stay a fair time and, as I was sure the spool was running out, I tried to switch off the camera. Accidentally I nudged it, so that the focus went off the nest, just at the moment when he flew away, but I filmed the chick rending the ptarmigan, jerking back morsels, and also trampolining about the nest.

I could not keep looking through the eyepiece all the time – the position became excruciating for my braced limbs. I lay back to read. By fixing a small mirror on the inside roof and angling it through a tiny gap in the camouflaged netting, I was still able to keep an eye on the eyrie.

The sun only shone on this eyrie in late afternoon so I had a long wait for perfect light. Around 6 p.m. I saw in the mirror that there was an adult eagle on the nest. I shot up to the eyepiece and pressed the button. There was a normal whir, then high-pitched squeaking. The film had jammed, probably because in the short jerky sequences taken earlier I had let too much loose film go into the take-up spool and it had looped in the works. When I looked through the viewfinder again, I realised it was the female on the nest this time. She had her back to me and was rending the ptarmigan and feeding bits to the eaglet. I knew this from the pumping up and down action of her rear end and tail. Slowly the truth dawned on me, and my heart sank. There were white creamy feathers beneath the tail, the plumage was not as dark as Atalanta's and the body was not as large. I could see her far better now in this blazing late sunshine than in the poor light during all the previous visit. Surely this was not Atalanta? I watched keenly, but not once did the female turn to show her head. She finished feeding the chick, took one step to the right, still facing away from me, and flew away, her wings moving almost as fast as the male's had done as she too went round the cliff.

When I failed to free the film by twiddling the spool knob, I opened up the camera. Most of the film had gone through and I threw away the gunged uptight loops behind the section that had jammed. I put in my last film, hoping the mother would return, but she did not reappear at the nest. I shot some more of the chick tearing at the prey, overbalancing after jetting another load of white liquid into space, and leaping about the nest.

As the light began to fade, I realised I was aching in every limb. In such a hide one must have some muscle or other permanently braced to avoid rolling and hitting the sides of the hide on the sloping ground. My watch told me I had passed my thousandth hour in eagle hides after a record 38-hour watch. Enough. I had won! I was climbing out after dismantling the camera from the tripod when the eaglet began squeaking loudly and gazing up into the sky. Kneeling behind the hide, I looked up too. High above the eyrie, almost stationary in the cool western breeze, hung the female eagle, just checking the eyrie from the air. I looked through the binoculars and could see again the creamy feathers under the tail, the smaller size, especially of the wings, which were not tattered. This was not Atalanta, for sure. My fears had been realised, for Juno could never have taken over part of her nesting territory. Something wonderful had gone from these hills for ever. My goddess was dead.

117

I knew there was no way I could carry that huge hide home along with everything else. I flattened it out, dragged it back to the cleft in the next set of cliffs, staked it and weighted it down with rocks and obscured it with more vegetation. I left it there, as a sacrifice to the gods of that wild glen.

On the trek home I felt weak and trembly, for I had had no real sleep, and every muscle was exhausted from so much bracing. Climbing the great 2,000-foot wall with such heavy double packs was torture. I took one step up, counted one, two, three, and then moved up the other foot. One, two, three, and then the next step. One, two, three ... Like this I moved slowly, terribly slowly, onward and upwards, trying to achieve some rhythm. These hills are waiting to suck me in, I thought, as they sucked in poor Moobli with inexhaustible patience. You never beat them. They allow you to fight them when you are young, seem to help you when you are in your prime and learning most, but finally they destroy you and suck you back into their depths. The greater your love and your debt to them, so does their gravity-soul make you heavier and heavier, and eventually haul you down. It is gravity that ages and kills us all.

It was an awful weary slow slog, and at times I thought this was the end – I would never make it to the top. I felt lightened by knowing I had attained my target of 1,000 hours in eagle hides, but I had to call a halt some time, and would sooner go out on a winning day. I reached the final crest, turned to look back over the lonely glen that, like Atalanta, I would never see again, and said simply –

'Goodbye. Thank you.'

And I passed from its sight.

The trek back through Big Corrie seemed incredibly long. Shallow slopes I hardly noticed before had turned into mountains. The packs became heavier and heavier, my knees as painful as five years ago; even my hips were hurting now and the landmarks passing more slowly than ever. Finally I reached the last precipitous downward steeps and fell three times. I lay there, closed my eyes, and actually passed out for almost twenty minutes. Once my foot went into a steep narrow pothole, my exhaustion so slowing my reflexes that I could not pull it out in time. If there had been a sideways twist to it, I would have broken my leg under such a weight.

By the time I was a quarter mile above the cottage, Moobli's grave showing as a tiny green dot, I was tottering like a zombie. I took only a few inches with each step, moving in slow motion, feet very sore despite all my hard treks and experience. My ankles were swollen, and the veins were distended so much all over my legs that I feared some would burst. I was never so glad to reach home in my life. Indoors, as I warmed some water for a bath, I found that the salty sweat on my chest had solidified into crystals. In the mirror, I looked my haggard self in the eye and said –

'That *is* the last time!'

And so it was.

11 · To a Marten's Rescue

Although I was still without any kind of commitment from a television company for my film, there were now more encouraging signs. A letter from the BBC Natural History Unit in Bristol promised a studio booking later in the summer when I could take all my material in for them to view it. 'No. Don't cut it yourself. Let's see it all,' they said. They were used to viewing rushes and a whole afternoon could be set aside for it. But I did not want to rely on this one spark of enthusiasm. I had written to BBC Television Scotland, the independent Scottish Television Channel and the small film company that Channel 4 had recommended. When I saw among the letters I collected from my usual mail collecting box in the village Post Office 12 miles away on the other side of the loch an envelope with the red BBC TV banner on it, I naturally expected it to be news from one of my earlier contacts. It turned out to be from a producer I did not know at the BBC in London. The idea proposed was a series looking at people who live alone and who, in various ways, 'have developed a positive and rewarding pattern of solitary life'. Although there were times when Wildernesse had certainly been very rewarding, I was not sure how positive my life was now – nor, remembering the BBC's earlier attitude to payment, how 'rewarding' this proposal might turn out to be in the future. I replied with a careful letter explaining my reasons for living alone in the wilds and suggesting a very modest fee.

I also picked up both good news and bad concerning eagles. Through the good offices of their field scientist Jeff Watson, the Nature Conservancy Council had asked the Forestry Commission to stop building – temporarily – the new road through the glen below Eyries 6 and 7. The Commission had agreed, and there was now a healthy chick in one of the nests, the first time I had known this one to succeed. The bad news came over Radio 4 in my van as I was about to scramble down the marshy cliff to the boat on my way home.

Lord Burton of Dochfour, a landowner in the Glenelg region of Wester Ross, was reported to be tabling a motion in the House of Lords that would effectively remove such birds as the golden eagle from the protection of the 1981 Wildlife and Countryside Act. He claimed that one eagle in his area had caused damage worth thousands of pounds by killing lambs in the last few seasons. With backing from the National Farmers' Union, the report went on, he had twice applied for a licence under the Act for the eagle to be shot but had been opposed by the Nature Conservancy Council and the Royal Society for the Protection of Birds. No licences have ever been issued to kill an eagle, and when both his were turned down the good Lord decided he was not going to be blocked by the law – he would get the law changed. After all, the bird had killed more than 30 lambs, so it was said, and some crofters had seen it swooping down and carrying them off.

It came to my mind at once that this area of Wester Ross is one of those where up to 40 per cent of all lambs born die in their first twenty-four hours, due mainly to poor ewe nutrition in the winter months. Elsewhere in Scotland 17 per cent is the average fatality – and this is an *agricultural* statistic. Some of those 30 lambs must have been picked up when dead and taken as carrion to the nest. I can tell you that if a pair of eagles fed one chick on nothing else but lambs, they would raise it to flying stage on about nine. My own observations of eagle eyries over an eight-year period, given in my book *On Wing and Wild Water*, showed that 7 live lambs taken were all that I could account for when even the doubtful cases were included.

The N.C.C. warden who spoke on the radio in defence of their decision said that there was simply not enough evidence in this case to sustain a licence being granted to shoot the eagle. After the Lords debate, Burton withdrew his amendment. Over the following three years 4 golden eagles are known to have been shot in the area, but by whom no-one has discovered.

After the last Killer Trek I spent a restful day or two at the desk before thinking again about the buzzards. A drenching wall of grey moved in from the north west as I boated over to the lagoon and hurried up the sloping tussocks. Fortunately the worst of the rain passed by, only a few large drops splatting through the leaves as I reached the trees. I tipped water off the hide roof, titivated the corner posts with moss and slid inside.

Only two chicks were in the nest, both sprouting their first light-brown feathers through the grey-white down. The little chick had gone, perished. The male swept in, dropped a vole and left – all so fast I had no time to press the button. I filmed one of the chicks gulping it down. Both were now the same size, which indicated that Medium Chick was a female and would end up larger than her bullying brother. Big Chick had larger eyes in proportion to the size of his head and so I could deduce it was the female that got the vole.

There was no fighting at all now, and BC even pecked a scrap of food from MC's beak with affectionate little beak fencing that looked startlingly like kissing! He picked up a dead twig, held it up for a few moments, and then dropped it at her feet.

On the next sunny day I dug over the vegetable garden again and planted cabbages and kale where earlier lettuces and radishes had grown. Some days before I had hoed out a thousand or more 'weeds' – grasses, dock, creeping buttercups – and barrowed them up to the large rotovator compost bin I kept in the woods. Each year the bin converted last season's weeds, leaves, kitchen and human waste into 25 cubic feet of soily compost. This I barrowed down to the garden, spreading it two inches thick over the surface. Even though I intended to depart for good before much longer, I would leave the place in good shape. I had not created this garden and its thick rich soil from the wilderness for nothing.

While I dug in the compost before planting I kept stopping to film things of interest. Fourteen humble bees lay scattered among the white clovers near the bird table as if dead. When the sun began to warm them up, they came to life and scrambled over the flowers, thrusting their thick tongues out for nectar even before they were warm enough to fly. The delicate white traceries of pignut were

replacing the fading bluebells and luring the marsh flies. Golden cannikins of creeping buttercup nodded as bright orange flashes turned
into pearl-bordered fritillary butterflies that alighted upon them
briefly for a honeyed sip. The orchids were late this year and only
just beginning to put forth their blooms.

I heard a shout from the loch. Three fishermen in a boat were
heading east along the shoreline. One was standing up and waving in
friendly fashion. My return wave was halfhearted, for the shouting
had come as a shock, and this kind of disturbance was occurring
more and more frequently. Of course I did not, and could not, mind
fishermen going past but I didn't want them waving and yelling. I
had no objection to hikers walking through so long as they kept to
the shore and did not tread down my flowers or spoil the pasture.
Indeed some hikers will recall being invited in for tea and a chat. On
fine days, however, groups or whole families would sometimes turn
up in boats and peer at me through binoculars or start taking photos,
never thinking that the water carried almost every word they spoke
to my ears. From time to time a boat would be tied up by the west or
east wood and the occupants would climb round until they were
above Wildernesse and sit up there on the ridges taking their pictures
of my place while I worked in the garden below.

I decided to boat out and cheer myself up with a visit to the buzzards, taking just the Olympus stills camera and the lighter tripod.
The wing and tail feathers of both chicks were half grown. Soon the
female flew in with a shrew. Half an hour later I was astonished when
she returned with a semi-fledged mallard duckling in her talons. I
had once seen the male swoop down at a swimming mallard family
but the youngsters had all dived out of trouble. The larger mother
bird must have scooped this one off the surface for it was still wet.
The two chicks had a tug-of-war with the duckling, which the
female (now the larger chick) won, though her brother clearly
thought he was still boss for he jumped over the duckling and seized
her neck in his beak, attempting to shake her about. She took no
notice and went on pulling at the corpse, keeping her back to her
belligerent brother, who soon desisted, looking most put out. As
usual with buzzards when the chicks are this size, the adults took the
rest of the afternoon off and after 3 p.m. I knew they would not be
back before dusk.

The tame gull I called Cedwig came winging over the boat on my
way home. I fed him the half sandwich I had left from lunch. He

disappeared when all the food had gone, but I knew where he was and turned my head slowly . . . Sure enough, he was standing on top of the engine, hitching a ride back to his islet. This time he got a lift all the way for his timely appearance reminded me to check his nest. His mate rose reluctantly as I landed, but I was glad to see that they now had three eggs in the old diver's nest. Another gull had risen from the island's eastern spit, so I went to look there too and found a second nest, also with three eggs. These gulls were certainly triers. Less than three weeks before, Cedwig's mate had lost an earlier three eggs – no doubt to the marauding otter. At that time there had been three pairs of common gulls nesting on the island but only the one set of eggs. It had taken three years of egg predation by the otter and, before I had started to feed them regularly, the martens too, almost to wipe out a sizable gull colony. Obviously the otter had not been back this way. Maybe it thought it too late in the season to range the whole loch for eggs.

Cedwig was more territorial now. I was filming Michelle searching near the rhododendron bush for the raisins I had scattered – a ruse I hit upon for enticing the martens out in daylight – when a heron whizzed over from the direction of the islets, Cedwig close on its tail. With loud cries the gull forced the heron to dodge in the air, where it made '*kraink!*' protest calls that startled the marten. I filmed her bolting away. The heron and the gull had both vanished when I looked back. I went down to the shore, and off flew the heron from near my boat. Cedwig, waiting on the water just off shore, sprang into the air and pursued the heron away to the west until out of sight.

On a dark and dreary but rainless June 22 I was planting the last of the winter cabbage seedlings when I heard the single note of what I took to be an oyster catcher – '*kleep*' – just off my shore. A quarter of a minute later the sound was louder . . . '*Peet!*' Could it possibly be the otter back? I went down to the water but saw no sign of any animal, nor any ripples or bubbles. I had seen oyster catchers on the islets, and so thought no more of it.

I was rudely woken around dawn by the shrieking of gulls, yelling as if they were on the roof. When I got to the window I saw three gulls on the garden fence posts but Cedwig was not among them. Further cries announced his presence on a favourite perch on the chimney pot. If they thought they were going to be fed at this hour they were mistaken. I went out and angrily shooed them away.

Later I boated out to pay a last visit to the buzzards. Four gulls began calling and wheeling round the near islet, sometimes diving towards the water on my side of it. I could see nothing through the glasses except a female merganser paddling along. The gulls soon landed back near their nests with their usual territorial calls. Just another of their extempore displays, I thought, until I spotted Cedwig landing on my boat in the lagoon as I was climbing up into the wood. How odd . . .

These should have been among my best buzzard pictures – if only the camera shutter had not stuck halfway across on every shot. Both chicks looked like feathery footballs on stilts. The male chick rooted out half a shrew from the nest wall and began rending it with his talons. His sister raised her tail perpendicular so she could reach back and preen the under feathers. When the mother came in with a vole at 3 p.m., the female chick pounced on it first, her wings opening, and swallowed it with three sharp backward jerks. As the chicks beat their wings hard with short quick strokes they rose in the air while still clinging to nest twigs like grim death with their talons.

I took down the hide and left the site pristine, concealing all the loose camouflage vegetation under nearby bushes. On the way home I went to check the gulls' eggs, which should be hatching soon. To my dismay, both nests were empty and no gulls were to be seen. There were no pieces of eggshell in the holes leading to otter holts either. Surely some blasted canoeist wanting to 'live wild' hadn't taken them for breakfast? I searched the whole islet, and in the end found the evidence – one new almost whole eggshell among heather at the highest point of the islet, another piece nearby, and another by a fresh and fishy otter scat further to the west. There was a new lay-out place too, still wet from the otter's body. So that *was* an otter whistle I had heard yesterday. How could I have been so stupid? I could have set up on the far islet and filmed it today. But I felt sorry for the gulls, especially after their second brave try to rear a family.

Early next morning I was woken again by the four gulls, all standing on the grass below my window. I gave them some food to help ease their misery, speaking softly to them. Obviously it was not food they were after – they were staging some kind of protest! What did they expect me to do about their stolen eggs? This was clearly the end of their colony, and also of the divers breeding. With nothing to hold them to the islet now, the gulls treated my garden as their own territory, conducting early morning rituals of yelps, chirps and screams before drifting up into the hills to feed. Ear plugs made it tolerable.

To my surprise, Chica turned up alone the following evening. She seemed as small and skinny as ever, darting about even more nervously and cramming her mouth with food before dashing away again. I little knew it was the last time I would ever see her. The other martens had not come for three nights, though Mickey's cheeky face appeared at my open window the next evening while I was listening to music on my battery record player. He took a whole slice in bits – the last morsel from my mouth – showing that he could remember for quite a while that I was friendly. He huffed and gruffed when I touched him, and I recorded the sounds on a little cassette machine. I could hear strange breathy '*shirree shirree*' calls that I had never heard before coming from the nearby woods. It occurred to me that they might be coming from young martens. After eating his fill, Mickey stuffed his mouth with bits and made off with his dancing, loping run. He moved more slowly, heavily, than usual. Was he taking food to his kits?

Around 4 a.m. I was woken by louder, more insistent '*shirree*' calls coming through the open window. The light was fair, despite the mist, so I put on trews and light trainer shoes and went out to follow the calls down through the woods.

A young marten, quite big, about two thirds of full-grown size, was perched on the outer end of a long branch of the huge Norway spruce. He looked as if he had got a foot trapped or his tail twisted round the end sprays of green needles. I could see his mouth opening against the light of the sky as he made a weak call every few seconds, though he did not try to pull his tail or foot out of trouble. It was as if he had ventured too far along the branch and was now scared of trying to turn back. I could saw through the branch, but then he might be injured in the fall. I felt that his parents could not be far away. They would hear his calls, and it would be better for me to return to bed and not panic him into any sudden moves.

At 7.24 I woke and went out again. The marten had gone. Good. He was probably fine, just nervous on his first few forays into the high arboreal world. I was stealing quietly round the spruce grove, ducking under the long plate-like branches of the tree which was a full fifteen feet round the butt, when I happened to look up at the ancient open bird nest box I had nailed to the trunk years ago.

A perky elfin face with radar-scanner ears was poked over the side of it, regarding me solemnly. I hurried for my camera and took some photos, then ran back for a ladder and a slice of bread and butter and raspberry jam. I also had the presence of mind to strap my little tape recorder on to my chest. When I returned, he was still there. I put the ladder against the trunk and climbed up. The marten put on a fierce display, giving '*chrehm*' gruff barks and whickering noises.

My heart beat hard with all the excitement and not a little fear. Slowly I inched my hand and the slice nearer and nearer. The marten gave short coughs and made a slashing bite towards my fingers. I took no notice, though the teeth could inflict considerable injury. I just kept saying, very softly, 'I love you, I love you, I love you', and moving my hand forward. He made another coughing slash but I kept whispering the words and moving forward until I got the raspberry slice over the edge of the tray of the nest box. To my delight, he licked off the jam between growls. It was so comical! The poor bairn had been almost starving, I supposed. Well, I would catch him and give him a really good feed-up.

Carefully I moved my hand forward again and once more he slashed, but I kept at it until I could fondle the back of his neck with my fingers, talking, saying how much I loved him, willing it to him in silent animal language. He now looked at me in such an amazing way. He *knew* I was no threat. My hand slid round his body and I lifted him out. He was chubby and lovely, not at all smelly, very young and fresh, and for a moment all I wanted was to be him – to be all that again too. I held him by the nape of the neck and against my chest while going down the ladder, then got the other hand under him and carried him home. Not once did he attempt to bite me.

Immediately he scurried between some books under my desk. I went down to the rhododendron bush by the path to carry up the den box. By golly, it had been well used, the hay all flattened and filled with sweet marten scents. I caught him – again he went soft and made no attempt to bark or bite at all – and put him into the box. I set food and milk round it and left him there, in my study, while I went for supplies. I also had to make a promised telephone call to the young producer at the BBC Natural History Unit in Bristol who was interested in my film.

After shopping, I shifted my racing bike really hard for twenty hilly miles to make up for recent lack of exercise, then rang the producer. He had booked a viewing studio for July 2 – a mere five days away! I explained that I could not possibly move out, get south, have all my films developed, and reach Bristol in so short a time. As he had to go away on a trip in a week's time we left it that we would keep in touch and look at my material later in July. By now a blitz of letters to find a TV network backer (in case Bristol failed) had produced results, and I had arranged to show my best films to both BBC and ITV in Scotland and to Anglia 'Survival' in London during my stay south. I knew I would not endure another winter at Wildernesse, and as a friend had offered me a temporary room in her large house in Surrey, I resolved to shift out my most valuable heavy belongings, including the makings of a wildlife museum, at the same time.

When I reached home I was astonished to find that the young marten had not stirred from the den box, nor had he eaten anything. Well, presumably he had enjoyed a marvellous sleep after his traumatic night and the best thing I could do was free him to return to Mickey and Michelle. I tipped up the box and had some difficulty getting him out. He set off slowly round the room. Again I talked to him, the same words, caught him in my hands and took him outside. I held him up briefly as I said goodbye and saw that the creamy patch on his chest had at least four brown spots on it. It also extended a fair way down his right front leg. All pine martens have different pelage patterns on their chests, so it is possible to tell individual animals apart, but I had never seen so many patches as this. From now on, provided I saw him again, he would be known as Spotted Dick. I would have dearly liked to keep him, and if he had eaten some food I might have kept him for a day or two. But then I had to leave anyway, for at least a month. I put him on the grass and he went off easily, trotting east through the trees towards the burn over which the martens had their den. He was fat, did not need my help, for he was certainly not ill in any way. He had just become temporarily lost. That night Mickey came grabbing bits and rushing off towards the spruce grove where I presumed Spotted Dick was waiting.

I decided that the big move would take place on June 30, when nineteen years of living alone in remote wild places with only boat access would be complete. For two days I lugged gear down to the big boat and shipped it across to Easy Bay, where I could get my van within thirty yards of the water and near its level. Twice Cedwig came flying over and landed on the roof of the boat's semi-cabin, which was so smooth that he had to keep flapping his wings to keep his footing in the breeze. With no eggs to help to incubate I think he was bored. Well before dusk he and his mate landed on garden posts to be fed. Mickey came each night several times, grabbing bits and rushing off with them. Why, if he had more than Spotted Dick to feed, didn't he and Michelle bring their whole brood to the table, dammit?

On the afternoon of June 29 I winched up the big boat, the loch water so far out that I had to re-set the wooden runways end to end no less than eleven times before I could chain it to the biggest ash tree above the shore. I then turned to the big engine. Was this to be the day when I could not carry it up in one go, the day when I would know I should quit this harsh life? I cheated a little, just lugging it a foot at a time from the boat bay to the foot of the steps, where I decided to leave it alone for a while. After tipping water out of the smaller old sea boat I found a new leak in the hull. I wiped it clean and turned it over into the sun to dry before making a fibreglass repair that would set overnight.

Back at the cottage, I made the final pack-up – a suitcase full of heavy diaries, books and letter files, show projector and screen, my lecture photos, all the still and movie photography gear and so forth. While doing this I realised I had not filmed the wonderful orchid fields above the cottage, for although three weeks late this year they were now blooming in profusion. I would need such material for brief cutaway shots in the summer sequences.

I had only one 200-foot canister of old film left, and my camera took either 100 or 400-foot rolls. Using the blankets on my bed as a darkroom, I shoved my hands underneath, made sure there were no gaps to let in daylight, and inch by inch wound half the film off on to a 100-foot reel. It took an extremely boring and finger-aching half hour. I then carried everything up and shot a pan of the colour studded fields, ending on three heath-spotted orchids. A brief search enabled me also to film a lesser butterfly orchid which moved nicely in the breeze, and after a short climb, an early purple orchid too. That done, I went to fibre-glass the leak in the old boat, ready for use on the morrow. I then turned to look at the big engine again. Darn it! I had forgotten something. I walked up to the cottage and brought back two old sweaters.

I stood the engine on a flat rock by the steps, put the bunched-up sweaters on my right shoulder, knelt down, pulled the engine on to them and tried to stand up. I could not move it. I stayed kneeling, my head bowed. Then this was the day – I knew I was beaten. All right, I had really known it for a long time now. I did not say a short prayer or anything like that. I stayed there for a time, thinking of the incredible years I had known here. I looked at the engine again and said –

'You have been my pal, and life-saver, for a long time. Don't give me a hard time now. I'm trying to make you safe until I return.'

I tried again. It was heavy but I lifted it quite easily and carried it all the way up to the cottage, breathing far more heavily than I needed to in case my heart conked out. Just as I was congratulating myself and was letting it down, it suddenly became terribly heavy and I was forced to let go. The engine fell forward and its top hit a stack of big logs, this time smashing the carrying handle off completely, leaving only jagged edges. I had to use gloves to manoeuvre the engine into the study where I hid it, along with my chain saw, behind the desk.

12 · Crashing into Trouble

I put out plenty of food for the martens and scattered two pounds of raisins into the long grasses among which the yellow banks formed by tormentil flowers were being replaced by the dazzling blue speedwells. That should keep them busy for some time and so keep them in the area. I carried the rest of the gear down to the boat bay and loaded it aboard the small sea-going boat under a dull grey sky. The water was calm. By the time everything was in the van it would be the heaviest load I had ever attempted to get over the 1,000-foot pass by the single track road to the nearest village. I decided to wait until 7 p.m. when there would be less traffic about on the steep inclines.

After turning off the calor gas and the water, I locked up and carried the last load down to the shore. My departure was delayed until two tourist boats had passed after stopping to allow those aboard to take photos of my place. I crossed without mishap, water occasionally slopping over the gunwhales. By the time I had everything stowed in the van there was hardly an inch of space left. I hid the boat engine in a mail sack behind a boulder high in the woods. I secured the boat as best I could close to the bank by a screen of young alders that would make it hard to see from the forestry track down which an increasing number of visitors were hiking these days, often stopping to picnic opposite Wildernesse and take photos, sometimes even setting up telescopes.

131

I had the driving window open when I set off just after 6 p.m. and flies were buzzing irritatingly on the windscreen. A wasp smacked into my eye and then began zooming about. I grabbed a stiff envelope and tried to scoop it out as I came up to a tight bend in the road with an 8-foot ditch on one side. Hastily I pulled back from it on to the road, but the verges were soft and the camber was wrong. The wheels began to slide sideways. I yelled with fear and anger as down, down went the van to finish on its right side at the bottom of the ditch.

A split second followed in which I was astonished to realise I was unhurt. The van lay in an area of mud and grass almost the same shape as itself and my elbow rested in the mud through the open window. Suddenly I was struck by the typewriter and two cases as they tumbled on to me from the passenger seat. Behind me the van's interior was a shambles. A mahogany box of tape cassettes had smashed into five pieces. I heard the engine still running as I realised I was imprisoned. The righthand indicator was clicking and flashing, and I could smell leaking petrol. One spark and I would be incinerated in a raging inferno!

In blind panic I fought my way through the debris and tried to get a foot on to the steering wheel, which slithered round. I had a terrible job opening the heavy nearside door directly above me at full stretch. At last I held it up and tore myself through the gap. I balanced on the running board and leaped to the top of the ditch, only then realising that the indicator was still flashing and the ignition still on. Now all my belongings, photos and vital notes for future books could be burnt up without me. All the films over which I had slaved could also be lost.

I scrambled back inside, switched off the ignition and the indicators and tore an arm muscle in getting out again, also scraping my scalp in the process while holding up the heavy door with my neck and head. Fortunately the rear door still opened, and I spent half an hour extricating the most valuable items and stacking them on dry shingle amid the shoreside trees. The bike, which was on the roof of the van, had suffered a buckled wheel, but a few whacks with the flat of my hand and some twiddles with the spoke spanner straightened the rim well enough for use.

I was three miles from the nearest phone box and the forestry track was rough and gravelly. It was a bumpy, wobbly ride on the damaged bicycle. The local police station was engaged for so long that eventually the operator put me through free of charge to the cops in the big town 40 miles to the east who said they would go on ringing the local station until they got through; they would tell the new policeman there to call me in the coin box. Twenty minutes later he did. He said he would send a breakdown unit out soon. Ten minutes passed, then he rang again to say he could not get one. The man who now owned the best local garage, in the village at the far end of the loch, lived in a new house and the phone had not yet been connected. Someone was now walking to the house to tell him. Fifteen minutes later the policeman called again – to say the garage owner was not at home! I thanked him and asked him to get someone to me in the morning. I would be by the van from 10 a.m. onwards.

Back to the van I pedalled. There was still a strong smell of petrol, so I extracted everything else of value and stacked it on the shore with what was already there. Then I went back up into the woods to fetch down the boat engine. I hauled the boat back into the water, carried all the gear down to the boat and dragged the lot back over the loch. I carried films, photos and diaries back up to the cottage but stashed the rest under a tarp in the big boat's cabin. I turned on the water, reconnected the calor gas, seized a bottle of vino and ate a hasty meal. As I sat in misery and exhaustion, with only the ruined old sleeping bag in which to spend the night, I felt sure my van was ruined. How long would it be before rescue came, and would it still even go? I'm afraid I said it aloud: 'I've had enough of this damn awful life!'

I celebrated entering my twentieth year in the wilds by rising at 7 a.m. and lugging everything back down to the shore again. The same laborious procedure a yesterday followed – amid light showers this time – and after three hours I was standing by the van, all the gear under a tarp. The petrol had stopped leaking, obviously because the tank was empty, but it had gathered in oily pools in every crevice of the under girders of the van's chassis. I spent time trying to mop it up. It was 11.30 before I heard the thudding of an engine. Up drove a monstrous breakdown truck, the biggest I had ever seen, with wheels so large that the top of the tyres were above my eye level. Out jumped a lad I remembered as a schoolboy. My heart sank, but he reminded me that he had been working at the garage for more than five years now. Well, he ought to know what he was doing.

We fixed his steel hawser on to the van's top front wheel stanchion and he rumbled along in his vast machine on the far side of the track.

Slowly the van came out but kept slipping back sideways. I had to help by standing in the ditch and pushing it upwards. I kept a very wary eye on the hawser, for one sign of a snap and I'd be out of the way like lightning. Finally, the offside front wheel hit a buried rock, came up, and the van was free.

What astonished me was that there was hardly any damage to be seen! All the glass windows were intact along the side that had hit the bottom of the ditch, and there was barely a scratch on the paintwork. Miraculously my dear old vehicle had crashed into the one short section of deep ditch that did not contain protruding rocks. Only the fibre glass roof section, which was hinged so that it could lift up and form an extra bed space, had been pushed over slightly, the fibres tearing at each end. Easily repaired, I thought. (In fact I could find no-one in Britain who would do the job, and it was finally repaired in a back street boat works in Spain three and a half years later.) The petrol tank was nearly empty but undamaged. Oil had flooded one cylinder. The lad removed the plug, blasted out the oil, and afterwards the engine started first touch!). With a new plug I was free to continue my journey.

It took two hours to clear up the jumbled mess inside the van, and a further two to carry everything up from the beach a second time and stash it away safely inside. I had asked the young man and the local postman, who had driven past, to get some petrol sent up to me from the head forester. I waited and waited, while more boats came down and paused opposite my home before going back. At length three gallons arrived in a van driven by the new forestry keeper whom I had never met, donated by a stranger who lived in the nearest hamlet, a man who had read my books and to whom the postman had told my plight. Some 'well wishers' were far from nuisances, I reflected wryly as gratefully I wrote out a cheque.

As I rounded the last bend before the hills leading up to the pass, I saw a buzzard hovering over the fields. It just happened the ciné camera, head and tripod were already assembled so I swiftly connected a battery, set it all up on the track and was onto the bird while it still hovered. It treated me to two wide aerial oblongs, each ending with more hoverings, then it made a spectacular dive down the side of a tree-lined knoll where I lost it in the gloom. A fine sequence to play before the vole foraging outside its burrow, and then the buzzard landing on the nest with a vole.

I made good time to a small quiet wood near Silverdale in

Lancashire, where I camped for the night. For the first time I had the oddest feeling, that I had *escaped* from Wildernesse, that what had once been my paradise was now becoming my hell.

'All men kill the thing they love' – the famous words of Oscar Wilde came to my mind. Ay, I thought, and the thing they love kills them!

If I could not find a backer on this trip, that would have to be the end of all 16mm filming for me on my slender finances. I did not know it then, but I was dallying in a world of very clever, smart-suited, smart-talking people, among whom a naïve hermit from the wilderness had about as much chance of survival as a salmon in the Sahara. Perhaps the most disconcerting encounter came when I rose early and drove to Bristol to keep an appointment with the BBC Natural History Unit on July 23.

Although I had been told not to edit my films as they were used to viewing rushes, and that the viewing theatre had been booked for the whole afternoon so that there would be plenty of time for them to see everything, the two producers I had been in touch with announced on my arrival that they were very busy and would be hopping in and out. Four other youngsters joined us as I handed my films to the projectionist. The sequences of the eagle hauling the roe-buck uphill were fortunately near the beginning for nothing interested them until then. I had stayed too long on one eagle, I was told. I should have pulled in and out more, showed the eagle's head in close up, just its beak rendering flesh, just its eye. I asked if they had any idea how hard it was to get as close as I had to an eagle at a carcass in winter. It had taken me ten patient years, and to change lenses when only 40 yards from a wild eagle would have driven it away for days. Even the most up to date professional zoom lens would need careful handling from a more distant hide if the birds were not to notice it.

I could see what they were criticising – these fellows who had had the advantage (from the point of view of filming techniques) of using a tame falconer's eagle for the 'Living Isles' series. I did not want to pretend that tame birds were wild, or that I had the best, the most expensive equipment. Perhaps my mistake was to have been cool over lunch to their suggestion that they might film me going about my routine. Perhaps I was too sensitive to their forthright way of telling me that though there were a few good things among my sequences of martens and buzzards at the nest it was not enough on

135

its own for today's sophisticated audience. I bridled at the suggestion that a film editor would throw my stuff out as unusable unless I provided more variety of shots and angles. Maybe they just didn't like the grizzled old recluse who answered them back.

No-one saw it all, and we rushed through the last two reels on a little steambed viewing machine upstairs.

I was not going to make the same mistake again. Over the next few days I spliced together some of my best sequences in a show reel, to capture interest quickly. I received a better reception for this from a big affable fellow at Anglia 'Survival'. He wanted to see it again in the autumn after he had discussed the material with his colleagues. I edited the show reel further still before taking it to an independent production company making films for Channel 4. To my surprise, a brisk, pleasant man of 40 looked at everything I had and said he would back me if I would provide him with a synopsis for a film which he could show to Channel 4. He made no promises, said I would need better equipment and more material, but if Channel 4 would finance him, we might come to terms. I was given a large scotch and left at 7.30 p.m. walking on air.

I drove up to Sandy in Bedforshire and showed my edited film to John Pattison Tomkins, the man behind the R.S.P.B. film 'Where Eagles Fly', the film that the men at BBC Bristol had constantly held up to me as a model. He too said that I needed better equipment, but he liked the eagles at the carcass, which they had been unable to get for their film. And that had cost a total of £67,000 to make – ten times my costs so far! He would have bought my sequences if he had known about them, he said after complimenting me on some of my wildcat and pine marten footage. He thought it was almost impossible to compete without the resources and a team – an assistant cameraman, a driver, a sound man, a crew of helpers. In his view I should have leaped at Bristol's suggestion of a film about me that included some of my own sequences.

It was a wet and blustery drive back to Scotland on August 15. Ten years earlier I would have done the whole 570 miles in one go, but, feeling oddly weak and shivery after 360 miles, I camped for the night in a tree-lined road north of Moffat. Growing old is a strange business. Only a day or two before I had felt fine after covering 9 miles on my bike in less than 30 minutes.

Besides, I had arranged two more interviews in Glasgow on the morrow and wanted to be fresh and alert for them. It did not begin well at the BBC's Scottish studios. The producer I was to see had been called away to a meeting and I was left with his assistant. Was this the old runaround again? He took me to some viewing rooms, secured a projectionist and at first looked bored when my stuff came up on the screen. Then he perked up with the eagles at the carcass and the buzzard chicks in the nest. By the time we were upstairs in the luxury suite he was urging on his chief with enormous enthusiasm. This time I was asked what sort of fee I wanted. I was amazed, after so cursory a look at my films, for I had never really expected a deal with the BBC in Glasgow.

They thought the best idea would be for them to make a film of me at work and to fit some of my own footage into that. With Bristol in mind, I was not going to say no a second time, but I added that I was more interested in showing Scotland's spectacular wildlife than in seeking fame for myself. But they took no notice and began talking about the possibility of a series of four half-hour films, each concentrating on one species or one season. If that were possible, I might make £10,000 on the deal, they said.

Once more I was walking on air, though I was brought back to earth at Scottish Television (the ITV company) where I was told that the union would not allow a one-man film made by a non-union amateur to go on the air. They suggested using a short extract, coupled with an interview, on an outdoor show hosted by a famous personality – the sort of thing I was used to doing just to publicize my books. It would not have returned one tenth of my costs.

Nevertheless, as I boated home to Wildernesse in a golden sunset, I allowed myself to believe that at last I had broken through.

13 · *Preying on the Mind*

I carried my belongings up to the cottage. The paths were overgrown and the little plum tree and the wild raspberry canes to the west were full of fruit. Pine martens are partial to raspberries and I wondered if they had not been around to strip the bushes. I put some jam on to buttered bread, cut it up and set the small squares out on the bird table. After sorting out my gear and putting the new unexposed film rolls in the calor gas fridge I went into the study with a drink. To my astonishment, Mickey was already there, gobbling up the titbits. In the past it had been two or three days before he returned following my prolonged absence. He must have heard the boat. Or had he scented me? I talked to him in the old way, and clearly he recognised me after a six weeks interval. He came at once to take food from my fingers.

The following night he returned to feed at 8.30, even taking a piece of bread that had a huge black slug tucking in at one end. He didn't bother to brush away the slug but delicately slid the morsel away from it and chewed it up. A much smaller marten arrived an hour later but it kept its back to me so that I could not see the chest markings. Surely Chica could not be back?

The answer came two nights later when, at 9.46, Mickey brought another adult. I could see her marks clearly – Michelle, once more restored to full size. When I heard scufflings outside half an hour later, I looked out to see four martens on the moss. One of

138

Michelle's two small kits had a full white or cream chest without a single mark on it, the other had a large brown spot which almost blotted out the cream chest patch. I named them White Chest and Centre Spot. What could have become of Spotted Dick, whom I had rescued from the tree? Did he not belong to Mickey after all?

During the six days of gales and rain that followed I worked on my eagle book. Afterwards I was more disturbed than ever by uninvited visitors. A veterinary surgeon, who had treated Moobli some five years before, arrived unannounced with his entire family, wanting to camp among the trees beside the cottage. I walked them all round, explained my attempts to film the martens and the delayed work on my book, and eventually visited their campsite on the other side of the loch. Then a small white boat I had seen passing in centre loch suddenly turned and crash-landed on my beach. I left the difficult spot I had reached in my writing and went down to investigate. It was an Australian lad who had read one of my books – in Taipeh, of all places! – and had decided to meet me while on a European holiday. As I had never mentioned the name of the loch in any of my books, nor the name given to the house which is marked on the maps, how on earth did all these people manage to track me down to this inaccessible place? It began to pelt with rain as I was telling him that this was no holiday for me and that he had interrupted my work. I took him inside for some tea and scones. When the rain stopped after half an hour, he went reluctantly back to his boat and took so long getting launched that it came on to rain again. In desperation I fetched one of my old jackets for him and told him not to bother to bring it back. I suppose I should be pleased that a stranger took pleasure in meeting me, but it had also taken two hours out of a working day.

Some days later two of the nearest farmer's yellow boats, filled with people, came cruising past, a large red and white parasol sticking out of one bow. I heard shouts and loud laughing as they reached the islets where, to my alarm, they turned and headed back towards my boat bay. They paused by my boats before continuing on beyond the west wood, where I heard the engines cut. There were more shouts and whistles. What in heaven's name could they be up to? I crept along the shore and peeped through the heather at the top of the knoll. Seven people were hiking up the edge of the wood (not actually on my land) to the ridge above my house where they stopped to take their photos of it. There was no sign of them when I went up there later to see if they were still hanging about.

All this may sound like unnecessary fretting to a city dweller who is used to human noise, but in this wild and isolated place it was more than a nuisance. It was decidedly unsettling. I could never know, as I heard that drone of engines approaching, whether the new batch would be friend or foe; I was alone, more than six miles from any sort of assistance, and I no longer had Moobli for protection. I could not relax or return to work until the latest invasion had passed.

Spotted Dick turned up at 9.10 p.m. on August 24 when I had no fewer than *five* martens running about on the mossy table. His four chest patches were unmistakable. The variation in pelage of three kits in one family was quite amazing. Spotted Dick was by far the most confident of the youngsters, White Chest the most reserved. Only Mickey took food from my mouth, while Spotted Dick came close to my fingers but waited for me to drop the morsel before he snatched it.

After more rain the burn waterfalls were belching foaming torrents far into space, as if attempting to reach the hills on the far side of the loch. I covered the movie camera with a plastic mac and took a dramatic sequence of them.

The rain often ceased after dark, so the martens continued to come. Spotted Dick and Centre Spot had a fine game of 'parachutes'. One would run to the top of the bird nest box and leap off, all paws extended, toes spread, to land on the other, which then dashed up to repeat the performance. They huffed and hemmed, rolled over, slapping each other with their fluffy tails. The long-suffering parents took it all in good part, dodging out of the way while they went on with their chewing. The kits loved the game so much that they were back at 5 a.m. playing it again! With the aid of two candles, a paraffin lamp and a torch, I had managed to film the martens coming through the window on to my desk, but these flimsy lights would not reach out to the spread of the mossy table. I could have tried a 12-volt spotlight to film the game but felt sure they would not play in the same way in such an artificial glare. Maybe I would be able to stage something in sunlight.

In drenching rain the next day I baled out the boats and fought my way across the loch to fetch supplies from the big town 40 miles away. I had run out of bread and the martens were not taking kindly to jam on months-old Weetabix. While shopping, I ran into Ro Scott, the N.C.C.'s assistant regional officer, who took me in for coffee. She herself was a botanist, with two assistants compiling material on flowers in the area, but the disquieting news she told me concerned a new fish farm which had applied to the local authority (a requirement recently made law after pressure from conservationists) to put 14 salmon smolt cages right up close to the islet on the south side of the loch where the second pair of divers nested. This site was a little less than half a mile from the two main cage installations of Marine Harvest Ltd. In the three years they had been there only one diver chick had been raised to maturity on that islet. If 14 more tanks were moved close to the islet, this pair's breeding was doomed, for there was no other suitable nest site in the western part of the loch. The N.C.C. intended to object, but the answer would be that the project meant more jobs in an area of high unemployment. I said I would think about whether it would be useful for me to be singled out as a crank against local employment. It might not be such a bad idea for the divers to be forced further east where they would be less disturbed, though the birds might desert the loch altogether.

'If the whole loch is an SSSI [Special Site of Scientific Interest],' why can't you stop all these fish farms wrecking everything?' I asked. 'What's the use of declaring SSSIs if you can't protect them?'

This was always a problem with the Nature Conservancy Council, which was originally set up as purely an advisory body. It performed scientific investigations and gave advice on conservation, but its recommendations could be ignored by government, and often were. It could do a good job – such as it did for the Somerset Levels, clamping down on farmers and declaring the West Sedgemoor area an SSSI in 1983 – but would then run into trouble. When the government finally gave in to the big money land-owning fraternity in Somerset, the N.C.C.'s chairman, Sir Ralph Verney, was sacked, along with other members of the Council who agreed with him. Years later, after an SSSI was successfully negotiated for the region, and the sum set aside for grant-in-aid shot up to £42 million, Somerset Level farmers reversed their clamour and begged to be included in the SSSI so as to benefit from the management agreement money. While the N.C.C. could now object to land and water use at planning stage, it still had no real power unless it could count on local popular support. In the case of the new fish farm planning application, permission was refused not due to the N.C.C. but because first-comers, Marine Harvest Ltd, made strong objections on grounds of unfair competition and the increased possibility of disease.

The other news I gained that day was that N.C.C. eagle survey field scientist Jeff Watson had been appointed the Council's assistant regional officer for Ross and Cromarty. He had bought a cottage and several acres of land. As I drove back to the lochside I realised for the first time that I had been less than intelligent about my own future. In all my 19 years in remote places I had thought only of getting on close terms with the wildlife, much of it now rare, and of writing about it in the hope that it would be better conserved. I had given no thought to old age, or the security of having enough money to *own* a property. Now it was like a losing battle, despite the growing public awareness – itself a cause of the decline, it seemed to me. If I managed to finish my film and it was seen by millions on television, how much more of a threat would that be to the very creatures I had sought to protect?

Four times I plunged down the slippery cliff to the loch with my purchases in the unending downpour. When I boated home I found the loch had risen so high that I could beach the boat on the grass, though I could not leave it there in the freshening gale. By the time I had retrieved the two wooden runways from where they had floated along the bank, the wind was so strong that I could not get the boat up on to them in the normal way. I could not hold the heavy boat out against the storm while I pinned down a runway and eased the trolley to the right place on it. Lashing waves made it impossible to hold all three together for long enough to begin hauling the boat on to the trolley. In the end I jammed the boat on the runway without the trolley and left it tied to bent trees on either side, to keep it head on to the incoming waves. I dug the rear anchor into the earth to prevent the boat from swinging sideways and hoped for the best.

It was 7.30 before I carried the last load indoors. What had once been a challenge, a test of survival fitness, had now become a tedious and even dangerous chore. Fortunately the expedient worked this time. Though the loch rose more than I estimated, and the bent trees ran out of spring, so allowing the prow to drift round slightly, both boat and engine were still intact, if in need of baling, next morning.

A dispiriting day on the eagle book was relieved when the marten family reappeared at about eight o'clock. For the first time Spotted Dick took titbits from my fingers, while White Chest seemed content just to run after the other two once they had something in their jaws. When sun broke through the clouds the following afternoon, I was astonished to see Spotted Dick and Centre Spot start to play games below my study window. Swiftly I assembled the movie equipment and filmed them racing about, leaping high and batting at each other with their front paws. That night Michelle allowed White Chest to drive her off a piece of bread on the table and came to me for more. Spotted Dick was clearly boss of the kits, and had not been 'lost' when I rescued him from the tree so much as adventurous. He was growing faster than the others. The five martens had gone through a whole loaf that day and were now my main interest in life.

The bad dreams returned at night. Once I dreamt I was an old man, forced to live in a small wooden back room in a tenement block with all my belongings strewn around me. I was looking for the bathroom when I saw people tumbling out of the smoking foundry building next door. Someone yelled up at me that the whole street was on fire. I rushed about trying to save my life's work, throwing out of the window the films that were yet unsold. Flames were licking up the outside of the building and the room was thick with smoke. The top of the house had opened and pages of my diaries were disappearing one by one up into an orange heaven. I prayed that every one would be burned rather than found. A burning ladder below me collapsed and fell back. People were yelling 'Don't jump, you'll kill yourself!' The ground looked damp and mushy from three storeys up and I reckoned my Hill-powered legs and weight-trained arms would break my fall. I stretched them all to earth, jumped – and awoke!

With a sudden burst of energy I worked compulsively all next day to finish the book. I left the desk in a brief spell of sunlight and was surprised to see a pair of eagles flying towards the Eyrie 1 peak. I shot indoors for the half-assembled film gear, clipped on a telephoto lens and a battery and struggled out with the lot. Juno had landed on the peak and was still there! I could see her hooked beak turning as I focused on to her and pressed the button just before she opened her wings and soared away to the right. I followed her as she circled round, appeared to spot some prey, then dived down with folded wings at great speed. She seemed to miss her target for she zoomed up again into the white sky. I just had the presence of mind to tighten the aperture from f8 to f16 in the strong light. She sailed to the west, then turned and came back to hover quite close to me. She hung in the air for a long time, and I was able to see that an eagle does not have to winnow its wings against the wind, as does a kestrel to perform this feat. Juno merely adjusted her wings slightly, her tail twitching this way and that, both sets of talons stretched towards the ground, working to keep her anchored in the sky. I could see her head turning from left to right as she scanned the ground. Then she looked up again and spotted something interesting to the west – maybe her mate – and drove her wings hard to give herself pace before easing into a jet glide on the south-east wind past the distant rockfaces. As she disappeared below a crest I kept the camera turning on the blowing grasses.

About an hour later I saw a female eagle with an eaglet tagging along behind, its creamy wing patches showing clearly. I knew it could not be Juno, who had had her eggs stolen late in the incubation period. This pair could have been from the nest out of my territory three miles to the east. Whichever they were, this poaching over Atalanta's former territory was further evidence that she was indeed dead. I saw the two again just before dusk, passing east below Eyrie 1 peak. Could there be a rare summer carcass of deer or ewe up there? If only this rain would ease up I could take a look. Farmers in this Highland region had suffered a disastrous summer. With the second crop of hay ruined and cereals flattened there would be no winter sileage.

The marten kits came alone that night. Centre Spot was hungry enough to pluck a titbit from my fingers for the first time. It certainly appeared that the adults were letting the kits take over the territory for a while, helping them to feel more secure.

In the soggy gloom next day I detected movements on the martens' table while I was typing the last words of my book. A fat-faced little field vole had made a burrow in the moss round the top of the run-up log and was foraging fitfully for scraps of food left in the thick green strands. It darted here and there, whiskers quivering, dark eyes bulging, gleaming, before dashing back into its hole. A few seconds later, out it came again. This was just the sort of film I needed to link shots of the mother buzzard leaving the nest to hunt to those of her hovering and diving down before returning to the nest with a vole in her talons. Maybe I could cheat a little too. The chance of filming so closely a vole in the wild was about one in a thousand. I set up the ciné camera, put on a 100mm lens, adjusted the aperture and focus, and took a fine little sequence of the questing vole barely four feet away through the study window.

At night all the martens but White Chest came. Mick and Mich engaged in little '*chrehm*' barking quarrels over morsels as I buttered and jammed yet another slice. Each time I said a sharp 'Na!', how-

The male eagle flew away from the nest with an unwanted twig of foliage.

When near the eagle eyrie red deer hinds stayed closer to their new-born calves than usual.

A red deer hind with rare twin calves, now too large to be at risk from golden eagles.

The martens' new kits – Spotted Dick (*left*), whom I rescued, and Centre Spot (*right*) who was shy but not too timid to come for food.

Cedwig, the tamest member of the common gull colony, took to calling from my chimney pot in times of stress.

He would take a slice of bread from my bird table and share it with his shyer mate on the loch.

The rare giant toadstool *phaedrus schweinilzi* appeared only once in the woods, growing from old larch roots.

Alone in early autumn, a young heron learned by trial and error how to fish the burn.

ever, they stopped fighting. It was like controlling young teenagers.

It was so cold over the next two days that my fingers turned white while I sat typing out my eagle breeding reports for the government. I lit the barrel stove before the target date of October 1 for only the second time in 19 years. The idea now seemed absurd: what more did I have to prove about this lifestyle? On my next supply trip I decided to row both ways across the loch, just to maintain body strength. I saw as I landed in the far bay that some tourists had been filming me. I pretended not to notice and drove away. The head forester told me, when I ran into him, that he had let some of the local hotels have keys to the barrier on the forestry road and proprietors were lending them to guests who wanted to drive out and look across the loch at Wildernesse! I was glad to hear he was changing the lock because poachers had been buying copies of the keys. He would let me have a new key. He said it as if he wanted to impress on me that access depended on his goodwill. It seemed to me that a half-seen door was already beginning to close.

I took the long route back from the town, which gave me a sight of the beautiful view across the sea to the islands of Eigg and Rhum that had first inspired me to live in the Highlands. While driving along the north shore of my own sea loch I saw what looked like a large eagle fly from a ewe carcass by the roadside. It had an odd sort of peppered plumage, with large flecks of dark brown and creamy white, and at first I took it to be a young golden eagle. When it landed on a rock only eight yards further in from the road, I saw that it most certainly was not. Just then I spotted an adult golden eagle perched on another square rock nearby. Never before had I seen in the Highlands two eagles at a carcass beside the road. I stopped the van and raised my binoculars. The adult goldie walked, ran, then flapped just a few feet before it appeared to stumble. Both birds just stood looking at the van. I wondered if agricultural poisons had been put into the sheep, which looked as if it had been hit by a car. After a few seconds, in light too poor for photos, the peppered eagle flew weakly towards the adult golden eagle.

I was fairly sure the young one was a white-tailed sea-eagle, and was the one chick which had fledged this season from the sea-eagles reintroduced into Scotland by the Nature Conservancy Council over the last few years. When I got home I searched through my books and confirmed that it had indeed been a young sea eagle. After reporting the sighting to the R.S.P.B. on my next trip out I drove back to the site and was glad to find no trace of a dead eagle. Nor had anyone heard of one being found. They had probably moved awkwardly because they were full up.

On a dry but dull September 11 I set off on the killer trek route to reach the 2,179-foot peak of Guardian Mountain to see what the deer herds were doing. I had no intention of completing the whole trek again but wanted to know if the stags had broken out of their bachelor summer herds and were taking their places among the hinds for the autumn rut. As I headed up the steep east side of the burn gorge, just past the level of Eyrie 1, a deep cleft appeared between the hills to my left. I saw a large eagle soaring towards me on the southerly wind, her wings held half backwards. I thought it might be Juno, and then suddenly her mate zoomed out to the south and performed a perfect golden ball dive. He saw me, circled airily, then tucked his wings back and shot straight for me at great speed. It was a frightening sight through the binocular lenses – the thick torpedo body and wings, the wedge-shaped head, the piercing orange eyes, hurtling so fast towards me. Even as I recognised the light plumage of the male Melanion I feared that he might be going to attack me. But at the last moment he pulled out of the dive, the air roaring through his long pinions as he braked, then corkscrewed away to the north west, where he performed another dive and sailed back to join his mate. I could see now that she was neither Juno nor the dark old Atalanta. Excited and momentarily scared by this remarkable encounter, I had the distinct impression that he was just having fun with a human he knew well, had decided on the spur of the moment on catching sight of me to shake me up a bit. He certainly succeeded!

I was wondering how their eaglet had fared – the one I had filmed at the end of the Killer Trek – when it sailed into view, joined its parents and all three went circling away together to the north west. It was smaller than its parents and clearly a male. I was glad to know that they were all well.

14 · Up with the Stags

No sooner had I bathed myself down at the sink than I was surprised by a knock at the door. When I opened it, standing there was the estate's new young deer stalker, Calum, and with him was the daughter of the landowner who had leased Wildernesse to me. Calum said that she had developed a taste for stag shooting, and that they had walked the hills all the way from the nearest farm, which was more than six miles away. As it was now 6 p.m. and too late to walk back before dark, would I help? I loaned them my old sea boat and the 4 h.p. engine. I gave them petrol and some tools, and despite the wind that had sprung up, they managed to get away.

Late the following afternoon I heard a boat approaching. It was Calum again, this time alone. He was returning my old sea boat and the engine. He said the engine had broken down near the end of their journey the day before but it had since been repaired by the neighbouring farmer. Calum also told me that he and the landowner's daughter would be out my way to stalk stags a few more times during the season. I could not escape from the suspicion that the estate was trying to lean on me for some reason. Why should they want to come all this way to walk over the small piece of land that had been leased to me? But my irritation eased when Calum handed over a heavy plastic bag. It contained two bottles of good wine, a gift from the estate owner for the loan of my boat.

I invited Calum in for a cup of tea, over which he told me some interesting things about matters that had made me curious. He remarked, for instance, that he had seen no grouse or ptarmigan at all on the hills this year. It confirmed my view that some of the eagle's natural prey had been in short supply. I also learned that it was not until after April 20 that he and the farmer, and the keeper of the glen containing the Killer Trek eyrie, had taken guns and terriers round the fox dens. That meant, of course, they could well have been near Eyrie 27 around the time that Juno's eggs had vanished. But Calum said they had seen neither foxes nor eagles in that area this year. He was sure the farmer and the keeper were not against eagles – in fact the farmer had never mentioned them. In any case, Calum said, he had little reason to dislike eagles because, unlike some farmers, he had not increased his sheep flocks to gain the new EEC lamb subsidy and was still ranching the same 1,400 animals over the 10,000 acres of the two estates. Why should I doubt Calum's word when in one season he had been the only one to give me help with my eagle hides? Besides, he didn't seem to know where Eyrie 27 was.

He was amused when I told him that one of his pheasants had adopted me. It appeared that the estate had released 450 pheasants into the forest five miles up the loch – a long way for one to have wandered to reach my place. Although he would be taking the landowner's daughter to get a stag or two while she was up on holiday, he said he was not stalking in earnest before September 30, when he would be taking out paying guests. Even then he reckoned to be culling no more than 13 to 15 animals, fewer than usual.

We talked of the many fish farm tanks that had been installed in the once pristine bay where for eight years I had anchored my boat. Calum told me that three years ago Marine Harvest had released some 45,000 smolts into the river which drained the loch, hoping to increase salmon stocks. Some of the fish that were coming back to spawn were thinner than the wild fish had been. The catches of wild salmon, he said, had been well down in the past two years. Before then the two syndicates that fished each side of the river had caught a total of 500 salmon with rod and line – the best year since records began. Usually the catch would be about 300, but last year had been very poor, with this season showing only slight improvement. I wondered if the scents being released into the water by the thousands of artificially kept smolts were interfering with pheromones that guide wild salmon to their own home rivers.

I was not surprised to hear that the farmer had landed the contract for feeding the fish in the tanks which were, after all, in the loch water adjacent to his tenanted land. Indeed the fish farm vehicles drove down his tracks. No wonder to me that he had called the fish farm installations 'progress'!

On my next supply trip the 4 h.p. engine gave out after only 200 yards. The plug in it was old – certainly not mine – and all coated in oil. A little later, after I had put in a new plug, the flywheel began rattling against the engine cover. The top nut had not been tightened up and would soon have come off altogether, perhaps causing more damage to the engine. If only one could rely on people to whom one lent things. I relied on this boat for safe passage to and from home.

Waiting for me among other mail at the Post Office was the first copy from my publisher of my latest book *Out of the Wild*, the story of all the wild animals I had looked after in my home – foxes, owls, badgers and so forth. I showed it to the head forester when I called for the key to the new lock on the forestry road barrier and hand in the old one. He flicked through the pages, showing particular interest in the photos of my three little foxes, and then gave me some news. The old naval Captain who had been in charge of the local fox hunting pack was retiring to Somerset and his successor was to be my farmer neighbour.

The local Hunt was not a sporting body but a fox destruction society, run with government subsidy for the purpose of controlling the number of foxes that could prey on live lambs in the spring. I had held several good-natured arguments with members of the Hunt, including the farmer, on the merits and otherwise of hunting foxes. In the book I had gone more deeply into the question, assembling as much scientific evidence as I could, and had come down firmly against foxhunting. While I did not want to point a finger at anyone in particular, what I had said might not please some of the more militant members of the Hunt, and a few might even take umbrage over the book.

By mid-September it was even more clear that the adult martens were leaving the kits free run of the territory, so that they would grow firm and fit and learn in safety how to forage and hunt. All three youngsters were coming through my window each night and even shy White Chest took food from my hand for the first time. Maybe Mickey and Michelle were scouting out new areas for their kits, ready for the time when it came to split up. This was something

I had found that tawny owls do. If so, it was another example of the kind of 'spiritual love' which is not supposed to exist in the animal world. Scouting out new areas while wild foods were at their best made utilitarian sense, at least. The adults could then either let their kits take them over or move there themselves.

The nights were beginning to close in, and I had to light the lamp by 6.50 p.m. Bracken on the Hill was turning orange before the final brown. The single live branch left on my ancient plum tree was bearing a record crop. Fat-bodied craneflies were everywhere, trying to stab their eggs into the soil. They swarmed through the open window at night and burnt to death on my hissing lamp. Once I counted 31 corpses that had fallen into the margarine carton. *Ugh!* After feeding the martens I had to close the window on them for a spell.

In a mountaineering programme on the radio I heard Chris Bonington telling listeners that the first thing one must do as a loner in the hills is to leave a message to say where you are going, so that if you do not return on time, rescuers will know where to look for you. I had been out on harsh hills in Canada, Scotland and Spain thousands of times over twenty years without anyone ever knowing where I was going. There had been no-one with whom to leave a message.

In hot sunshine on October 18 I made the laborious 1,500 feet climb up to Big Corrie with the heavy load of film equipment in search of rutting stags. After stalking one fine beast with six hinds on the highest north-eastern plateau I stopped to assemble the tripod and camera behind an outcrop. Gingerly I moved into position, only to find that the deer had fled. An empty glen stretched away below me. As I scrambled back down I heard a scuffling to my right round a bluff, and then I saw the deer charging away to the west. I had not moved carefully enough, and felt dispirited. I left the gear and belly-crawled to a spot where I had seen some hinds lower down. There I found a stag with an escort of five. I crept back for the camera and set it up on a boulder. This time I was more successful and took some useful sequences of the stag with his harem.

I searched all the dips and dells around Big Corrie with the binoculars. There were plenty of stags to be seen if you knew where to look, and I heard their distant lion-like roarings. They had certainly not been over-culled this year. Calum must have kept to his schedule to take fewer than usual and to stop shooting a week before the end of the hunting season. I heard no shot at all that day. I scared off another group in the basin of the corrie with poor stalking. It was difficult to move quietly with so much weight to carry. I began to think I was losing my touch. Scanning the ridges again, I located six more stags but they were too far away. My heart was no longer in this terribly hard work in these relentlessly punishing hills. After enduring the brutal knee-crushing trek down the tussocky steeps I discovered that I had lost all the mechanism for the guide shaft control on the fluid head, and that meant hiking up again to search for it goodness knows where. I felt feather-light without the great pack and was lucky to find the device before too long lying in the tussocks.

While I bathed at the kitchen sink, I heard on the radio that Orson Welles had died. A recording was played of the Hollywood genius talking about his career. 'I approach movie making innocently,' he said, 'to get it right, as a child.' Well, I had something in common with the great man! 'I spend two per cent of my life actually making films,' he went on, 'and 98 per cent hustling for the money to make them.' It could just be that I was tackling it the wrong way round.

The Indian summer continued for some days and I took the opportunity to dig over the whole vegetable garden and repaint the iron roof. On October 22 the first flock of redwings flew in for the winter and fluttered round the rowan berries. I filmed them and, after finishing the roof, lugged the film gear up into the hills again for more stag material. I was only 200 feet up when I spotted what looked like a pair of buzzards hovering over steep ground below Eyrie 1. I glassed them and saw that they were in fact eagles, much higher than I had thought. By the time the movie camera was set up they were gliding away towards Eagle Rock Mountain. I was sure it was Juno and her mate. I had seen a small adult eagle sailing over Eyrie 1 the day before. All these sightings were a clear indication that Atalanta was now dead and that other eagles were prospecting her territory for areas of their own. Boundaries must inevitably change when a dominant female dies.

Near some trees flanking the burn gorge just below Eyrie 1 I spotted two young stags with four hinds, two yearlings and a calf born this year. I took some trouble stalking them and was rewarded with some interesting film. The dominant young stag was in full throes of the rut. His tongue leered from the side of his mouth in a look of frustrated passion. He sauntered among the hinds, pausing to look at this one and that, and occasionally to throw up a tuft or divot with one of his eight-point antlers. He glared at his rival and roared as he ran towards him. Suddenly he tripped on a tussock and fell. Looking very nervous, the other stag took his opportunity and walked away.

The attacker appeared weak from his lack of interest in food, but after a minute or so he struggled back to his feet, ran in a short semi-circle as a further warning to his rival, and then walked towards a hind that was lying down chewing the cud. He manoeuvred himself so that he was standing at right angles to her head and fixed his gaze upon her eyes. He seemed to be trying to hypnotise her into getting up and standing for him. She lazily blinked her long-lashed eyes and went on chewing. Eventually the stag turned away, took a few steps, gave another roar of frustration, then slowly sank to his knees between the tussocks. Before long he was dozing.

I found the first dead deer of the year, a hind, below the main waterfall as I was returning home. The carcass was wedged between two rocks. It had been scavenged by foxes, or perhaps even by the martens.

Quite soon afterwards I met Allan Peters by the Forestry Commission deer larder and he told me about his own stalking season. He had taken mainly Germans to the Hill this year, and the economics of it all were fascinating. At £8.40 per hour one rifle had brought him £178 for a total of 24 hours of stalking. Three stags per guest had cost them each £580, and for that he would be allowed to keep only the head and antlers, the actual venison meat belonging to the Forestry Commission, which sold it off on the open market. In addition, each guest paid 25 pence per mile for motoring, whether by car, van or the caterpillar-tracked Argocat. The stalker was also due the traditional tip – in Allan's case £25. When you add to all this the cost of hotel accommodation, food, drinks and travel, a week's stalking could cost the hunter well over £1,500 at 1986 prices. Even so, this was far less than the cost of the equivalent in Germany. Allan told me that he and a co-keeper would wait until they had six stags' heads before they boiled off the skin and flesh so as to present the trophies to the hunters as they liked them – clean and with lower jawbone attached. This operation would consume one whole 32lb bottle of calor gas.

Despite the continuing warm sunny days, the nights were now bitterly cold. The colony of pipistrelle bats in my roof often flew at dusk, fattening up for the winter on the last of the flying insects. When I found the bats flying in near frost conditions in the dark, I recalled a scientist saying on one of the Radio 4 nature programmes how research had shown that bats needed a certain warmth before they flew. I never cease to wonder at how much twaddle is spoken over the air by so-called experts. I have been told that some naturalists are jealous of a man who can just wander out into the hills with a notebook and camera, can live alone simply and make a living from writing about what he sees and hears, without any other employment. Whether this is true or not I have no idea, but if I find that scientific thinking does not match my own observations, why shouldn't I say so without any sense of rivalry? I am not competing with others; I do what I want to do, what I truly believe in, and if I am mistaken it's no-one's fault but mine.

For days I had been in a state of turmoil about whether to last out one more winter here or to winter in Spain and start the search for the lynx, the bears and the Spanish wolves. I had hoped for a film deal by the summer that would number my days in this hard life, and here I was at the end of October with no more certainty about the future direction than at this time last year. What had become of the enthusiasm I had been shown at the BBC in Glasgow? Could I survive another winter as severe as the last one?

The dreary, rainy weather returned on November 1, and I awoke on the following morning to a blizzard, the snow covering everything. I spent the whole day packing up, four hours of it winching, levering, manoeuvring the big boat up to the stoutest ash tree, to which I lashed and locked it. After that I hadn't the strength to risk carrying the heavy engine on my shoulder when every step would be risking a dangerous slip on the snow. Instead I pushed it in the wheelbarrow, then took the small boat across and loaded my things into the van before returning for a last night with the martens. I had decided to make one last round of calls for my film and then head for Spain whether I had a deal or no.

The martens enjoyed a feast. Spotted Dick was now bigger than his father. He moved beautifully, sleek and muscular, while Mickey had the look of a fat old man who had enjoyed an easy life. He went more slowly, moving awkwardly down the sloping logs from the mossy table, as if unsure of his footing. I wondered if the youngsters would send their parents packing from the territory. I left them enough food for a week, emptying all the remaining bread, jam and honey, as well as other scraps on and around their table.

It was a risky crossing the next day. A damp south-west gale had blown up after a calm period and I had to weight down the plastic tarpaulin over my cargo. I made straight for the far shore and turned west for the half mile to Easy Bay, ready to dive for the beach if the hull split again, as it had in mid-loch when last I had carried so heavy a load. Dusk had fallen by the time the boat was secure and I had the van skidding over the patchy snow on the pass.

The news at the BBC in Glasgow was, to say the least, disappointing. After a wait of four months I was told that the network did not want my film, or to make any kind of deal – for the time being anyway. The executives in Bristol had exercised the final veto. The Scottish producer held out the possibility of a regional film made on a much reduced budget, and then attempting to sell the finished product to the whole network, but as he was already working on another animal series I doubted the idea would come to anything. I spent time re-editing my film before taking it once more to Anglia 'Survival' in Park Lane, but they had lost interest in Scottish wildlife. I contacted a producer at Central Television, who years ago had wanted to come and film at Wildernesse, but it turned out that his schedule was full for the next three years. My one hope now was the independent producer for Channel 4. I would write a treatment, or a working script, while I was in Spain and send it to them.

I settled down to three months of writing in the isolated clifftop villa I rented in south-east Spain, maintaining a strict routine of long mountain bike rides in order to keep reasonably fit. It did not take long to complete an outline script for my Highland wildlife film which I posted off to the Channel 4 production company, before starting a new book that was to tell the life story of my beloved Alsatian Moobli. I was puzzled by an acknowledgement of my film script but no comment on it, and no promise of backing beyond a note saying they looked forward to hearing from me when I got back to Scotland.

Before the time came for me to return and give a lecture on golden eagles at Cambridge University in early March, I decided to trek among the mountain wildlife reserves of Extremadura, to see if a book – and maybe a film – on the wildlife of Spain was a viable idea, making it worthwhile residing in the country for some years. I had been a visitor many times while my father lived out his retirement in Spain, but I did not want to tackle so large a subject unless I could get as close to the wildlife as I had in Scotland. It was an astonishing two weeks in which I encountered not only bears, the huge black vulture with its 9-foot wingspan, rare imperial eagles, black storks and red and black kites, I also discovered that the Spaniards were operating what I considered to be the most enlightened conservation policies to be found anywhere in Europe. Furthermore, no-one had written in depth and from personal observation on Spanish wildlife for more than half a century. I would call the book, aptly I thought, *In Spain's Secret Wilderness*, for though the Brits and the Germans had flocked to the sunny coastline of Spain since the war, few knew anything of the nature hidden away in Spain's mountainous interior. The project, I felt sure, would give me a new lease of life, now that my work in Scotland was really over.

Due to dense traffic, I arrived a few minutes late for the lecture in Cambridge. I had spent a long time on my notes and sorting through my slides and felt rather nervous when I was ushered hastily into a packed lecture theatre in the university's Department of Zoology, where a sprinkling of older faces told me at once that it was not only students making up so formidable an audience. With no time to decant my slides into their machine, I declined the forward podium and operated my own projector at the back, forgetting of course that, once I had got through a rather stodgy fact-filled preamble and called for the blinds to be drawn for the first slide, I would be without any light by which to read my notes. There was a moment of panic and then, with a few encouraging whispers around me in the dark, I saw that there was nothing else to do but take the plunge and ad lib. After all, it wasn't as if my own observations were anything but burned into my memory after writing two books on the subject. Soon the audience began to respond. I relaxed and was enjoying myself, though I knew I was going on for too long. My watch crept past five o'clock when, I had been told, some students would have to go to their 'supervisions', though as the blinds went up there seemed to be no fewer present than when I had started. I answered some good and interesting questions and was given an enthusiastic round of applause – a rare response I was told at the end. Afterwards Dr John Treherne wrote generously to thank me, saying with a euphemism typical of him, but not of most dons I had encountered, that my talk had been a 'knock out'. They wanted me back.

My pleasure did not last long. The Channel 4 production company did not want to go ahead with my Highland film after all. My film footage didn't match up to the writing in my script. The real reason for the change of mind, months after seeing my films, was revealed in the next paragraph of their letter where they referred to the BBC 'Living Isles' series, the first three parts of which had contained most of the kind of things I had put into my script. Despite the fact that I had not seen any of these Bristol-produced programmes, there was little possibility now of raising finance for another Scottish film. I was back where I had started!

Soon afterwards I received another letter bearing worrying news. As a matter of courtesy, Marine Harvest Ltd – the fish farming company operating on my loch, which I had discovered was a part of the mighty Unilever empire – wanted to inform me of their plans to expand and establish a new site for pens near to Heron Island, on which the rare black-throated divers had often nested. This alarmed me. I made several attempts to talk to the fish farm manager on the phone and eventually succeeded in asking him about the precise location of the pens, for anything placed within a quarter of a mile of the island would seriously upset the breeding success of these rare and protected birds. I was assured that they had been in touch with the Nature Conservancy Council, which had drawn attention to the breeding site, but their smolt pens were to be placed in a bay nearly three quarters of a mile away – if planning permission were granted. I had to be satisfied with that, though I couldn't help feeling it was probably just the beginning of the end for the divers in this spot.

The Channel 4 producer was sympathetic when I talked to him on the phone. Maybe the BBC had gained something from seeing my films, and might well have used the hired tame eagle to shoot their sequences for 'The Living Isles', but there was no copyright in ideas. Why buy my stuff, I was asked rhetorically, when they have much better equipment and film crews on the staff to keep busy? I talked to Hugh Miles, who was then filming ospreys at Loch Garton. He told me he was having to finance his own film about British birds of prey because he had been unable to get any money out of Anglia 'Survival' or the BBC for it. If ace cameraman Hugh

Miles couldn't get backing, no wonder I was out in the cold. We arranged to meet in the summer when I could show him what I had been hawking round.

Without much hope or enthusiasm, I bought another 500 feet of unexposed film (£81.64 for 15 minutes, more than three quarters of which, taking averages, would end up in the bin) and headed back to Wildernesse. There was still time to get better shots of eagles at the nest, and maybe, as a bonus, the divers too. I gave myself until June 30 – when I would have spent 20 years alone in the wild places with only boat access – to come to a decision.

15 · Explosive Predicament

The first clue that my premonition of trouble had substance came when I ran into keeper Allan Peters near the end of the long journey home. He looked unusually ill at ease. The story he had to tell was extraordinary. Some weeks before, the local foxhunters had got some hounds trapped in a rocky cavern close to Eyrie 28 and had been forced to use dynamite to get them out. It was no good expecting the eagles to use that eyrie this year.

I felt as if I had been hit in the gut. The eagles had lost their eggs in the lower Eyrie 27 last year and it was highly likely they would have used 28 this spring. Surely the story was preposterous – dynamite blasting would kill any trapped hounds, not free them. Allan said he had not been to see for himself but he had been assured that the story was true. Huntsmen had been struggling up there for several days in awful weather and had lost several hounds – he didn't know exactly how many. I knew that the fox dens in that area were some hundred yards below Eyrie 28, so it was still possible for the nest to have remained unharmed. The whole thing seemed so unlikely that I had to fight hard to resist the notion that it was somehow a spiteful way of getting at me.

For the lone wilderness dweller almost everything becomes a matter of survival and so he is prey to different fears from those that sometimes beset urban life. What if my boat had been tampered with, or Wildernesse itself, in my absence? High winter waves had lifted the boat higher on the grassy loch bank but it was unharmed. The water pipe from the burn at Wildernesse was broken in the middle and two of the corrugated iron roofing sheets had been ripped off the porch and lay beneath the kitchen window. Both were explained by the long winter freeze-up and ferocious gales rather than any malicious intent.

On the way up to inspect Eyrie 28 I located a new eyrie, a fairly shallow nest of sticks on a triangular ledge 200 yards to the east of Eyrie 33, which had blown out. Here was Eyrie 42, held in place by two slim young rowans. There was no sign of warm grasses lining the inside, so it was unlikely that eggs had been laid in this nest. But why had eagles made a new eyrie? I knew for sure that there had been no nest in this spot before. Eyrie 28 was intact when I climbed down to it, though it was clearly unused for there was no new material in it. I looked down to the foot of the great crag on which it perched. There was a huge gaping hole at the bottom, a fissure about 12 feet long and 18 inches wide. Sandbags could be seen among the newly exposed rocks, while a trail of rocks and boulders lay strewn down the steep hill which sloped away from the foot of the crag.

Clearly this was where the huntsmen had blasted, not among the dens lower on the hillside. It was hard to believe that all this was the result of trying to free trapped hounds. Any hound or terrier in there would have been blown to bits by an explosion that caused this much damage. After scrambling down, I found a fuse wire, a detonation coil, a broom handle (perhaps used for tamping in the dynamite) and more sandbags. Some of the bags were filled with sawdust, others with white grass. Having worked as a blaster myself in Canada, I was puzzled by bags which seemed to serve no useful purpose. It certainly looked as if an attempt had been made to blow up the whole cliff. Even if they had not been *intent* on destroying the eyrie – which, after all, could have been accomplished much more easily without resort to explosives – the disturbance over several days, not to mention the blast, would have been enough to put an eagle out of residence for ever, whether she had laid eggs or not. I toyed with the idea of a report to the R.S.P.B., or even the police, but I needed to ascertain the facts first. If anyone had been intent on spoiling known eagle nest sites, the lower Eyrie 27 would have been taken out as well, but that was untouched, and also unused this season. What puzzled me most was that on more than a score of visits I had never spotted even the smallest crevice in which hounds *could* get trapped. And if the eagles had built the new Eyrie 42 after the blasting operation, why were they not now using it?

I decided to take a look at Juno's best two eyries on the other side of the loch. The head forester had told me at the end of my journey home that they were planting 50,000 new young trees in a compartment by Eagle Rock Mountain where previous plantings had failed. I had made the point in my talk to the locals that these clearings, where new trees would not take, were excellent for wildlife conservation if not so for forestry economics. The compartment that was to be replanted ended about 150 yards below Juno's best eyrie, number 30, and was not much farther from her second best, Eyrie 34.

After the hard mile ascent from the loch shore, I scrambled along the steep little cliffsides above the burn and climbed over the 7-foot forestry fence. I worked my way along the edges of a gorge and up the tiny grassy steps of the steeps until I came to the spot where I could scramble down to the great boulder that had disguised my hide four years before. At first the nest ledge on the far side of the gorge appeared to be empty, but as I raised my binoculars a part of the dark ledge moved. It was an eagle, and it was Juno! The same huge orange eyes and superb golden nape. She stood up slowly, yawned with her great hooked beak wide open, casually unfolded her long wings and floated off on the south-west wind right down the gorge. I could just see the big dry cup in the centre of the nest twigs, but as Juno always made a deep bowl I couldn't be sure there were any eggs – though clearly she was not sitting there just for the sake of the view. My spirits lifted. This had always been the best site for photography. And there was no sign or sound of work being done in the nearby forestry compartment.

The martens returned within sixty hours of my homecoming. After a five months absence, Mickey took food from my hands but his larger son, Spotted Dick, was now too shy to do so. Deep raven croakings shortly after dawn sounded menacing as they echoed between the two woods. Later, while I was searching to see if they had a carcass, I saw two eagles in the sky above Eyrie 1. I dashed indoors for the movie gear, carried it a short way up the north hill and began filming. By then there were three eagles swooping about. I had no doubt that they were Melanion, his new young mate and their eaglet from last year. I watched Melanion climb

160

high, then dive down on the female as she turned over to touch talons. The eaglet seemed to stay on one side as if it knew, or had been 'told', that its days with its parents were over. Suddenly, its white wing patches showing clearly, the youngster turned south, set its wings back in the jet glide position and swept across the sky, faster and faster, until it was travelling at tremendous speed. I filmed this 'farewell' to its parents, a ritual I had seen many times before, as it shot across the firmament like a meteor and vanished from sight.

Fearful bangings began on the forestry track that ran along the opposite loch shore. Huge dump trucks kept driving past my parked van and two bulldozers were working round it. When I went over to move it out on a supply trip, the workmen were polite and levelled a heap of gravel so that I could drive away. They were repairing winter storm damage, I was told.

I made enquiries about the blasting of the crag and was assured by everyone I met in the village that the account I had been given by Allan was correct. The incident had been written up by one of the foxhunters in the parish magazine, though nobody had a copy of it to show me. It seemed that blasting had been tried as a last resort when all barking from inside the cavern had stopped and the hounds were going to die anyway from starvation. The rescuers had spent several bitterly cold February days – before any eagle would have laid eggs – trying to get one terrier and several hounds out by other means. No-one on the Hunt that day, the story went, knew there was an eyrie in the vicinity.

When I collected my mail in a heavy sack I found that the Nature Conservancy Council had declined to send all my usual licences for photographing rare birds at the nest – a legal requirement I wholly supported. The letter said that 'in order to minimise disturbance' they were giving me photography licences for only two species while they were happy to grant me EXAMINATION licences for all species in my application. This was absurd. I could photograph all these large birds from a distance of 40 yards, but to examine them I would have to go right up to the nest, thus causing far more disturbance. Why should I have my activities curtailed by civil service bureaucrats in London who knew nothing, it seemed to me, of rare Highland species? Scottish wildlife should be in the care of Scottish experts.

I was required, in addition, to consult with the N.C.C. head warden in the area before visiting any nest. But as I knew where most of the nests were and the warden did not, I still held most of the cards.

It was proving to be the coldest, wettest spring I had ever known at Wildernesse, with rain every day from April 24, except for two fine days early in May which enabled me to get out once more. While Eyries 27, 28, 33 and 42 had not been put to use by an eagle, I found a weak and dying lamb that had been missed in the last gathering and no less than five dead sheep in one mile of trekking. Only five common gulls were left of what had once been a thriving colony on the nearest islet. I rowed to the farther Heron Island for signs of the black-throated divers that I had heard mewing in the early mornings but had not seen. They were not there, but recent storms had broken off many pine branches that were useful for disguising a hide. As I motored home Cedwig the gull, who had been calling from my chimney each morning, turned up for a ride on my engine back to his home islet. How he remembered from year to year that he could do this I shall never know. I took him all the way home so that I could examine the islet's shore for signs of a diver's nest. There were none.

As I was hauling the big boat on to a wooden shore runway I managed to pull something in my left hip. I had never done that before. It swelled up and hurt like hell, so that I could hardly get out of bed next morning for the pain. Slowly it eased off a little as I spent the day answering letters. While hobbling after sheep to get them out of the east wood at dusk, I saw the diver pair in the lagoon just off the gulls' islet. Perhaps they were going to nest there after all. I left them alone on the next day, which remained dreary and drizzly. It was so cold that my hands went white and I had to light the stove.

More disturbance followed on May 8, and I felt it to be essential to guard the divers. A small boat drifted past and I followed it through the trees to ensure that it did not go to the islet. Two bright yellow two-man canoes were in front of it, also heading east. There was one diver in the water south-east of the islet. It preened its belly feathers for a while, then dived and came up by the islet. I saw it stumping awkwardly on backward-placed black legs up from the shoreline to what was obviously a nest. Two more canoes went past some time later and I dashed down to the south-east land spit, but they did not stop and the diver remained on the nest. When two more canoes passed at four o'clock, the diver was put off her nest. I saw her swim up to her mate to receive a fish from his bill, then she went back to the islet. With all this disturbance so early in the season I felt I ought to get a hide up quickly. At least I might keep off the marauding otter. I really needed a helper to row away the boat so that its presence at the islet did not frighten the divers or attract humans.

There was no sign of the divers next day when I searched for them with binoculars. I hauled the old sea boat into the water, transferred the oars from the big boat, and was about to set off when I saw one of the divers swimming to the south west of the islet. It must have heard me moving the boats and left the nest. I decided not to row across. Later I saw both divers in the water, exposing their white belly feathers to one another in a brief sunny spell. Then one dived and returned to the nest.

South-west gales brought more lashing rain the next day. The loch water was rising fast, and I could no longer get across the raging burn to check the divers' nest by sight from the shore beyond the east wood. On May 11, after a torrential downpour all night, I saw that both boats were under water, the 20 h.p. engine also submerged. I went down to them and started to fight. It took five hours to get those boats out and the engine dried and going again. After frantic baling I hauled the small sea boat out first, then stood in the big boat, boots filled with water, to get the engine off. I nailed a framework of four by twos between the trees so that I could hang up the engine and rotate it. Countless times I pushed it upside down and back while slowly I dried it out with rags. All the pipes had to be undone and blown through many times as the rain continued to lash down on to the plastic shelter I had hastily erected. Eventually the engine fired; I had saved it. The struggle to get the big boat out of the water took almost as long. Once again I baled like a maniac, dashed to the prow to haul it up a mere inch at a time, then dashed back to bale again before the waves refilled the boat over the stern. My hands were torn, I pulled muscles in my back and waist, and the hip started hurting again.

At 5 p.m., the loch now far higher but calm and sunlit, I relaunched the smaller boat and rowed past the islet, keeping well out from the shore. There was no sign of the divers. I landed carefully at the west end and crept between the trees to where the nest site was. Or HAD BEEN, for it was now under two feet of water. The eggs must have been washed away. There was no way a diver – an ancient survivor of the toothed birds of the Pleistocene era – would have the intelligence to carry her eggs to a higher site. Indeed there was no higher site to which she could have carried them. All the islet shore was under water. Then I saw the divers paddling past the second islet, displaying the usual bereavement behaviour by putting their heads back behind their wings. I rowed home with a strange feeling of sadness, for I was sure now that Juno had failed too.

I mooched about miserably for several days in the dark rainy weather, fitting new anchor ropes to my boats, chasing out more sheep, finding another dead deer. If Juno had failed I would begin packing up straight away. I even telephoned a London lawyer who had wanted to buy the remainder of my lease.

On May 17 the rain relented, and in hazy sunshine I boated over to Eagle Rock Mountain with the movie gear and the hide. As I stumbled over the forestry drainage trenches, the male eagle came across from the right and veered away over the bluff containing the low Eyrie 34. Soon afterwards Juno circled among the trees of the gorge before sailing into the Eyrie 30 ledge. I could hardly believe it; she must have a live chick in there by now.

So as to avoid putting the eagle off the nest I turned north west to keep a rise of land beteen me and the eyrie and entered the forestry compartment that was supposed to be replanted. There was no-one about. By the time I had dressed the huge hide with heather and foliage the sky had darkened and it was raining again. If I could not put up the hide, I had at least to see if there was a chick in the nest or not.

After making a cautious approach, I peered round the side of the boulder. There was no eagle to be seen, but a huge and bloody lamb lay on the eyrie. I had to admit that the eagle had probably killed this one. There was much less wild prey about this year. The nest bowl contained an oval whitish thing which looked like an unhatched egg and a bigger pure white object that was just as still. It was surely a chick, though it looked like a dead one. On the other hand, I knew enough about eagles to think that it could be asleep. While it was cold for May, the ledge was well sheltered.

I was unsure what to do – strip the hide and take it down after all my labours or leave it flat on the ground, tied to trees in the forestry compartment, in the hope the eyrie was viable and I could use it later? I decided to leave it. On the drenching trek down, I saw Juno return and circle above the eyrie. Then, to my surprise, she headed west, swooped down, and a ptarmigan shot away, its white wings flashing. Juno did not pursue it.

Soaked to the skin all down my back and below the waist, I endured one of the coldest boat trips I had ever known for the four miles home. Before reaching my shore I checked the near islet. Only Cedwig and his mate were still nesting, the other pairs having given up and gone. This once-thriving colony had been reduced from forty pairs to just one.

The bad weather continued, but there were still plenty of chores. For the first time the kitchen drain became clogged and I had to unearth the entire 30-yard stretch of pipe and the cess pit I had made and clear the stinking gunge away. After a long search I found no occupied buzzard's nest, and was struck by such violent hailstorms when I went to look at my farthest east eyrie that I had to shelter behind great triangular fangs of rock that reared from the earth like teeth. I did not see a single eagle. All I could make out on the nest was a double twig of reddened bone with dark feathers (probably the last of a crow) and one unhatched egg. I had to perform some nifty and sensitive work with the throttle when my boat almost capsized in a storm on the way home. When I saw the waves smashing on to my shore, I took the boat to a small bay to the east of my land. It was only the third time I had been kept out of the usual mooring place.

The atrocious weather meant that I could not spend my birthday in a hide watching eagles, though I spotted one flying over the ridges. Maybe Eyrie 42 was being used after all. I missed filming a buzzard which perched in a birch tree above the carcass of a little tup through pressing the camera button when it was in the reverse position and all the film became scrunched up inside. I missed an eagle when I went to look at Eyrie 1 and the tripod legs became jammed shut. But hearing a scratchy song on my return, I found the singer atop a hazel sprig – a whitethroat, the first I had seen at Wildernesse.

Not until May 28 did the sun emerge again for reasonable periods. I puttered over to Eagle Rock Mountain. The water was now so high that I could slide the keel right up on to the grassy bank above the gravel shore and tie the bow rope to a tree two feet away. After the long weary climb, I managed to roll up the hide, vegetation and all, and heave the great bundle over the 7-foot forestry fence, almost sustaining a hernia as I followed it. Bit by bit, I lugged it over to where I had left the movie gear, taking care to crouch low so that I could not be seen from Juno's nest. I dumped the hide and peered round the great rock.

The ledge was empty. The 'sleeping' chick was definitely a dead one and its pulverised down was splashed with brown debris from the rain. Juno had failed. Her nesting was wrecked not by human cause but by the weather.

Next day, when the rain held off, I forced myself to boat out again and stretch my aching limbs up to Eyries 27 and 42. Neither were being used, though there were two downy incubating feathers on the new nest. There were no eggs in its unusually small grassy cup. I filmed the results of the foxhunters' blasting below Eyrie 28 and slowly, wearily hiked down to the boat two miles away. As I left the glen I held up my hand in salute and said, 'Thank you . . . Goodbye.'

Like most things in my life, my time in Scotland was ending in anti-climax. I could fill in a month till June 30 – when my twenty years would be up – with a few bits and pieces of the remaining film on mergansers and sandpipers, maybe an otter. But I knew it was really over now.

16 · Birth in the Kitchen

It was hard to shake off sour feelings not only of defeat but of persecution. The wilderness paradise I had sought to nurture all these years seemed to be dissolving around me in the continual deluge and I felt bewildered and hurt by the lack of response from those who could have helped me with my film. *Out of the Wild* had received surprisingly good reviews and, along with the other books, succeeded in attracting many more tourists to the area (despite my never naming the spot in any of my books) who seemed to take as much pleasure in gawping at me going about my business as in the unspoilt nature that was beginning to suffer from their innocent presence. I wanted to be taken seriously by those who had the power to influence the course of conservation in Britain, and to give those who lived in cities some inkling of the pleasures of a natural life. I had no wish to become some kind of minor matinee idol. I thought I had left all that behind twenty and more years ago when I escaped from the bright lights of Hollywood. The suspicions I harboured that even some of the local Highland inhabitants had taken against me were the hardest to bear. In this frame of mind, it did not occur to me that they could be little more than self-inflicted wounds.

Allan Peters scoffed at the idea that dynamiting the eagle crag could have been done to get at me for the anti-foxhunt sentiments I had expressed in my book. He had not heard anyone say anything unfavourable about it. My sense of proportion was momentarily restored when an old friend in the big town to the east told me one day of some of the tragic domestic and business problems facing people I thought I knew quite well and imagined were leading reasonably contented lives. I had become too isolated for too long.

On the car ferry between the local village and the big town the rabbi-bearded, bespectacled face of the N.C.C. head warden appeared at my window. We talked about the weather and how the eagles had failed. He told me that although five of the white-tailed sea eagle pairs which had been introduced into the western Highlands were nesting this season, one set of eggs had failed to hatch due to the rainstorms. When I thanked him for sending me a copy of his excellent paper on the checkered skipper butterfly – for which I had given him some detailed reports from my side of the loch – he apologised for the absence of my name among the usual credits. A typing error, he said. I told him not to worry; I was getting used to the cold shoulder from scientific bodies. The British Trust for Ornithology were pleased to accept 76 eagle nest histories over ten years without including me among an extensive list of attributions. All I had ever been given by that organisation was a petty and disparaging review of my book *A Last Wild Place*.

The warden gently rebuked me. Surely I could not be worried by such things. Many naturalists he knew had told him how they envied me my freedom, living in the wilds all the time, with no office routine and no boss, a famous writer making plenty of money . . . I put him right on that last score straight away!

'They're welcome to try it. There's plenty of room out there,' I said. 'What stops 'em?'

My mail did little to cheer me up. A famous television wildlife presenter, who had shown interest in seeing my films, was going to be busy filming in the Mediterranean and could not see me until October. (I never did succeed in showing them to him.) The London lawyer wrote saying he was no longer interested in buying the rest of my lease unless it could be extended.

There were still more letters from readers (usually forwarded to me by my publisher) asking if they could walk in and meet me. I should have been gratified that I was getting through to some people, but all I could think of was the increase in disturbance for the wildlife. Some of the letters I received were very moving, saying how my books had changed the lives of the correspondents. They only brought home to me how much I needed my own life to change. The best news in this batch was that a Spanish publisher wanted to bring out an edition of *A Last Wild Place* in translation. I took it as an omen that I ought to move to Spain.

After a day spent digging over and composting my vegetable patch, I took advantage of a sunny spell to row over to the two islets. Cedwig and his mate were off their nest. Their eggs were gone. I had not seen or heard the otter but its lie-out places were certainly being used. The divers were nowhere to be seen. On the smaller island I found a dead mallard duck lying on its back. It had come off a nest on a small brow where I found seven cold eggs. What on earth had killed it? Something had certainly broken its neck. A few yards farther up on the crown of the islet I came across a red-breasted merganser's nest with eight eggs. I saw the bird in the water below, eyeing me apprehensively. She had almost completely covered the eggs with down, billberry fronds and holly leaves. I found no trace of a new divers' nest. I picked up the dead duck and two of her eggs and took them home.

I put the duck in a plastic bag and placed it in the calor gas fridge, ready for posting to the wildlife analysis unit in Edinburgh. The eggs I set in the incubation contraption I had made from a stout tin in which was a layer of gravel and a nest of thick cotton wool. This device was propped over the warm outlet valve of the fridge's calor gas flame at a height that maintained a more or less even temperature of 100°F. Although I reckoned the eggs had been cold for too long to hatch now, I did remember to turn them every day.

After lunch I boated the three miles to Heron Island, my heart leaping when I saw both divers in the lagoon. I went well past them in a wide semi-circle and set up the ciné camera among larches on the mainland. But the divers vanished round the long sandy point. With them gone I could make a quick safe search of the island's shoreline. I had little hope of finding a nest. What I did discover were dozens of merganser eggshells, halved or quartered, all scattered over the beaches and moss-covered rocks at the western end. I could find no pine marten scats to account for the destruction, nor even those of mink, which I had heard were spreading among the lochs further south where escapees from mink farms had begun to multiply. It must be that otter again, I told myself.

I struggled through deep tangled undergrowth to the eastern end of the island and there found a perfect otter holt under the huge roots of an upended Scots pine. The entrance was screened by long heather and there was a runway to the beach. Following a well-worn second runway, I came to another holt, a big hole under a rock which was obscured by foliage. In the entrance was a large chunk of fish. It had been skinned, so I couldn't identify it. No diver, merganser or duck could nest safely on that island while the otter was alive, but what I had seen was natural predation so it was not for me to interfere.

I waited at the edge of the mainland wood 90 yards away in the hope of filming either the divers or the otter, but after two hours I gave up and went back to the islet nearest my home. I had to fill in the time somehow before pulling out, so I set up a hide between dwarf pines from which I might be able to film the divers, the otter, *anything* . . .

A ferocious north-east gale blew up, making it necessary to brace the hide with cords. I climbed the rocks to tie one cord and gashed my scalp on a sharp, projecting broken branch of a pine tree. Blood flowed profusely. It seemed like a knife attack on me from the wild. Enraged, I smashed the branch off with a karate blow which gashed my hand. Cedwig and his mate, who had started to come over to my garden more often for scraps, regarded all this with passive equanimity. Morosely I boated home and doctored my wounds as best I could.

I was woken early next morning by glorious sunshine streaming in through the window and rowed over to the islet, where I sat in the hide until 1 p.m. All I managed to film was Cedwig and his mate chasing off another pair of gulls and some courting pied wagtails. It was a far cry from eagles at the nest. I rowed back for a hot fish lunch, hacked down some brambles and new bracken to improve the front pasture, then returned to the islet. I had pulled on the oars for no more than 250 yards when a mighty wind sprang up – this time from the north west. There was now no way I could tie the boat up on the islet's western side without the waves smashing it in minutes. It was as if nature, the whole place, were telling me to GO; that no matter what I tried to do in this last season I would not achieve it.

Somehow I struggled to the lee on the eastern edge and tied the frayed old ropes to a tree. I sat in the hide while the wind increased to Force 9 and filmed nothing at all. When the cords began to snap, I gave up, took down the hide and tried to row back against the wind with all the gear. It was impossible, and I had to sit there for an hour, waiting for the wind to die down. Within half an hour of completing the painfully slow crossing there was a dead calm!

I *was* defeated. Looking up at the hills, I knew I would never watch eagles in them again. I wondered how in hell I had ever done any of it. Yet, all around me, Wildernesse looked beautiful right now, as if saying 'Goodbye . . . remember me with love.' Something told me that I would never sell any of my hard won wildlife film, though I didn't want to believe it. A sign came on my next supply trip, on June 9, when the BBC television producer in Glasgow told me on the phone he had failed to get even a local regional deal for me. But, he added happily, he had been given the green light to make the animal series that finally became 'The Animals Roadshow'.

I was in depressed mood when I returned home and entered the kitchen. Suddenly I was startled by a loud cheeping noise. I listened, trying to make out where it was coming from, and finally located it to one of the mallard duck's eggs in my weird incubator atop the fridge.

'*Peep, peep; Peep, peep!*'

I did not know before this that young ducks could call to their parents from inside the eggshell. I made a similar cheeping sound in return. Immediately it answered me. I realised quickly that its parent would not cheep back at the egg, so I made my best imitation duck sound.

'Quack, quack!'

After I had 'quacked', the tiny creature became quite excited and kept on calling. I grabbed my cassette recorder and taped our conversation. Now that I knew it was going to hatch, what on earth should I do to look after a wild duckling? I took down my file marked 'DUCKS' and read that they were very hardy and would eat almost anything organic. I cooked an egg, mixed brown bread with milk and butter, added a little iron and vitamin powder and a few chicken scraps. I boiled a little rice and an extra potato with my supper. In case it hatched overnight, I placed the duck's egg in a larger pan, surrounded it with thick cotton wool and set it back on the fridge vent. I saw that the chick had pecked a small hole in the shell and the egg tooth at the end of its beak was now showing through. As it sensed my movements its cheeps became louder.

The hole was enlarged next morning but the chick had not yet emerged. As soon as I picked up the egg, the chick peeped and struggled, all bunched up inside the shell. I peeled away a small piece. The chick wriggled violently, and suddenly it was out. It lay on its side, gasping and kicking with legs that were grotesquely big for its size. It did not want to open its beak, so I made a warm moss bed on top of the wine incubator and put a water supply near it. There I left the duckling while I boated down the loch in glorious sunshine with all the ciné gear.

Tortuously I heaved the lot up to a height of 700 feet, from where I could look across the whole panorama between Eyries 27, 28, 33 and 41. Conditions were perfect, though the north wind was cold. I was glad I had brought gloves. I waited from 9.30 until 2 p.m. and not one eagle did I see – just two meadow pipits and some moulting hinds too far off to film. It was like a curse! Fed up, I carried the heavy load back down the almost sheer slopes like a slow motion puppet. So steep was the ground in places that one could break a leg if one slipped under that weight.

I had forgotten the little duckling until I was opening the door on reaching home. As I went in I called –

'Quack, quack!'

'*Peep, peep-peep!*'

What else would I call the duckling but 'Peepie'?

Only the ignorant pour scorn on this habit of mine of giving names to the creatures that, over the years, have shared my home. And also others that have not. So long as it is not a harsh sound, it matters little what the name is, but there can be do doubt whatever that an animal or bird will respond differently, become more trusting, once it is given a name.

When I put Peepie on the carpeted floor, the duckling walked about with a sort of shuffle and dug its beak into the pile. I could not get it to take any food. By opening its beak gently, I got a few scraps down its throat, but it seemed to swallow because it had to do so, not voluntarily. My duck notes said that newly hatched young have enough nutrition stored in their bodies to last for three or four days. I kept the little thing warm and talked to it. I held a tin lid of water near and dipped in its beak. Feeling the liquid, it tipped up its head and swallowed some. It did not look as big and strong as photos of first day ducklings in my book, but I recalled wild ducklings on Heron Island not going to the water until the second day. Peepie would be stronger tomorrow.

Around 9 p.m., however, the little scrap became far more lively and kept jumping out of everything I made to contain it. It did not like the warm wine incubator bed nor the saucepan nest over the fridge light. It tried to beat its way out with its tiny, stubby embryo wings. I made another complex for it inside a suitcase. But Peepie was becoming stronger by the minute and positively leaped over the 7-inch sides. The duckling ran to the door, flailing away on its tiny paddles, then turned and saw me and came waddling back to stand at my feet, looking up. It was such an endearing action that I picked up the little mite. Now I could see the light browns, fawns, greys and even yellows in the downy plumage (in which there were already tiny feathers) and the little primrose cheeks below the dark eyes. I was sure it was female. I put her down and let her run about the floor until she was tired. That seemed to do the trick. As soon as I caught her dozing beside one of my mountain boots I made a new bed and even provided her with a substitute mother – a wooden decoy duck used by hunters. I put this lifelike effigy on to a bed of hay inside the suitcase, and padded the sides with cotton wool which I had rubbed in dry earth to make it a more natural colour. I managed to ease a little egg yolk down Peepie's throat, then set her beside her new 'mother'. She peeped in dying diminuendo until 9.40 and was then quiet for the night. To keep her warm, I lit the paraffin stove and shut the kitchen doors.

She started peeping away next morning as soon as she heard the door open. She was still under the brooding feathers of the mother duck. She was fine, though I was surprised she still would not feed herself.

Of course! The idea struck me in a trice. Baby ducklings go to the water with their families by the second day at the latest. I thought briefly of taking her down to the loch and standing guard over her in the water in my wellingtons. But surely I could not put this tiny warm thing into cold water. I wouldn't swim in the icy loch in June.

Instead I heated some water, mixed it with cold until it was just below my body temperature, filled the largest saucepan (which was about 15 inches across) and popped Peepie in. To my delight, she immediately paddled about happily. She dipped her beak down, tasted – WATER – and promptly tipped her head back and swallowed some. She did this twice more, then set off paddling round the edge of the pan, cheeping excitedly *'Peep peep-peep! Peep peep-peep!'* very quickly, as if she had suddenly realised that this was her natural element. When I dropped in a few crumbs, bits of egg yolk and cooked chicken, she dipped her bill in and out, grabbing tiny morsels and swallowing them. But she took so few that I did not believe it was enough to sustain life. After a minute I force fed her a few fragments but again she disliked it, so I stopped. I didn't want her to fear me.

I could not supervise Peepie all day because I had to go for supplies. I dried her off with a towel and set her back under 'mother' duck, with a tin of water and plenty of food nearby. As she clearly disliked the shut-in sides of the suitcase I set down the complex on the carpeted floor. If she wished, she could run about on a soft surface and then go back to her artificial mother.

My return was delayed by a chance meeting with Allan Peters, and together we had gone to look at a buzzard's nest which contained one chick. When I opened the door, Peepie ran to greet me like a little dog, cheeping loudly. Still she would not feed herself from the floor. I set her on the wooden shelf where I peel my vegetables. I was sure mother ducks did not feed chicks beak to beak, but I thought I would try it and put some morsels of chicken and crumbs on my bottom lip. Pursing it out like a beak, I went close until Peepie was out of focus. All I received for my pains was a sharp nip from her spatulate bill, strong enough to surprise me, but she swallowed nothing. I made a new warm bath for her. This time she would not feed in the water, and just kept trying to scramble out. In the end I eased a few oats, two rice grains, a scrap of egg yolk and some potato crumbs down her throat with a plastic probe, and poured in half a teaspoon of water, so that she had to swallow.

Suddenly she scrambled across the boarding of the shelf and launched herself into space. Luckily I was fast enough to catch her in my hand when she was a foot from the concrete floor, though, being so light, I doubt if she would have hurt herself much. I let her go, and all the time I was preparing supper she ran happily about the floor on her pigeon-toed paddles, always ending up right beneath my feet. I had to watch carefully where she was, and where I was treading, for she now had no fear of me at all. She would even run on to my hand if I held it near the floor. As she peeped away, and sometimes I quacked and sometimes I peeped too (she was supposed to have brothers and sisters, wasn't she?), I realised that I was becoming really fond of the mite.

As darkness fell I got Peepie under her surrogate mum where she settled down, apparently fine, peeping gently to me once I went back to the kitchen to fetch my cooked stew.

When I opened the kitchen door next day, my heart sank. Her

tiny body lay between a spare pair of boots on the concrete floor. Had she spent the night there? Swiftly I picked her up. Though her webbed paddles felt cold, too cold, she greeted me with her usual cheeps. But still she would not feed herself. Becoming desperate, I poured some warm water into the big pan and put her in, and, to my relief, she again paddled cheerfully around. I dropped in the usual food fragments and this time she did peck them up. She also realised that, by stirring the water with her paddles, she could swirl the food *up* to within reach of her beak. A forward kick against the sides of the pan could create even more turbulence and suck the food to the front of the beak from behind her. After seeing this example of fast learning, I felt sure she would be all right.

As the dark clouds had rolled away by 11 a.m., I set Peepie by her 'mother', launched the boat in glorious sunshine and burbled down to the mainland wood opposite Heron Island. Cautiously I stalked through the wood right round the bay, keeping well inland, and set up the movie gear on a big rock behind which I could hide most of myself. It was a long wait of some five hours. I did not even glimpse the otter, and when the divers appeared they kept their distance, right over at the west end of the island, really too far to film. The one good thing to happen was that a fishing boat scared a pair of red-breasted mergansers over to my side. They did not see me as I filmed them climbing out on to the rocks, where they waited until the boat had passed, then launching themselves into the water again.

I was hungry, and suddenly remembered little Peepie. I staggered with the heavy gear over the tussocks to the boat and went home. On opening the kitchen door, I saw she was once again on the concrete floor, tucked between my boots. Why on earth had she not stayed in the warm artificial 'plumage' I had made for her? I quacked, peeped and talked. There was no reply. I picked up her body. It was icy cold. She must be dying of hypothermia, I thought. I felt awful as I warmed her in my hands and felt her begin to move. I set her back in the saucepan's cotton wool bed on the fridge light and stayed in the kitchen while writing up my diary. In half an hour she seemed fully recovered.

Peepie then began to paddle about the floor as before. There were a few stumbles, but she scuttered right to the top of a plank I had set so that it bridged the floor and the top of the kitchen table. She had another warm swim. She ate a little, but far too little in my view, so I eased two morsels of mince down her throat, washed down with a little water. I dried her off then set her down close to her surrogate parent, tucking her into the wool and hay.

I had been struggling for some time over a complicated passage in my book about Moobli, and for some reason I now found the words beginning to flow again. It was gone eight o'clock when I went into the kitchen to prepare supper.

To my dismay, Peepie looked weak, standing by the duck on the carpet, her eyes closed and swaying on her feet. The crick in her neck, which I had noticed after she hatched, was more pronounced, and I wondered if it had made swallowing difficult. Her development must have been arrested when the egg was cold between the death of her mother and my finding the nest, so she was a weakling from birth. The other egg I brought home had not hatched at all, and its contents were now just swishy fluids. If Peepie could not survive the rich diet I was giving her she would surely die.

I set her gently back into the 'mother duck' bedding, and with the stove providing heat, I returned to the desk, hoping that a good sleep would help her to recover. After that long cold time on the concrete floor, it was possible she had caught pneumonia. Well, I suppose that a few days of life – when I had spent time with her and she had been happy – were better than no life at all. And that had been her fate before I found the nest.

When I went back into the kitchen at 9.20, Peepie was dying. I held the tiny quivering body and she laid her head over my forefinger. The awful loneliness of my life closed in again and I gave way to morbid self pity. I was ending up a lonely old man on a hill. Soon I would leave, yet had nowhere to go.

I kissed the duckling's dear little head and part of me wished I could go with her. I had failed her, and could not bear to hold her while she was dying. Carefully I placed Peepie's scrap of a body back in the bedding, then began to pace round the cottage, outside in the dusk. When I went back five minutes later, Peepie died before me. One dark bright eye opened, the head shrank back, the beak parted and slowly closed, there was one small kick of her feet, and she was still in death.

I carried her still warm body up the north hill in the gathering darkness and, with a trowel, I buried her above Crowdy and next to Moobli. It all ends in death, I thought, as I felt my way back down the hill. All we really leave behind of any value is the result of our activities. Late as it was, I forced myself back to the desk.

Stalking master stags in the rut was difficult with the heavy movie gear, which made a silent approach impossible. The young stags that moved in when the masters had finished with the hinds looked like amateurs.

The crag below an eagle eyrie that was blasted by foxhunters to free their hounds (*left*).

Fish farming installations (*right*) create disturbance for rare loch-nesting birds. When smolt tanks were pushed too close to the island, the divers left their nest for long enough to allow a predator to get in.

After losing their first eggs to floods, the black-throated divers tried again on Heron Island. I was lucky enough to witness (*below right*) the moment of laying her fourth egg in late June.

All that remained of the divers' second attempt to rear chicks after the noisy installation of the last smolt tank too close to the island. Maybe a parent of these gambolling otter cubs was the culprit.

17 · *Witness to a Diver's Secret*

The death of Peepie lowered my spirits even further. As always at such times, my only refuge lay in more work.

I rowed over to the far islet with the green Fensman hide and set it up between the two pine trees whose branches swept down to obscure its front. Having seen the divers there this morning, I would try to be settled into it shortly after dawn the following day to film them. I was there by 7.10 a.m., but the divers did not show up. Instead I filmed some red-breasted mergansers courting – which seemed odd for the females had already laid eggs. The brightly-coloured males performed a wonderfully weird ritual, suddenly stretching their necks up into the air at an angle of 50 degrees and opening their red beaks, for all the world as if someone had shoved a hatpin up their backsides from beneath the water surface. Then they pulled their necks back, as if completing a huge burp, and resumed a normal swimming posture. Occasionally they indulged in 'speedboat chasings', shooting off after a rival in a flurry of water, with flailing feet and splashing wings, only to pull up immediately on reaching him and gulp water, with their heads momentarily under the surface. I had never seen this spectacular behaviour before, and it looked very colourful through the lens.

As nothing appeared by midday the following day, and it remained sunny and hot, I boated down to the lagoon opposite Heron Island and set up again behind the big rock in the mainland wood, hoping to film the otter moving on the runway from the island holt. After waiting for half an hour the sky began to grow darker and darker, until it was so black that I could not have filmed an otter or anything else that put in an appearance. It started to rain, quite heavily. I had packed the gear and was halfway round the curved bay when the deluge struck. The rain cascaded down as I hurried to the boat. I loaded everything in and took off just as lightning flashed and thunder cracked overhead. A snake-like head and neck bobbed up in the water between me and the shore as I rounded the long sandy point. It disappeared again, and twenty yards further on the water beside the boat suddenly boiled. I had a glimpse of a diver's head, dagger beak and orange eye, as the frantic bird turned fast and dived away. When I looked back, both divers had come to the surface. I had almost run them down under water. Such a shock would do nothing to aid their chances of nesting again, though I was sure it was already too late in the season anyway. I was sorry to have scared them, but I had no way of knowing they were there. Even less chance would there be of the trippers' boats avoiding them.

Fishing and tourist boats were buzzing about on the loch on the next fine day, though none of them came into the lagoon while I was setting up again behind the rock opposite Heron Island. I saw both divers at the far west end of the lagoon, preening as they swam, frequently turning sideways to show their white bellies – a part of their courting behaviour. Then one swam along the edge of the island, as they do when they have eggs, while the other came towards me until it was quite near. I kept watch for the otter until the divers were back at the west end of the island. One stood in the shallow water beating its powerful pointed wings for my whirring camera.

Suddenly the female diver was climbing out of the water and performing her flop-walk routine over the shoreline rocks and grass to what was obviously a new nest. I kept the camera going while she turned something with her beak, then settled down to incubate. It was amazing that they were nesting again so late in the season, and lucky I had been there at that moment.

While I was filming I saw one of the fish farm boats pushing a smolt pen into the bay to which they had said they would expand, just over half a mile away. Now I had to move fast: no hanging about like last time. As I hurried round the bay with my heavy pack and reached my boat (which was well out of the divers' sight) a young man rowed into the lagoon. I watched closely, but he turned out to be just an inept young fisherman, and when his small engine burst into life and puttered over to the loch's south shore, I left too.

I sped back to my own islet to collect the hide, which I had left partly erected on the special wire frame I had made for it. I could not mess about; speed was essential if I was to succeed. The divers must have heard my engine for they were gone from the lagoon when I got back there. I went straight to the beach below the hide site, erected the hide in a matter of minutes, hastily camouflaged what little of it showed above the rock with foliage and shoved in the movie gear. As the nest site was still in sunlight and the divers had not returned I stole over swiftly and saw just one egg in the shallow nest scrape. Wasting not a moment, I leaped into the boat and sped away noisily so that the divers would know I had departed. Before I had covered half the lagoon I saw both birds swimming back into it from the west.

I could hardly sleep for excitement. My only fear was that I myself might have disturbed the divers too much, but these birds knew me, had often brought their chicks to my boat bay and stayed there when I went down to them. I was reasonably sure that, after all my years of experience, I had judged everything correctly. Leaving all the valuable equipment in the hide was risky, but it ensured that I could now get into the hide without disturbing any bird on the nest. I woke before the alarm was due to go off at 4 a.m. and after a hasty egg and toast breakfast was on my way.

While still a full half-mile from Heron Island, the sun an eastern topaz in the cloudless sky, I stopped to plug the rowlocks of the big heavy boat with plastic and then rowed silently into the small shingle bay on the opposite side of the island from the divers. Landing as quietly as possible, I stole up the beach and hid the petrol tank. A cold north-east breeze produced plenty of rustling noises to cover my stalk over the island to the hide. The low sun was behind the hide, so dazzling the eye of any diver on the nest. I slid in, making sure the black muslin was in place. Gingerly I lifted one of the panels.

There was no diver on the nest. I could not see if the egg was there or not as a small flat rock obscured the view, and I dared not leave the hide to take a look. Perhaps the diver had gone for a short swim while the early sun kept the egg warm. Two hours passed, and when I looked up from my book I saw the grey shape of the diver just offshore. She kept drifting in, taking a look at the nest site and drifting out again. I began to think that the egg was no longer there.

179

Over an hour later I heard a mewing wail and saw a diver on the far side of the lagoon, preening and turning her head sideways. It did not display any bereavement behaviour or look towards the hide. It drifted west, turned and began to come back. Suddenly a jet aircraft screamed over, very low and making a terrible noise. The bird dived and disappeared.

By 2 p.m. I was so fed up that I wanted to get out and see for myself whether there was an egg or not. Both divers were bobbing up and down on the bright wavelets only a few yards away. I filmed them, one diving after the other. At 2.40 I saw the female near the shore by her nest. My heart began pounding, but I willed it to stop doing so in order to prevent communicating nervousness beyond the hide to the diver. My left knee was hurting, as if there were a metal ball in the joint, but I forced myself quietly into position. Away she drifted again, and I was about to sit back with my book when she drifted in once more. I had the movie lens trained on the start of her runway, and as soon as she appeared in the lens I pressed the button.

I filmed her climbing laboriously out of the water, pausing, then flop-walking, step after awkward step, up to the nest site. I kept the camera going as she turned round, sat down, got up again, turned the egg with her beak, then flopped down on to it. I almost yelled EUREKA! I had never filmed the divers before but at last, at last, one damn thing had come right in this disastrous season. I took another three-minute film of her incubating the egg, relaxed and looking about. After an hour she became more alert, peered this way and that, then left, shoving herself down to the water on her belly with her legs. After filming all that I changed the 800mm lens for one of 400mm, to give me more of the background, and prepared the stills camera.

At 5.10 p.m. I heard soft muted '*gowawl*' calls and saw both divers at the shoreline looking up at the nest site. I took a marvellous sequence of them together, paddling about, one diving, the other stumping up to the eggs, turning them with open beak and settling down on them again. That ended my last film, so I carefully removed the ciné camera and then struggled to fit the stills camera on to the tripod with screws that did not fit. In the end I had to secure it with masking tape and string. I noticed the diver's strange breathing rhythms, an adaptation for long dives underwater. For 71 seconds she did not breathe, then she took three quick breaths with beak slightly open before becoming still again.

Often she dozed, her eyelids closing from below. After a time the other diver came to the shore (the one I guessed was the male) and made '*oom*' sounds. He kept tilting up his beak as he made these calls, as if saying 'come on, come out here'. Eventually the female gave in to his wishes and propelled herself down to join him in the sunny waters. I could see them through the bushes and little trees beside the hide – preening, showing their creamy bellies and the male presenting his mate with a small fish.

I went back to my book for a short while, and when I looked up again, the other diver was on the nest, having reached it without making a sound. I was sure now that this was the male for the head and neck were thicker, bigger, and the top of his head was longer and less rounded than the female's. His beautiful black front neckband went almost straight round his neck, whereas the female's neckband divided in two at the top, with a heart-shaped patch between. To me it was a clear distinction, and went against the 'sexes alike' phrase used in most textbooks when describing this species. It was also the first time I had known for sure that black-throated divers share incubation duties. I took many more photos with the sun sinking low.

After 13½ knee-busting hours, I decided to leave. I had to be very careful as I sneaked out of the hide with all the gear except the tripod. I then had a hot, hard and dusty crawl back through the tunnel of foliage, the bilberry leaves softening the rustle of the heather twigs, and managed to get to the boat without the diver leaving the nest.

The lure of glorious sunshine the next day was strong and I abandoned my correspondence for another spell at the divers' nest. The site was empty when I arrived but twenty minutes later, after setting up the stills camera, I saw the female heave herself up to the nest. An hour and a half passed, and then she began to behave very strangely. She started to jerk, rocking forwards so that her breast scraped a flat rock, as if she were about to vomit. Her black legs were raising her rear each time. The rocking became faster, her posterior lifted up, the tail feathers parted and lifted, the whole rear swelling until it protruded in a sort of square. Then I saw that it was opening up.

I took what I believe to be unique pictures of an egg coming out. It did not just drop on to the nest. Her ovipositor, or laying membrane, descended with the egg and laid it just outside the nest scrape. This diver had managed to lay two more eggs after the first clutch had been washed away – surely something new for the record books.

181

She did nothing for the next half hour while her posterior slowly retracted to near its normal size. Then she stood up, hooked the new egg next to the first one with her beak, turned and settled on them both. I wondered if she had been unable to move in that half hour or whether she had been waiting for the shell to harden before shifting the egg.

I decided to take away everything except the hide, which I left in place so that I could keep an eye on the divers from time to time and see that the eggs hatched safely.

'Well, that wraps up Scotland,' I said aloud as I boated home. Like a boxer, I had wanted to quit after a winning bout, but had begun to think I had gone on too long. Now, after these two fabulous days, I could quit a winner! Though there was not all that much to sing about, with no takers for my film and no new home.

As I was passing the sandy point I saw three boats pulled up and about a score of people sitting on the beach. Suddenly two of them stood up, then a third. I heard someone shout 'wonderful books!' and they all started clapping their hands. I looked round but could see no-one on the loch to whom they might be calling. Then it dawned on me that perhaps they might be applauding my writings. I waved to them. It no longer mattered if I was to be besieged by well-wishers. I was leaving soon, and victorious.

A large backlog of work kept me at my desk for several showery days, and I was unable to boat back to check the divers' nest until June 26. The loch was flat calm, and I rowed in so that the divers would not hear my approach in the unusual stillness. When I drew nearer, I saw to my horror that the Marine Harvest fish farm had put in three more tanks. They were strung out, with wide spaces between, so that the last one was only about 300 yards from Heron Island. They were far beyond the little bay for which (I assumed) they had been given planning permission and in which I had been promised the tanks would stay. Their noisy installation must have caused the divers a lot of distress. My heart sank.

I slid over the wet ground, better hidden than before by the taller bracken, and peered over the nest site. Both divers were out on the water opposite the nest and I had to wait until they drifted farther west before inching my way down to the hide, assailed all the time by biting midges. Once in the hide I lifted one of the side flaps and lifted the binoculars. Both divers were putting their heads behind their wings for short periods, the sign of bereavement. From time to time they removed their heads and preened their pale belly feathers, but in what now seemed to be a sort of displacement activity. If only I could see the eggs without leaving the hide.

After about an hour I heard a boat engine approaching, whining with high revs but moving slowly. Surely the fish farm couldn't be moving another fish tank in, even nearer? The divers swam off. There was silence for a few minutes, then the engine began again, moving slowly away. After another ten minutes I heard the *'gowawl'* gull-like notes again. The divers were back, but keeping to the far shore and still hiding their heads. Why did they not return to the nest? After a while I heard the fish farm boat whining back again. The great birds dived, came up twenty yards to the east and swam away. The engine noise was very loud now, but I could not see the boat because the tip of the island obscured the view. At least it wasn't yet *in* the lagoon. After a short silence the boat went slowly away.

When the divers returned, after about forty minutes, one swam towards the nest site, looked at it mournfully, then paddled very fast to its mate on the far side of the lagoon. I had the distinct feeling that the eggs were gone, especially when again they displayed bereavement behaviour. I heard a raven calling in the mainland woods but could not see it. Some young crows were giving weak harsh *'skretch'* calls among the old standing pine snags nearby, but nothing landed near the divers' nest site. Almost another hour passed before I heard the fish farm engine returning. It sounded even nearer than before at the end of its journey, the racket like that of a plane about to crash land on the island. Another silence, then once more it started up and slowly faded away. The divers took longer to reappear this time. One swam towards the nest but went away again before it had got closer than twenty yards. It was now 2 p.m. and I decided I had better find out for sure.

I pulled out of the hide and walked to the nest in full view of the divers. To my surprise, they swam nearer and nearer, as if they recognised me as the friend and protector I had always tried to be. The nest was empty. *Hell!* When I looked closer, I saw that one egg had been dragged to the waterline, and the inside skin of the broken bits of shell was still fresh. No human had done this. I didn't think it was the work of the otter either. It had always taken the eggs right away. The second eggshell was more intact and lay three yards away, the inside cleaned out. I looked out at the divers. They were close together now, watching me as I examined the broken shells.

I said softly, 'I am very sorry for you. Very sorry. It is awful for you.'

They came even closer, listening, as if it were possible for them to understand human speech, or at least the emotion behind the sound of the words.

I turned away, sad and angry. The poor birds failed when floods swept away their first eggs; now their brave second attempt had failed also. And I could not absolve the greedy fish farm from blame. The racket of installing the tanks so close to the island had kept putting the birds off the nest, so enabling a predator to move in and get the eggs. I stayed awhile, telling the divers how I felt for them and they remained near me, not diving or moving away. Then I packed up, dismantled the hide and left.

As I boated away I saw that two new tanks had been added to the previous four, the last one situated only about 230 yards from the island. It was not as close as it had sounded but it was far too close for the divers to have any chance in the future of nesting successfully in their favourite little bay.

18 · Endangering Life and Limb

If the fish farm had exceeded the terms of planning permission – they had certainly broken their promise to me – then the latest siting of tanks seemed a deliberate act of provocation, wilfully endangering a protected species. This could mean war. Or else turning a blind eye and just leaving, as I had planned, because my work in these hills was really over. I was in no mood for a battle, but even less did I feel I could just abandon the divers. And it wasn't merely a question of standing up for a pair of beautiful birds that I was fond of and that could not protect themselves. One has to take a stand somewhere. The whole environment of this loch was under threat, and there were many other such lochs and wild mountain ranges making up the western Highlands, one of the most precious natural assets left in industrial Britain. I had come to the wilderness to care for it, to pay it back for the insights and the spiritual uplift it had given; could I now shrug, run out, and allow the decline to take its course?

I resisted the impulse to boat down to the fish tanks at night with an axe. That would be seen as no more than vandalism. I remembered my reaction to the dynamiting of the eagle crag. Besides, the divers had lost eggs to predators in the past, before any tanks were installed. Hasty vengeful action would not help the birds now, for I could not prove it was the installation of the tanks that had allowed the predator to get in again and demolish their eggs. All the same,

185

you would have thought that even if the fish farm were adhering to the letter of the law, and had any care at all for these rare birds, they would have postponed the movement of tanks for a few short weeks until nesting birds on the loch had reared their siblings to a stage when they were able to fend for themselves. Greedy commercial interests had to be made aware of the consequences of their activities and answerable to the community for what they damaged in the process. In my view, this holds good for hoteliers and others concerned with the tourist trade as well.

The disturbance from visitors was worse that summer than I had ever known it before. Fishermen and tourists trolled in their boats to and fro below my study window, often slowly and noisily, some waving their arms above their heads whenever they caught a glimpse of me. Sometimes they chattered loudly, and once I heard ringing across the water: 'Can you see Moobli?' Some youths arrived in canoes, wanting to camp in 'a wild place' – among the trees right next to the only cottage in nine miles of empty lochside. They said they didn't know who I was. I showed them to a spot half a mile away where they could put their tents. When they left in the morning, they waved, and one called out 'Thanks Mike!' On another occasion I stepped outside and immediately heard a camera click. The young man near my porch said it had been the main mission of his holiday to get a natural picture of me. Two boats with straining engines at top pitch came down the loch, sounding as menacing as the droning rumble of Nazi war planes, and stopped right outside Wildernesse. They took off again when I appeared.

You could argue that I had brought it all on myself, that my books had much to do with the disturbing invasion, yet in those books I had sought only to tell people about what was worth preserving in our natural heritage. I had no quarrel with the fish farm so long as it observed the law relating to wildlife in the area and did not threaten the natural environment. I could not be responsible for the way in which some of my readers conducted themselves after I had been so careful to avoid naming the loch or revealing any of the precise locations in my books. I gained nothing from the invasion, though some local tour operators seemed to be doing well out of my presence. One who ran cruises from the head of the loch into 'Scotland's Last Wild Place' told me a year after I had left that there was a never-ending stream of people who wanted to see where I had lived. 'I sometimes think they were the only customers I got,' he told me. At least the bulk of the visitors arrived after mid-July, when the nesting was over. Besides, if people didn't read about lochs such as mine and go to see for themselves that the last wild places were worth preserving, within a generation we would have much more than the odd fish farm encroaching on an irreplaceable natural resource and ultimately destroying it.

I had already moved some of my belongings south, to the home of my friend in Surrey, who had agreed to let me store my things in her cellar while I was pursuing wildlife in Spain. Where I would end up I had no idea. Before setting up a new permanent base I would need to find a buyer for the remaining seven years of my lease, but my departure now did not mean I had to rush into relinquishing Wildernesse. I would give the fish farm until the start of the next breeding season in March to move the tanks back to where they should have been, and meanwhile muster support from such bodies as the N.C.C. and the R.S.P.B. and others locally.

First, I would go to London, to see my publisher and to get all my films developed. I loaded the big boat on June 30, twenty years to the day since I had first ventured into wilderness life in Canada, and headed out. On the way south I called in at the Nature Conservancy Council offices in the big town 40 miles to the east and reported the incident with the fish farm and the divers. They promised to send a warden to investigate and, if the tanks were too close to the islands, try to persuade the fish farm to move them back. The R.S.P.B. in Edinburgh thought the whole business over the tanks was 'very sad'. Highland officer, Roy Dennis, said he would write a letter to the planning authorities, asking them to ensure that the tanks did not exceed their limits and were kept at a safe distance. Even if they were marginally beyond limits, he pointed out to me, one could not think of prosecution without proof, and it would be very hard to prove that installing the tanks had put the divers off their eggs to the extent that a predator was let in. He cited the instance of a man who was prosecuted for stealing greenshanks' eggs and who was heavily fined. The man's defence, or complaint, was that the Forestry Commission could bulldoze a dozen greenshank nests while preparing the ground for planting and get away with it. Yet he had taken just two eggs and it had cost him £600. This sort of thing is all too common and highlights a weakness in the 1981 Wildlife and Countryside Act, and other conservation legislation since.

When I returned to Scotland towards the end of July, I learned that the N.C.C.'s head warden and the new young warden for my area had boated down the loch the previous Friday and had decided that the fish tanks did not infringe the terms of planning permission and were within the outlined zone. Since I had been provided with the same map as they were using I could not understand how they had come to their conclusion. I could not discern any definite zone outlined on it. I telephoned the warden, who was out, and spoke instead to his assistant. He agreed with me, that the tanks were too close, but it was outside his remit as a reserve warden to make a lone protest. It was up to his superiors to do that, and he thought it unlikely they would do so.

For a long time I had thought that the Nature Conservancy Council had no real teeth. It was set up as an advisory body, but no one was obliged to heed their advice. The whole loch was designated a Site of Special Scientific Interest, and if they could not protect that, what in heaven's name could they protect? What was needed, in my view, was a National Wildlife Bureau, or better still a Ministry for Countryside and Wildlife, with legislative teeth and representatives on all planning authorities, not just an Environment Ministry in whose book wildlife conservation had lower priority than city parking meters.

Now, of course, while I am still writing this book, the Tory government has seen fit to replace the Nature Conservancy Council with three regional conservation bodies with more autonomous powers, known as English Nature, Welsh National Heritage and Scottish Natural Heritage. Staff in the field, where conservation counts, are to be increased by up to 40 per cent, but I cannot see that the remit of these bodies is likely to be any more effective, constituted as they are in the main from bits of the old Nature Conservancy Council and the Countryside Commission. Why can't we have an organisation that can *instruct* people, with full backing of the law, on how they may or may not conduct their affairs in the interests of conservation – as is the case in Spain?

In my homecoming mail was a letter from the secretary of the Fox Hunt, who had heard that I was 'building up a head of steam' over the dynamiting incident. I telephoned her to say I appreciated her offer to make the long hard walk out to Wildernesse to explain what had happened and why. She sounded a genuine person, and I looked forward to our meeting.

I wondered whether to advertise the remainder of my lease for sale. I tried to do some more work on my book about Moobli, but was in two minds about everything until this fish tank business was settled. In early August I wrote a polite note to the fish farm asking them to move the last two offending tanks back to the correct half-mile distance from the islets. I enclosed a copy of the detailed report I had written about the whole incident which I had been obliged to prepare for the N.C.C. under the terms of my photography and examination licences. I sent copies of my request to the R.S.P.B., to the N.C.C. head warden, and to Ro Scott, the N.C.C.'s assistant regional officer in the big town to the east, who had also taken action on the part of the divers by sending a formal request that the fish farm keep boat traffic away from the nesting islets from March to July and keep clear at all times of any divers seen in the water.

Later in August I heard from Roy Dennis of the R.S.P.B. that he was sending a diver expert to look at the situation and confirming that half a mile was a safe distance to prevent disturbance. He had advised the area planning officer and the Highland Development Board of the problem, and sent me a new leaflet which, he said, was the start of a campaign to heighten concern for the future of this bird in the Highlands.

On my next supply trip I looked across at the fish tanks from the forestry track. One of the pens, just one, appeared to have been shifted. The tank nearest to the islet looked as if it were a little farther away. Perhaps the gale had pushed it about. In any case, this last one and the two nearest to it were still, in my judgement, far too close to the nest sites.

One evening I went out for a breath of air in beaming sunshine at the end of a day of misty rain that had kept me at my desk. A lone eagle was soaring over the crests to the north east. It turned, circled, showing me its immature wing and tail patches, then dived down behind the ridge with wings up and talons extended. Some seconds later it soared out again, looking bulky, and this time came down on my side of the ridge. Suddenly I spotted a young fox rolling in the grass below. Could the eagle have dropped it? It landed two or three yards from the fox as it got up and tried to run away, stumbling over tussocks awkwardly, as if it had been injured. It was a big dark fox cub, and I watched it shoot under some rocks, with the eagle flap-flying and jumping after it. I ran inside for a camera and by the time I emerged again there was no sign of either the eagle or the fox. A few minutes passed before I saw the young eagle come over again. This time it dived down on a hind, which dodged slightly, jumped over a small rockface and went back to grazing. The eagle swept towards me, circled to the east, and I took a photo of it landing, wings up, on a near crest. It was certainly a youngster of this year for its hunting skill was not developed.

The divers were being unusually vocal for the time of year, several times waking me early in the morning with weird childlike screams. I often saw the female red-breasted merganser with her five flightless chicks. She at least had escaped the otter, or whatever predator had killed the mallard. I startled a young sandpiper in the eastern bay. It jumped into the water and swam across all the way to the far side of the loch, sinking lower and lower as it went. Having gained the shore, it climbed out and ran off over the rocks. Until then I did not know that a sandpiper *could* swim. It was clearly less buoyant than a duck and would have drowned had it been forced to swim much further.

I took refuge from the shouts of the sightseers on the loch one afternoon in cutting up a larch tree that had fallen across the burn. Because of its many branches, I was afraid it might form a dam. I power-sawed fifteen 2-foot bolts out of it stumbling with heavy saw over boulders and fallen branches in the water. Then I carried them all to a high bank and from there pushed them, three at a time, in the wheelbarrow the 150 yards uphill to the woodshed. Rain put a stop to both the tourists and me. Sweating, I took my blisters to the kitchen for a cup of tea. I couldn't help reflecting that life at Wildernesse had been one long fight, just to stay alive. I did not want to fight the local farmers or the fox hunt, or for that matter the fish farm. I had done more than enough here. The more I researched the wildlife of Spain, the more eager I became to get to grips with it, but I needed a little more cash if I was to set up a new base there in a less harsh environment.

One symptom of my weakening link with the Highlands was the purchase of a small black and white television set that I could run off the van's 12-volt battery system. The only trouble with it was that I could get a clear picture in only one spot – at the top of the 1,000-foot pass on the way to the village, where I could park directly underneath a small TV booster station. After a supply trip on August 28 I was sitting there watching Sebastian Coe, Steve Cram and Tom McKean perform in the European Athletics Championships when a man in a smart cloth cap loomed up in the window and knocked at the door. Irritated, I asked him to come back in ten minutes – unless he wanted to watch the programme too. He could come in if he kept quiet!

The man turned out to be one of my keenest readers, Eric Jones, with whom I had corresponded. He was the helmsman for the Beaumaris Lifeboat in North Wales, and was up in the Highlands looking for a place like mine. He was fond of wildlife, had no wife or children, and could obviously handle a boat in dangerous waters. It took me seconds to say I might be willing to sell him the remaining years of my lease, which would give him time to make up his mind about Scotland without too much expenditure. If he could walk in along the forestry track to the loch shore opposite Wildernesse by 5 p.m. I would collect him in my boat and show him round.

Not only did Eric turn up on time, he also fell in love with the place as we walked the woods. He agreed to pay the modest sum I was asking, for which I would pass on the 7-year lease, both boats, the big engine, some tools and books and the bits and pieces of furniture which I left behind, including kitchen equipment. The old desk which had belonged to James Barrie at the time when he was writing *Peter Pan*, on which I too had pounded out nine and a half books, would not be left behind.

We did a deal, subject to approval from the estate, and agreed to put everything in writing. It was late by the time we had finished talking and I invited him to stay the night. I boated him across the loch next day and drove him the three miles to his car on the other side of the locked forestry barrier. We were met by the local police constable, who was extremely annoyed with Eric. When he had failed to turn up for supper at his hotel and was not in his bed there in the morning, the hotel manager had got the police to send out a search party, in case something had happened to him in the hills. This seemed to me extraordinary, and I said so. No one had ever sent out a search party for me in all the years I had tramped about in 300 square miles of these hills. None the less, Eric was commanded to report at the police station on his way through.

As I drove back I saw the estate boat – like mine, for I had recommended its purchase – close to Wildernesse. Were they coming to see me about my letter to the fish farm, or perhaps bringing the fox hunt secretary? I launched my boat towards them at speed, but they just kept going on up the loch. Three days later the young stalker Calum, again accompanied by the estate owner's daughter, landed the estate boat on my rocky shoreline. They were polite and cordial and made no mention of the fish farm except to say they had stopped releasing fish farm smolts into the river so as to augment wild stocks. I was amused to hear my words quoted back to me – that it was uncertain what effect the artificially bred fish might be having upon the wild ones.

I was lying abed, listening to a favourite radio programme on the morning of Sunday September 7, when a shadow passed the window and I heard a knock at the door.

'Hang on!' I called out, dressing hastily.

When I opened the door, in bounded a huge Alsatian, one that could have been Moobli's twin, followed by its owner, the fox hunt secretary, who had kept her promise to pay me a visit. She was a good-looking blonde woman in her early thirties. She could certainly hack the Hill for she had trekked in the hard way – the length of the glen below Guardian Mountain and up over the tops to reach me. She handed me a large fruit cake, as a 'peace offering'. Rather archly I said I had not been aware of any war. But I thanked her and made some tea. Her account of the hunt took some time to relate and she stayed for lunch. In brief, this is what I heard.

The hounds were chasing a fox up to the high ridges, followed by the huntsman who was ahead of those on foot. He came upon the hounds gathered on rocks about eight feet above the fissure, looking down and barking with excitement. He was sure the fox had gone into the fissure and so put in a terrier either to kill it or flush it out. Then he heard other whuffings and whinings coming from deep down the hole. When he counted the pack, four were missing, probably all in there. It was thought that they might have found another small entrance lower down, hidden by deep heather. Several hunt members did everything they could think of to tempt the terrier and the hounds out again, but it sounded as if they were in some sort of cavern, the walls of which they could not climb.

Several of the men went back there next day and tried to shift some of the rocks, which took hours of work with crowbars, but still they could not get the animals out. On the second day they took in a rock-cutting machine on the estate's caterpillar-tracked Argocat and succeeded in cutting a fairly large hole, but the fissure extended downwards much farther than they expected. The dogs could not be lassoed with ropes because they could not be seen. For two more days they worked with the cutter and a pneumatic drill, but the animals were still beyond reach.

The farmer thought the task was hopeless, and only then was blasting suggested to him. Of course everyone appreciated that the blast or broken rocks could kill the hounds, but they would die anyway, slowly, from cold and starvation. Blasting, I was assured, had been a very last resort. If it shifted enough rock there was just a chance of getting one or more dogs out alive. In the end it had been a consensus view, with which she, the Hunt Secretary, had agreed, that dynamite be tried. If it failed, at least the animals would be spared a lingering death.

With the aid of a local road blaster, they blew off smallish pieces of rock at a time. When this seemed to be taking too long, they tried bigger blasts – three, as far as she could remember. Everyone thought that these had killed the animals. But on the seventh day, when the blast debris was cleared out yet again, they could see the ribcage of one hound still rising and falling. They could not give up then. Lights were fetched, and they worked on until midnight in temperatures below zero, finally freeing a three-year-old bitch hound called Melody. She was weak and could not walk, but she eventually recovered.

Though no more sounds were coming up to them, the huntsmen worked for two more days until they could just see the other three hounds wedged together in a crevice. They were all dead. Neither fox nor terrier could be seen.

It was a tragic story. Those men, who had endured nine days in atrocious weather, must have cared very deeply about their animals. The sacks of hay and sawdust I had seen were not attempts to contain the explosion but had been tucked into gaps in the rock to keep the animals as warm as possible at night.

The Hunt Secretary revealed that from a pack of thirty hounds they lost on average six each year. Some picked up poison left illegally on the Hill for foxes and crows, others were caught in snares or fell over chasms while chasing foxes. A few got lost and were never found. It seemed to me that foxhunting was as cruel to the hounds as it was to the foxes. I saw no reason, despite the heart-rending story I had just heard, to change my view that it is wrong for the government to fund or subsidise packs of foxhunting hounds.★

She told me she had found foxes in snares still alive after five days, dying in lingering agony from ghastly wounds. At least hunting disposed of the fox quickly, or else it got away, she argued. It was her view that if hunting were to be banned, farmers would still try to control foxes with snares, terriers, guns or poison. She told me that she and her husband admired eagles and understood exactly what I had felt on finding the eagle crag had been blasted. They had helped the R.S.P.B. and the N.C.C. to find and monitor eyries for the government survey, just as I had.†

When I pointed out to her, as I had done in my book *Out of the Wild*, that two independent agricultural scientists had recommended suspending fox control for a period of years, so that lamb predation could be measured, farmers had refused to put this idea into practice. She agreed that in sheep-rearing areas the farmers' lobby was very strong, but she believed that many of those who joined a Hunt did so because they did not want to feel left out in the community. Although she could not agree with everything in my book, she said that everyone she knew liked it and all the other wildlife books I had published.

I walked with her to the top of the nearest ridge. She seemed an honest person and I was glad she had come to talk to me.

★ Further proof that the need to 'control' foxes is exaggerated came a few years later. In 1987 the League Against Cruel Sports funded a three-year experiment on the 70 square kilometre estate of Eriboll, in north-west Scotland, during which no foxes were killed, by hunting or other means, between March 1987 and March 1990. Extensive studies by agricultural scientist Dr Ray Hewson found that there was no increase in fox predation on lambs, nor in the number of foxes or breeding dens in that period despite the absence of any sort of control. The fascinating details of this study, which also includes interesting new facts on foxes in Scotland as a whole, are contained in *Victim Of Myth*, obtainable from the League Against Cruel Sports, 83-87, Union Street, London SE1 1SG.

† At the time of writing, the government initiated a second golden eagle survey, ten years after the first. Sticking my neck out, I can tell them the result – Britain's golden eagles are in slow decline; and it may not be so slow at that.

19 · End of a Highland Odyssey

Two evenings later, while I was watching one of the divers paddling along near my boat as dusk was falling, two figures stumped loudly past my window and knocked on the door. One was a blonde woman, her companion a tall unshaven man. Both were German, and in halting English said they were lost. As guests of a nearby landowner, with whom I was less than friendly, they had started out from the west of the glen below Guardian Mountain and were trying to reach the neighbouring farm from which, they had been told, they could get a lift back to where they were staying. It seemed impossible; the farm was over six miles down the loch! Had they maps? Yes, they said, but the path over the mountains was very difficult.

They would not come inside. The woman asked for a glass of water, and I gave them both some water. They wanted to know which was the path along the loch shore to the farm. I escorted them to the end of the west wood and showed them which way to go. Before long they were back. They could find no path: would I boat them across the loch to the forestry track? I walked back to the cottage, put on my rubber boots, picked up the boat bung and went down to the loch shore. The man had already tried to launch my boat but found he could not shift it. I shoved it out, they got in and I took them across to Easy Bay, half a mile past the spot where my van was parked above the 80-foot cliff. Not once did they apologise for disturbing me, nor did they offer to pay for the gallon of petrol.

195

I was glad to see them off. For some minutes I watched them march briskly along the forestry track towards the barrier without looking back. They still had a long way to go. There was something about this pair that I did not trust. I was thinking of the fish farm, which had still made no reply to my letter. They were probably quite innocent tourists, but it is a fact of wilderness life that one's intuitive responses to people are immediate and enlarged, much more so than in urban situations, where the arrival of strangers is much less threatening. Of course, one's first impression can sometimes be mistaken, but not often. At least this pair could not complain to the locals that they had been let down by a nasty, unsociable old man down the loch.

Some weeks before I had been disturbed to see a man canoe along the far side of the loch, land on a shingle beach below my van and begin climbing the cliff. I hurried down to the shore to launch my boat. Then I saw him down on the beach setting up a pup tent. I watched him walk to a sloping rock and reach down with a mess tin to scoop up water. Suddenly he missed his footing, slid down and ended up on his bottom in a foot of water. Having scrambled up and slapped himself down, he reached for more water and took it to his tent, where he gathered rocks to make a fireplace. When I saw him fall as clumsily and comically as that, I felt I had little to fear.

My heart jumped when I saw him climbing again, but it was only to a small bluff a few feet above the beach, so that he could take a picture of his canoe, tent and fire. My instincts told me he was not a man to worry about and that my van would be safe.

Even so, when I awoke early in the morning, I decided to ferry across some more things to take south and see what he was up to. The canoeist had gone. He had left no litter, but I found a note tucked under my windscreen wiper.

Dear Mike, I loved your book *Alone in the Wilderness* and have been trying to have a similar experience in Scotland. No bears! Good luck . . .

I could not read the name. The considerate ones never call uninvited. Had he come all the way from Canada, where I had tracked grizzlies, to find this small pocket of wilderness? I should like to have talked to him.

While on my way to post the lease document to Eric Jones on September 17, I saw that the fish tanks were still firmly in place.

Well, they had until the end of winter, whether or not I was then living at Wildernesse. I still needed the estate's approval for the sale of the lease.

On my return from the village with supplies I saw across the loch a large black mass floating close to my shore. Hastily I raised my binoculars. It was the fish farm boat pushing along four great tanks in the direction of the lagoon between the islets. Surely they would not be so foolish! Were they going to pretend they had never received my letter?

I thought I heard yelling from two figures in the boat. Heart thudding, I carried my supplies down the cliff, loaded them into the boat and quickly cast off. By the time I had reached mid-loch, the tanks were passing the islets, but their engine cut as I reached my boat bay. I scrambled through the woods to the lagoon shore and heard the engine start up again before I got to the water's edge. When I arrived at the beach, the tanks were already 300 yards past the islets and heading for new stations two miles away to the east. What a relief! Even so, I felt as if the fish farmers were slowly closing in and one day would take over the entire loch.

I am not against *some* fish farming but it has to be regulated. Clustered pens have proliferated through much of the Highlands beyond all reasonable limits. While it has undoubtedly brought economic benefits to the region, it is now endangering too much that is irreplaceable and should be curtailed by planning authorities which, in my view, must be required by law to consult and heed the best independent conservation advice as well as all local interests. Considerations that should be given special weight are these:

Disturbance to rare wildlife species.
Destruction of the visual beauty of the loch.
Upsetting the tranquillity of the loch.
Pollution risk, and the effects on wild fish stocks.
Risk of passing on disease to wild stocks.
Possible loss of access and privacy to local dwellers.
Interference with wild fishing interests.
Precedent for further development.
The effect of farm lorries on single track roads.
Alteration of the aesthetic appeal of an entire formerly wild area.

At the same time, I cannot deny it could all be far worse. A water sports centre in the same part of the loch – which would be likely on an English lake, and virtually certain on similar American or Canadian waters, would be ten times as disrupting as any fish farm.

I was woken at 3.20 a.m. some days later by a banging, brushing sound on the window pane. To my astonishment, there was the little female badger I had looked after in the house five years earlier after finding her with severe neck and ear injuries. She reared up at the pane showing her hoary white belly, then jumped on to the old box-cage trap below the martens table. I shot out of bed, opened the window quietly, and saw her scoffing spilled marten titbits, her head facing away from me. I tweaked her tail gently. She whirled round, but did not attempt to bite. She just stayed there, very still, as if waiting for me to feed her. I had nothing ready to give her, and fool that I was, I put my hand out to stroke her. She turned abruptly and dived off the box-cage, catching her rear feet on the edge of the trap as she went down. I did not know that badgers could be so athletic. I knew it was Bessie, the ears still short even though the white tips had grown back. She was still small in size. I hoped she had not hurt her back feet on the trap. I threw some food out for her, and later I found her digging whorls in the east wood.

The sudden fierce weather, a reminder that winter was coming, seemed to galvanise the martens. They had been coming all summer, though among last years kits, White Chest was the rarest visitor. This season there seemed to be only one new cub, a tiny one with a very small chest patch, but bright enough to squeeze several jammy morsels in its mouth at once. It went against all the text books to see Mickey and Michelle with so many of their grown-up offspring still on the same territory.

One night, all but Centre Spot came at once, three of them tumbling over each other as they rushed through the window to gobble up food from my desk. None quarrelled with any of the others, and it seemed a veritable explosion of martens! I had no worries about leaving as far as they were concerned. Eric Jones said that the highlight of his visit had been Mickey taking a jammy bit from his hand. He promised to look after them well, just as he would tend Moobli's grave on the north hill and keep the path up to it clear. He had even said that I could return whenever I wanted to film the eagles, or do anything else, and that he would be glad to help me. Of course I could in no way impose on his generosity, but it had been the spirit in which

198

the invitation was made that finally clinched the handover for me.

I braced myself and telephoned the estate owner, my landlord. To my surprise, he agreed immediately to my passing on what remained of the Wildernesse lease to Eric Jones. He expressed some surprise that I should wish to leave, but if that was what I really wanted, and Jones's references were satisfctory, he had no objection. He did not even require a meeting with Eric beforehand, though he would, naturally, meet him in the course of time. The ease and speed of it all took my breath away as I felt Wildernesse and a whole era slip from me.

October 14 was handover day. I showed Eric how to work the boat winch and runways, the water system, and all the other primitive arrangements. I felt little emotion. Now the decision had been made, all I wanted to do was leave. I helped him with the big engine, which he thought of exchanging for a smaller and lighter one he could handle more easily, said a sad farewell at Moobli's grave, then went down to the oak and spruce grove in the east wood where I had camped on first seeing Wildernesse thirteen years ago. A lifetime away, it now seemed. I just touched the big oak, the spruce and gazed around at the woods and cottage and said simply –

'I loved you very much. I always will. Thanks for everything.'

And that was all. I felt relief that my ordeal was finally over, that I was free once more. Somewhere lurking was a dull sort of anger about what was happening to the wildlife I had come to love. But that wouldn't be changed overnight. I did not look back.

Before the long drive south, I was overcome by a desire to see again the little sea island of Eilean Shona, 26 miles away on the Atlantic coast, where my Scottish odyssey had begun over seventeen years before. A golden sun was sinking to the horizon, casting a shimmering, radiant path across the sea between the island and the little stone sea pier where I had so often launched my boat. I sat on the warmed stone of the pier in silence, grateful for the past, not yet fearful for the future, knowing only that the rest of my life would somehow still be bound up between man and the last wild places. I would try Spain first . . . Oh, there was still time enough to work out a new future, time enough to decide.

Epilogue

The story of my move to Spain and of my adventures in pursuit of Europe's rarest wildlife belong to another book, but at my remote villa in the heart of the Murcian mountains there was no lack of contact with the Highland loch. It seemed my life was still inextricably tangled up with it.

By early February I had heard from more than one source that the offending fish tanks had not been moved. My letter to Marine Harvest Ltd had not been answered and, it seemed, the advice of the N.C.C. and the R.S.P.B. had not been heeded. It was time, I decided, for a sterner attack, and so I wrote a very hard letter to the fish farm, stating my demand for the tanks to be moved by the deadline of March 31; failure to give me adequate assurances would result in my exposing the issue in the media and pursuing the matter with their parent company, Unilever. I sent copies to Ro Scott at the N.C.C. and Roy Dennis of the R.S.P.B.

Expecting little in response, I was delighted to hear, almost by return of post, that three pens had been moved and now they were *all* over half a mile from the divers' islet.*

I made a brief return to Britain in the spring for a large number of

---

* Eventually, due to over-production and the dumping of farmed salmon on to the market by the Norwegians, prices fell and huge losses were sustained over fish farming as a whole. In mid-February 1992, as this book was going to print, Unilever announced that they were putting Marine Harvest Ltd up for sale.

media interviews for the publication of *On Wing And Wild Water*. Suddenly there seemed no lack of interest from television companies in the idea of a film about my life. Among others, the BBC 'Arena' series kept discussions going for some time before they fizzled out. I was not surprised when the Moving Picture Company had their script for a film about my lifestyle – to be made by David Cobham, who directed the feature film of 'Tarka the Otter' – turned down by the BBC Natural History people in Bristol. The prestigious Oxford Scientific Films called me after hearing a radio broadcast I had done, and viewed my films with interest. There were some good things in them, they said, but I could have achieved so much more with equipment costing ten times what I had paid for mine.

A year later, when Scottish Television contacted my publisher shortly after *Moobli* appeared in the shops, I had become sceptical and disinterested. I went to see them in Glasgow out of a sense of duty rather than enthusiasm.

I was pleasantly surprised when producer Erina Rayner turned out to be an attractive young woman of pioneering New Zealand stock, while director Les Wilson was brisk, efficient, had a wonderful sense of humour and looked as if he could last more than a few rounds with Mike Tyson. My kind of people! I told them that my trekking and wildlife studies were a way of life, a mission for me, and I left them some of my philosophical notes. We got along well, but I felt sure their ideas would bite the dust like all the others.

All through the winter, Scottish TV kept in touch with me in Spain, telephoning friends who lived 40 kilometres away and who relayed messages. A hitch came when I discovered that Eric Jones had sold the rest of the Wildernesse lease, but the new tenant, Tony Millard, was another of my keenest readers, and he readily agreed to my return with a film crew to my old home. In early April I found myself back on the shores of the loch, acting as boatman to one half of the television crew while Tony Millard came over daily in my old boat to ferry over the other half. What followed were eight days of great fun and eight days of sheer hell.

Les Wilson and cameraman Jim Peters really put me through my paces and had the old horse on the run for most of the time. I had to row for miles, up the windy loch or along serene lochans with 'Hiawatha' scenery. I had to track through woods, up hills, and make my special 'invisible' hide, lie in it, show how I filmed the divers, buzzards, deer and so forth. They took me up in a helicopter to the very top of the 'Killer Trek' and made me re-live my eagle days – telling me to climb gorges, rock faces, jump peat bogs, struggle over raging waterfalls, and trek through the awful terrain, all with a heavy pack, hide, and the tied bundle of four hide-strengthening wands I had always used as a walking stick. No sooner had I done one good 'take' than Les would shout over the walkie-talkie from his comfortable seat in the air-battering helicopter –

'Well, Mike, that was okay, but would you do it again for Take Two? Go back to your original position.'

This could be nearly two hundred yards down an almost sheer cliff, or on the other side of a dangerous waterfall. I had never been up in a 'copter before, and it was incredible to see the terrain of the terrible trek, the jagged peaks and great tawny bowls below them, gyrating like tea leaves in a giant cup. They filmed me at campfires by the burn, with reflections of myself, the flames and the moon in the limpid pools. I had never met a cameraman with a more sensitive touch than burly Jim Peters and I learned some valuable lessons from him.

I was asked to talk about all aspects of Highland nature in my anecdotal commentary – more like a fireside chat – and to convey a little of my philosophy for the film. While I thought my performance was lacking, the team produced a beautiful little film called 'Wild Cathedral' which went out over the whole ITV network in July 1989. I was astonished to find myself splashed across two pages in the *TV Times* and to hear later that the film was so popular that it was repeated several times in the Scottish region. Only five or six minutes of my own film was included, but I was paid a gratifying fee.

It was during the filming that I heard from Allan Peters about an ingenious scheme he and forestry conservation officer Tony Hinde had devised to help the divers in the breeding season. Tony and his assistant Mike Canham had come to the conclusion that rising loch levels washing out the divers' nests after heavy rain was even more of a problem than disturbance, so during three cold days in February Allan and Mike had constructed a floating island on which the birds could nest in greater safety.

Two polystyrene rafts, 6 feet by 4 feet were clamped together with two H-frames, top and bottom, over which they spread carpet underlay, with wire netting stapled all round, binding the contraption securely. The sides of the raft were chamfered so that the birds would have a gentle slope up which to walk. Over the top of this artificial island they spread turf to resemble the normal island terrain. Allan and Mike wanted it to look as natural as possible before they took it out in mid-loch and secured it firmly by ropes to two stout anchors, one at each end. The anchors would hold the 'island' steady in gales, but the ropes would be left with enough slack to allow the island to rise with the level of the loch water after heavy rain. They sited it well away from the shore, between the natural islets and the loch's south shore, where they hoped no otter would venture.

It was a clever idea, but I was sceptical. Surely no bird as wary as the black-throated diver would actually lay eggs on such a contrivance? When I returned to Spain after my performance with Scottish TV, Tony Millard wrote to me from Wildernesse to tell me how the divers fared this year. He told me that a pair were nesting on the near islet, where he had seen them waddling up to the grassy area below the stunted pines. Then one morning he heard his dog barking down by the shore and went to investigate. 'A group of six canoes were pulling up at the islet,' he wrote. 'I made a quick dash across the burn and got them to move on. I hope I got to them in time.' The weather was changing and Tony said it had been raining for the past twenty-four hours. He was keeping his fingers crossed. So – 1,500 miles away – was I.

Then, on July 10, Tony wrote again with some astonishing news. 'The divers didn't return to the islet,' he said, 'but went across to the floating platform the Forestry Commission put out. On June 18 I saw the pair with two chicks swimming near the float. It must have been their first time in the water they were so small. Then, on June 26, all four were over by the islet, the chicks growing well. The last time I saw them was on July 1, in the little inlet past the west wood. I sat behind the big rock and watched them diving for fish and feeding the chicks.'

So the new 'island' had been a success after all. In my first nine years at Wildernesse, the divers had raised seven chicks to swim and fly. In the following five years they had not reared a single chick to maturity. Now that trend has been reversed. In the following three years the divers used the platform again for nesting and successfully reared two chicks each time.

Allan Peters had also been watching over the loch as assiduously as Tony and it was he who confirmed that a second diver pair, down by the green isle, also had a healthy chick with them. Without doubt, these had been the best diver seasons for seven years. By wrongly placing tanks too close to Heron Island four years earlier, the fish farm had helped to cause a hiatus in the breeding lives of my closest pair, but provided they did not extend their operations again, and with help from a second platform island to be installed by Tony, it appeared that no lasting harm had been done. Tony is not an over-emotional man but I was moved when he wrote to say 'these marvellous birds make your heart skip a beat.'

Another letter from my home loch brought tears to my eyes. It was from Niall McKillop, who has given me permission to reveal in his own words the extraordinary tale he had to tell. He had been running a passenger boat service to the seal colony on Sgeir Dubb, five miles down from Loch Linnhe, which finally folded when the appalling summers I have described in this book caused a severe fall in trade. A hotelier in my area had helped him to set up a small tourist boat on my loch, running trips from the hotel pier. When Niall wrote to me three years after my departure, he had just read my book *On Wing and Wild Water*, which had solved a mystery for him. This is what he said:

I already knew the loch well, having first fished there with my father when I was seven years old – thirty five years past – and from '81-'86 had fished the loch every Saturday throughout the season.

In June 1983 on a black brooding day of no wind but heavy threat, I was trolling slowly close to the shore. I was deep in thought and there was nothing on the loch that day which could disturb my trance. A light drizzle started and I put on my old Barbour hat which normally I didn't like wearing . . . I puttered on, looking upward to the hill, hoping for a glance of the bird in which we share a passion. Without warning, my heart leaped in shock, and at the same time I came out in a spontaneous cold sweat. What felt like a hand had been placed gently but firmly on my head. I did not jump or take a swipe at my head, for almost immediately I heard the quiet swish of wings and turned slowly, lifting my eyes; to see the clean pure white of a common gull lifting slowly from my hat, then drifting forward to land unsteadily on the slippery gunwhale about six feet ahead of me. That was my first meeting with the common gull I named Jonathan, and I can only assume that it is the same bird which you called Cledwin. [Author's note: In fact, I named him Cedwig]

204

I began to look forward to our meetings. Sometimes he would sit on my head, but only if I was wearing a hat. If I was eating when on the move he would stay on the gunwhale, sometimes running on the spot, wings akimbo, to try to retain his footing. I marvelled at the pure whiteness of him and at that perfect circle of scarlet which ringed each eye . . .

In 1987 I began running short cruises from — [in] a 26ft ex-Admiralty cutter carrying twelve passengers as opposed to the 96 I had been permitted to carry with the large boat on Loch Linnhe. I had purchased a rather splendid ensign staff for the boat which was capped by a large carved and painted thistle, and this, after my Barbour hat, became Cledwin's second favourite perch. He would never go to the gunwhale which was broad and flat, presumably because of the proximity of my passengers. Nor can I find any reports of the bird landing on any of the several boats owned [locally] and regularly on the loch. I took great pains to ensure that my winged friend was not disturbed whenever he paid a visit, keeping the passengers still and quiet. He became something of a celebrity and on two occasions I declined offers from newspapers for stories in case something might happen to him.

In July 1988, round about the eighth or ninth, I had gone down the loch on my own (no passengers because of rain) hoping for a break in the weather which would allow me to confirm that the chick from an eagle nest I knew was on the wing . . . The weather worsened and with rain and wind moving quickly east from Moidart I turned, leaving the eagles for another day.

Just after that, Jonathan appeared but could not land with the wind behind him. I pulled the boat round head to wind and, surprisingly, he came past me and landed on a thwart and stood gazing at me as I allowed the boat to fall off the wind again and take me back quickly.

He didn't look too good. There was nothing in his physical appearance that concerned me – he was as clean and beautiful as ever – but he was in some way, different; it was as though he was depressed or troubled. I was not altogether surprised therefore when Cledwin remained in the boat all the way back to the pier. I had never attempted to touch him over the years, although he would take food from my hand, whether soaring in from the side or scrabbling on the gunwhale of one of the Stage House's fibreglass boats. On this occasion, however, I felt justified in taking a closer look and after I had tied the boat up (which did not seem to bother him) I went back aboard and edged slowly towards him. To my great surprise he made no attempt to move and even when I lifted him gently on to my knee he made not the least objection.

He seemed of good weight. I checked him over and there was no sign of any infestation of mites or nits, nor any obvious reason for his condition. The only thing I could find in any way untoward were stress marks on two adjacent primaries on the right wing which appeared to be of the same age and, I figured, would be moulted that year in any case.

I put the boat on a mooring, leaving Cledwin in a shallow locker with the lid open and some corned beef and fresh water beside him.

I returned the next day to find him as he had been left, sitting on some old canvas. He was very weak, and the corned beef had not been touched. One of the stressed primaries had been shed. The day was better and I had a few passengers for my ten o'clock run so I put Cledwin in my dinghy in a cardboard box and left the boat on the mooring, away from village dogs and cats.

When I returned at twelve-thirty, having worried myself sick all morning, I found, tearfully, that my beautiful friend had died.

I disposed of him fittingly, digging a good deep hole near Sandy Point, topped by a heavy, pure white stone. I will look at it in years to come and remember him, Jonathan Seagull, so I called him. One can put no price on such relationships, no matter how absurb or ridiculous they seem to others. Their value is written not only by the sense of privilege one feels at each time of meeting, but hopefully by the memories those times will give in years to come. Cledwin died in peace, and we both will mourn a true friend . . .

How this letter tugged at my heart, far away in Spain. And how memory is rekindled when I receive reports from Allan and Tony about the eagles, the divers, the martens and all the other Highland wildlife I watched over and loved for so many years. When I left Wildernesse I swore I would never return to Scotland. Now, five years on, I would not place any bets on it. My mother was a Highlander through and through, and I find I cannot just banish a hankering for the land of my blood.

Postscript

When I left Wildernesse in October 1986 I felt truly finished on the Hill but, as readers of *In Spain's Secret Wilderness* will know, the dry warmer climate worked wonders, and for the next five years I climbed far higher mountains after even rarer wildlife than I had in Scotland. While I was not trekking after eagles, vultures, lynxes, wolves or wild bears, I laboured to edit the seven hours of film I had shot in the Highlands into a cohesive movie. I also wrote a commentary.

Returning homeless to Britain in March 1991, I took advantage of a friend's offer of a room in London and spent exhausting weeks finishing the film and driving from one studio to another to add a commentary and convert it all into a 90-minute VHS video called *Eagle Mountain*. Having spent about £12,000 making the film, I was unable (despite long searches) to move back to the western Highlands as house prices had gone up steeply during my years away in Spain. Then, at last, I found a new Scottish base, not far from the border, and can now offer the videos for sale.

Eagle Mountain tells the story of a magical Highland mountain through all four seasons. It has many unique sequences – golden eagles at the nest and their beautiful courtship 'air dances' an eaglet swallowing a complete stoat, a female eagle hauling a whole deer uphill on her own. The black-throated divers are seen diving, courting, and at their nest in sequences never filmed before. Pine martens are shown hunting in the wild, at their den, even coming through my window to take jammy titbits from my hands. All the comic, and tragic, sibling rivalry at buzzard nests is included, as well as hunting and nesting peregrine falcons, courting red-breasted mergansers, seals in the sea, swimming otters, water voles, and even a hunting wildcat. This is the real stuff – no tame birds with their jesses removed and taken into 'wild' situations – all was actually filmed as it was taking place naturally in the wild. Through it all, I show the lives of the red deer herds, including their foraging fitfully in winter snows and dramatic stag fights in the autumn rut.

I have produced only enough copies of the video – 500, and half that number have gone already – to recover most of my costs. A copy will be sent to anyone writing to me by the first day of July 1993 at the latest and enclosing £18 (this covers first class return post) c/o The Post Office, Hawick, Roxburghshire TD9 7NQ. Please allow one month for delivery.

Mike Tomkies
February 1992